CONVERSATIONS ABOUT DEATH

ALSO BY SALLY CANT

The Heart and Soul of Celebrancy

CONVERSATIONS ABOUT DEATH

A Practical Guide to
Talking about End-of-Life Care and Dying

SALLY CANT

COPYRIGHT © 2015
ALL RIGHTS RESERVED
First published in Australia 2015 Sally Cant
www.sallycant.com.au
www.celebrantstraining.com.au

All rights reserved. No part of this book may be reproduced, stored in a retrieval system, or transmitted in any form or by any means – electronic, mechanical or otherwise, without the prior written permission of the author.
Every effort has been made to ensure that this book is free from error or omissions. However the authors, the editor or their respective employees or agents shall not accept responsibility for injury, loss or damage occasioned to any person acting or refraining from action as a result of materials in this book whether or not such injury, damage or loss is in any way due to any negligent act or omission, breach of duty or default on the part of the author, the editor, or their respective employees or agents.

National Library Catalogue
Creator: Cant, Sally, author.
Title: Conversations about death: a practical guide to talking about end-of-life care and dying / Sally Cant.
ISBN: 9780992314217 (paperback)
ISBN: 9780992314200 (ebook)
Subjects: Death.
        Death—Psychological aspects.
        Funeral rites and ceremonies.
        Palliative treatment.
        Terminal care.
        Terminally ill—Psychology.

Cover Designed—Bespoke Book Covers
Cover Photo—Megan Aldridge Photography
Publishing Consultants/Interior Design—Pickawoowoo Publishing Group

Publisher
People With Passion Publishing
For enquiries, write to: rights and permissions via publisher.
info@peoplewithpassionpublishing.com.au

Dedicated to
Ben, Dan and Jess - my amazing children

CONTENTS

Foreword xi
Acknowledgements xvii
Introduction 1

CHAPTER: 1. WE KNOW WHEN LIFE BEGINS BUT DEATH CANNOT BE SO EASILY DEFINED 13

On what basis do we determine death? 14
What is the point of death if someone is suffering from
  Alzheimer's or dementia? 15
Is there a soul? If so, what happens to it at the time of death? 16
Differing views of death 17

CHAPTER: 2. WHY IS IT IMPORTANT TO HAVE AN INFORMED CONVERSATION ABOUT DEATH AND DYING? 21

Reasons why you should have the conversation 22
The risks of not having a conversation 23
Can people influence the timing of their death? 25

CHAPTER: 3. HOW TO MAKE THIS CHALLENGING CONVERSATION EASIER 29

Why is it so hard to have the conversation? 29
Unpacking some of the difficulties 32

CHAPTER: 4. THE IMPORTANCE OF RELATIONSHIPS AND OTHER CONNECTIONS 43

Why do large-scale tragedies affect us? 45

What effect does not seeing eye to eye have on a conversation? 48
The benefits of strong, close relationships...49
How do people react when informed of a terminal illness? 50
Who are we after a death? 52

CHAPTER: 5. RIGHTS, CHOICES AND THE LAW: WHAT WE NEED TO KNOW 57

PART 1 - WHEN A DEATH IS IMMINENT 58
Concerns around quality of life 59
Palliative Care...62
A nurse's story 65
The World Health Organisation (WHO) definition of Palliative Care 74
World Health Organisation Definition of Palliative Care for children 75
Advance Care Planning 78
Documents 80
Enduring Power of Attorney (Medical Treatment) 80
Advance Healthcare Directive –
   Living Will – End of Life Directive..81
Refusal of Medical Treatment Certificate..................................81
Physician Assisted Dying (PAD) 82
The Medical Treatment Act..88
Euthanasia 93
Dying at home..95
The baby boomer approach to death and dying 99

PART 2 - WHEN A DEATH HAS OCCURRED 102
After death choices 103
Who needs to be contacted when a person dies? 105
Keeping the body at home...109
Having a home vigil 110
Transporting the body 112
Organ donation 112
Mortuary care...115
Embalming and preservation 116

Preparing the body 119
Pre-paid funerals.. 121
Things to do before the funeral 123
When the body is with the Coroner 126
Amanda's story 128

PART 3 - DIFFICULT AND UNEXPECTED DEATHS 134
What can we experience when an unexpected death occurs?..........134
Suicide 141
Large scale deaths.. 142
Rhiannon's story.. 143
Paige's story 147
Fiona's story 149

PART 4 - FUNERALS AND FINAL RESTING PLACES 157
Don't be rushed into having a funeral 157
What does a funeral look like and why is it important? 159
The difference between honouring and celebrating? 160
Funeral options 162
Engaging a professional independent celebrant 165
Funeral company or not? 167
Advantages of using a funeral company 168
Disadvantages of using a funeral company 169
Doing it yourself 171
Advantages of doing it yourself 171
Disadvantages of doing it yourself 171
Using a funeral advocate... 172
Disposal of the body 172
Burial or cremation.. 173
Cemeteries, Cemetery Trusts and Crematoria 176
Can a cremation or burial be organised by the family?......... 178
Are burials on private property allowed?........................ 180
Can a cemetery cancel your interment right? 182
Natural burial 183
The story of Moora Moora's community's sanctuary 188

CHAPTER: 6. THE CHANGING LANDSCAPE OF FUNERALS 195

A funeral director's perspective on current practices 199
Have you ever considered having a living wake? 209

CHAPTER: 7. CONSIDERING THE IMMEDIATE NEEDS OF THE BEREAVED 217

Viewing the body 221

CHAPTER: 8. GRIEF – A LITTLE WORD WITH A BIG PUNCH! 229

Preparatory grief 238
The death of an adult child 240
Grief when a person is suffering dementia or Alzheimer's disease 241
Grief when someone dies suddenly 243
Grief from a tragic death 245
The loss of a baby 246
Children and grief 250
General tips 252
Oscar's story 254
Susan's story 259

CHAPTER: 9. HAVING THE CONVERSATION 263

Now we are informed let's have the conversation 263
Conversation starters 267

CHAPTER: 10. THE ROAD TO RECOVERY: MANAGING AND ADAPTING AFTER A DEATH 277

Looking after yourself 281

CHAPTER: 11. LIVING THE LEGACY 291

APPENDICES. CEREMONIES AND RITUAL: WRITING 'THEIR STORY' 299

- Storytelling 300
- Creating a ritual 305
- Planning a ceremony or ritual 307
- What does a ritual look like? 308
- Structure of a larger ritual or ceremony 311
- The informal ritual or ceremony 314
- Bobbie's story 315
- Examples of Ceremonies 321
- Ceremony for Nicholas Jonathan Pryce 321
- Ceremony for Baby Maya Anne Sonners 336
- Ceremony for Mary Moore 342
- Ceremony for Kathleen Reekie 354

REFERENCES 371

- Organisations and their roles 376
- Finding the right therapist 380
- Coroners offices 381
- Cemeteries 381
- Natural burial grounds 382
- Cemeteries Acts 382

INDEX 383

ABOUT THE AUTHOR 388

FOREWORD

The death landscape, particularly within the Australian context, is slowly being excavated by an increasing number of groups of passionate people unfulfilled by the way dying and death is being handled. Sally Cant is one of these advocates who has significantly contributed to bringing about a death revolution. She has gathered knowledge through her experience and research over many years and finally, this book, Conversations About Death presents an open invitation for your participation in reclaiming the manner in which death is being processed; to bring it back home to those who are most impacted when death comes to someone we love.

Many of us have limited knowledge of the options available surrounding death and funeral practices.

Upon the death of a loved one, most people go to a funeral director and let them take the reins of control. After all, that's what you do, right? Ultimately the formula presented by mainstream funeral direction consists of a suggested date and time for the funeral, a choice of coffin and floral arrangement (often from a brochure), up to three songs, and 20 or 40 minute allocation at the cemetery chapel. With the uniqueness of every individual, their final send-off comes down to a few limited choices because, at our most vulnerable time and without the knowledge of what we could do, we don't envisage that there are other, more fitting options and as a result do not ask.

When I discuss funeral options with my clients, particularly around the dressing of the dead, it astounds me how often am I asked 'oh, can you do that?' I often find that in the past they have been dissuaded from spending time with their loved ones after they have died, or worse, are made to feel that it would be something that is too traumatic to endure. However, it has been through simple education and facilitation that I have had families perform dressings, just as they would have only a few generations ago, without utilising a funeral director. I see irony that, when our family pets die, we are often in the room when they are euthanised; we dig the grave, wrap them in a sheet or towel, lower them by hand into the soil and then fill the grave. Many of us then plant a seedling over the ground. We want to respect that life lived by being hands-on at this time. Yet when it comes to our human family, we are often ostracised from the process.

Death and birth, whilst being the most inescapable and natural events to occur to all living beings, can bring up many complex emotions. Inevitably life is punctuated with the deaths of those we love; they become major life events for those left in the world of the living, and can fundamentally alter us.

My first experience with death was when my teacher, after being diagnosed with an aggressive cancer in the first trimester of her pregnancy, died shortly after the birth of her second child. I was young at the time and had little comprehension of death; it was surreal and I didn't know how to process what had happened. I didn't think much amount about death over the next few years... for it wouldn't come back to visit for another decade... little did I know that 15 years later my calling in life was to be firmly rooted in the death industry.

When my Grandfather died I feel guilty to admit that what I felt the most was relief. I didn't know that it was OK to feel that way. But for him, any love of life had ended in the months and years prior and in some way I understood that he was finally free.

Privilege and gratitude are the qualities that should be encouraged in the presence of death and dying; privilege in that we have encountered someone meaningful in our life, and gratitude that our paths crossed. Life is immensely fleeting, and our experiences with other people are quite miraculous when you consider the odds of connecting. Death reminds us of the fragility of life. It is a mirror to our own transient mortality. The simple and conversely miraculous nature of death has changed my life, and will also change yours.

I first met Sally in 2009 when I attended one of her funeral celebrancy courses. It was a few months after the death of my Nonno (paternal Grandfather) – a death that set about a formative series of moments in my own life which resulted in me wanting to see what else I could offer others in the face of death.

When he died I was somewhat surprised to learn that we would be having a full Catholic Mass (predominately to be conducted in Italian). As one of the only family members to not speak Italian I was somewhat at a loss as to how I could be involved in celebrating the patriarch of our family as he moved from this realm into another. I was studying fashion design, predominantly interested in bodies and dressing, metaphors of fragility, vulnerability and mortality – so when it was suggested that perhaps we could dress him for his funeral, I took the opportunity. To see him, or rather his vacated body, was an enlightening experience. To see the dead, to witness the stillness of them, to touch their cool skin and to feel the rigor of the junctions of their body was to understand what being dead means. And it surprised me. While I was nervous about seeing him, this dissipated very quickly. In its place came pride and honour to be able to dress this man who had known me longer than I had known myself. While he was clearly no longer in his body, it allowed me to say goodbye to the physical form he had taken and to comfortably send his shell back to the earth.

A few short months later his sister died and his daughters approached me to assist with her dressing. At this point I realised there was immense power in this ritual and I felt called to share my experience with others.

To think that the handling of the deceased body used to be a standard experience in western cultures only a century ago. How quickly we have lost the skills. However, in order to help others I needed to be educated about sensitivities and protocols around what to say (and not say) in the presence of the dead, and where to place the emotions that would inevitably come to me.

How does one stand in a community of those who are grieving and not end up in your own puddle of tears? I contacted Sally to help me. Sally's comprehensive funeral celebrancy course covered an array of topics around death and dying.

During the training one of the key elements for me was being instructed to write a ceremony. I decided that I would write for my (then living) Grandmother. I felt nervous writing the eulogy for someone who was still alive, but while she was still 'with us' her dementia seemed to have taken her mind years earlier. She didn't die for another year, but by that time I was as prepared for her death as I could be. In writing her eulogy I reflected on her life and her role in my own life. If I had not already prepared for her death through the writing of the eulogy, I would not have been as well prepared to bear witness to her actual death. To this day being with my Grandmother as she passed over is one of my most treasured experiences of my life, as special and miraculous as when I have witnessed a birth. Sally gave me the confidence and tools to navigate this juncture and I will be forever grateful for such empowerment.

When beginning my doctoral research into dressing the dead (how we dress the dead, and indeed why we dress them) there were few texts that delved into the topic. As I pushed further into the Australian context of death and dying there was even less literature. Robert Larkins' Funeral Rights was a great place to begin as the logistics of what could and could not be achieved under the current law was explained. Through my research I was fortunate enough to encounter many people working to change the process of death and dying in Australia. In 2014, after an extended trip in the United Kingdom where I worked at Clandon Wood Natural Burial Ground, I came to the realisation that I needed to return to Australia and formally link all those interested parties. Sally was the first person I called to form a group that later became known as The Natural Death Advocacy Network (NDAN). Since then Sally and I have resided on the National Executive of NDAN and remain committed to the changing movement in the industry.

Recognising that no single person or organisation can own death and dying we began to gather and share information to a much wider audience with the aim of educating and advocating an understanding of death and dying in Australia. This includes, amongst other aspects, end-of-life care of a loved one, your rights choices and the law pertaining to death, and creating a funeral that is authentic, relevant and meaningful to your family and community.

You may not realise it, but we are in a moment of far-reaching change for the death and dying industry. There are death doulas, DIY funeral facilitators, wool coffins and shroud cremations all within a few keyword internet searches. For example, I was recently invited to farewell a gentleman in a cemetery overlooking the mountains. With a smoke ceremony, digeridoos, and open fires; his shrouded body was lowered into the ground by his family; his grave then filled with eucalypt leaves and when full, one of his favourite species of native tree was planted at the head of his grave. It was in all manners of the phrase, a 'down to earth' ritual. Yet only a few years ago, this type of ceremony would, most likely, not have been considered (or indeed been allowed).

'Conversations About Death' removes the need to research widely on the subject of death and dying. In this book Sally has carefully integrated her research and vast experience of working with grieving families confronting end-of-life care and death. She has woven case studies, facts and formal information (rules, regulations and laws) with useful, practical tips and advice. I recommend that during the reading of

'Conversations About Death', you have a set of sticky tabs and highlight the sections that most speak to you! Knowing your options will bring you empowerment, knowing the law will show you where it can be melded, and having your own conversations about death will improve the way that we live with death and dying.

Dr. Pia Interlandi

ACKNOWLEDGEMENTS

Writing this book has been a challenging personal journey for me and I wondered at times whether I could see it through. However, I am convinced that there is a real need for a book such as this, that tells the story of dying and death in a completely open and honest way, from the perspective of one who has had much direct personal and professional experience in the field. I am deeply grateful to the many people who have contributed in very different ways over the years.

While writing this book I lost several friends to illness and each time this happened it would set me back as it was simply too tough at those times to write about death. It was during those times, however, that I experienced an amazing generosity of spirit from those families who, in the midst of their own grief, wanted to contribute to my project. My thanks to Ginny Bydder, her husband Michael and sister Jackie Kairau for allowing me to include Ginny's and their experience in this book; a great friend so sorely missed. I know she has been beside me continuing to drive me forward to complete this project.

Many others have taught me through their own grieving and I want to express my tender respect for you all. To my two nieces, Rhiannon Mason and Paige Pehlivan, who have shown such strength in contributing their own stories to this book, I am so blessed to be your aunt and your friend. A very big thank you also to Sherinda Shea, Amanda Pryce, Susan Simpson, Fiona Gilroy, Tennille and Mark Welsh, and Scarlett Lewis who all lost loved ones and were willing to share their experience of loss even though at times it was very painful and raw. I learnt not only from your contributions, but also from the challenges you presented to me. Words are inadequate to convey my deep gratitude for your time and courage.

To all the people who completed a questionnaire that was helpful when deciding on what should be included, I thank you for your time. To Dr Rodney Syme of Dying with Dignity, Victoria; Michelle Hook at the Cabrini Health Palliative Homecare and Consult Services; Anne Gleeson and Steve Lamb from MacQueen's Funerals, Terang, Victoria, I extend my heartfelt thanks; you were all happy to assist in specific areas of this field where my knowledge was limited. I am indebted for your assistance.

To my students of celebrancy, thank you for your support and reciprocal learning. I will be forever thankful that I can continue to facilitate courses that assist you in reaching what is often a long-held dream of becoming a celebrant in this most important field of work.

I want to thank the many people who have opened their lives and relationships to me as clients, entrusting me with the funerals of their loved ones. My heartfelt thanks to you for engaging me at a time that was truly heart-wrenching for you. You bestowed on me the honour of assisting you to put together an authentic way of celebrating a life.

To my friend Nancy Cato for your wise counsel. I'm so grateful for your honesty which allowed me to put a halt on my writing until I had it on track and who prodded and cajoled me in all the right directions. You made a significant investment of time in contributing thoughtful and insightful comments that vastly improved the quality of this book. Thank you my dear friend.

To my beautifully skilled editor Claudine Bjorklund, this book would not be the book it is without you. You came along at just the right time to refine the manuscript. I thank you for your friendship, your passion and encouragement, and for your integrity and sense of quality.

Acknowledgements

To Catie Wood, a friend of 20 years, who read the draft and gave me feedback whilst undergoing her own battle with cancer; you remain a true friend and an inspiration.

I am immensely grateful to all those friends who daily give me love and support, along with a good dose of humour. To Josie Arnold, Wendy Barton, Liz Gray, Catherine Bearsley, Bobbie Symons, Wendy Kirke, Lynne Jansen, Michelle Kiernan, John Terry Moore, Di Kleinert, Veronica Pappas, Wendy Haynes, Jill Harper, Dudley Raine, Glenda Coswello, Pru Hux and Martin Bramble: thank you from the bottom of my heart for keeping me sane and for the unique place that each of you has in my life.

This book was planned, discussed and penned in many and varied locations; the magical place of Sanur, Bali in 2012, sitting with Susan Stretch and Frank Schippers over a cold drink on the balcony of their villa; to my second home in Kallista with my best friends Cheryl and Paul Dakis (where staying overnight each Sunday feels like I've had a weekend off); travelling through nine countries of the Eastern Bloc of Europe in 2013 talking to people and learning about their death practices, (especially Kristina, a student and new mum, while chatting for over two hours in a Budapest park overlooking the Danube); the Western Australian home of Josie and Lindsay Arnold (after breaking into their home, and surviving to tell the tale!). This much-travelled manuscript has been with me every step of the way.

I thank all the other people and organisations for enthusiastically embracing this work. I dream optimistically that it will assist each and every one of you in some way.

Finally, an enormous thank you to my family: my truly amazing children Ben, Dan and Jess (it is my greatest joy to be your Mother) and their partners Zoi, Jess and James and my Grandson Lachlan; my Brother Jim and his wife Frankie, and my nieces and nephews, what can I say? I am a very lucky person indeed to have you all in my life.

I hope this book will make you curious and inquisitive and give you an appetite for more learning and, of course, be a resource that gives you comfort, guidance, solace and, hopefully, even pleasure.

INTRODUCTION

The fear of death follows from the fear of life.
A man who lives fully is prepared to die at any time.
— Mark Twain

Death. Why death? It is the one inevitable thing we know will happen to us all. Sooner or later every single one of us will die. That's the reality of life. Death is something we share with everyone and every living being. We are born, we live and we die. That is the natural cycle. But is it our instinctive fear of death that prevents this subject from being discussed openly? Is it any wonder when living in a death denying culture that so many of us view death as remote and lacking relevance?

Perhaps it is too hard to deal with because many of us don't want to think about our own mortality. This book is intended to empower you to openly discuss death and dying with people close to you, to allow those conversations to happen in a relaxed and easy manner, before any impending death or illness. It will explore elements of death and dying, and enable you to think about the possibilities of how the end stage of life will play out. It will help you to discuss the choices available, talk about how a life might be celebrated and consider what special requests the dying person might want followed through after they have died.

The primary aim of this self-help book is to:

(a) Provide general information about end of life, death and dying;
(b) Provide information on choices, rights and the law at end of life and death;
(c) Prepare you to have an informed conversation about end of life, death and dying.

This is regardless of whether:

- There is no imminent death and a more general discussion is had;
- Someone close to you is diagnosed with a life-limiting illness;
- A death has occurred.

One of the many issues this book will look at is what choices people have when faced with death themselves, or with the death of a loved one. Unfortunately, most people have no idea of the choices available to them when it comes to death and dying, so I will endeavour to prepare you by providing information for that discussion.

Being able to have an open conversation about death and dying and the issues surrounding it, provides an opportunity for the dying person to let others know their wishes at life's end. It gives us an opportunity to really talk and to tell each other what we mean, each to the other, and what we will miss about that person. It's an opportunity to thank those closest to us. It makes the task of those left behind so much easier when the death occurs or is unfolding.

This book will also help you to think about the experience of sitting with other people's grief, learning from people who are dying and learning more about yourself as a result. I believe as a society we would be healthier if our attitude to death shifted.

As Morrie Schwartz pointed out, in his movie *Tuesday's with Morrie*,

Introduction

"Mortality can teach us much about life, if we let it!" His famous line is "When you know how to die, you know how to live."

Talking about death with a dying person can give an extra sense of love and can demonstrate that we matter to each other greatly. It also gives an opportunity to prioritise what we spend our time and energy on. Dying is a natural rite of passage, a completion of our life, and the sooner we can accept death as natural, the more we will be able to live in the present.

My main hope is that by reading this book you can feel more relaxed, open and comforted by talking about death. It is not something to be afraid of; we all know it is going to happen. We can plan a lot in our life but one thing we cannot plan is when death will occur – or can we?

The publication by renowned Swiss American psychiatrist Elisabeth Kübler-Ross in 1969, *On Death and Dying,* was an important turning point in attitudes towards mortality. Kübler-Ross's interviews with cancer patients brought the dying process out into the open and returned to it something of the social acceptability it had lost. Along with this more open discussion about death came a more open discussion about grieving.

There has been a lot written about death and grief but most authors come to it from a medical, physiological perspective that may not be easily understandable and useful to the general public. Some books on psychology are very academic and not so helpful.

This book is meant for the general public as a tool: to start those conversations about what things a person may have been considering for themselves and their families regarding their death; to understand generally what's happening in the field of 'death care'; to know what changes are being made; and to be informed as to what might be possible for the future. In doing this, it will educate us on what is possible, how to have healthy conversations and how to 'sit in' another person's grief and assist them in a positive way.

Even though this book is about death, I would also like it to be about life. It is for every person who wants to get the topic out in the open, to be discussed freely. My hope is that this will be a topic that is discussed easily within a family when no one is unwell, ageing or dying, but that may be wishful thinking. It is more likely that death will be discussed when someone is facing their mortality, or experiencing the death of a loved one and wanting to work out how to sit comfortably with that person and have a frank conversation with them about death. This discussion will lead to knowing and being able to follow their wishes and their thoughts on how to celebrate their life.

The book is also for those who are caring for people who are dying as well as for those who are facing death and, perhaps more importantly, for those left behind who are trying to recover from the experience of the death of a loved one.

Conversations About Death is a resource for things we all need to think about; for having a discussion about death; for considering the options we have; for how we cope; and how we celebrate and get back to some sort of normal life again without that person in our life.

In the beginning when we lose a loved one, it isn't so much a matter of moving on as just getting through each day, of coping with life's day-to-day demands. I hope that you will find the book helpful at any time, but more so at times when death is either imminent or has already occurred.

I have worked in the field of death care since 1995 and have been fortunate to work alongside many people. It is an honour and very humbling although naturally at times it can be very stressful and not so joyful. However, at the heart of these situations it is our love for each other that thankfully shines through.

The idea for this book came about after several incidents. Over the years I have been approached by a number of people I know, as well as

Introduction

those I don't, the media and various colleagues, all wanting me to write about my knowledge and experience of the industry and the choices people are faced with during the death and dying process.

The idea of writing the book was further cemented after reading *The Alchemy of Loss* by Abigail Carter who lost her husband in the World Trade Center terrorist attacks. The *Alchemy of Loss* is the story of her transformation; tiptoeing through the chaos that is life after loss. Abigail found it very difficult after the death of her husband Arron to find any resource to help her in that time of need. When she was finally able to hold a funeral she did not know where to turn for help. Her book really brought home to me the uniquely personal nature of grieving. *Conversations About Death* remained in the back of my mind for many years. Finally, Abigail's story prompted me to the realise there was a place for my book.

Abigail said in her book: "I was resolved to celebrate Arron's life, rather than mourn it. I wanted to remember him the way he really was, happy and silly and alive."

I read Abigail's story when it was first published and it remains on my desk to this day. I use it as a resource when teaching students about death and funerals. It reminds me that there are so many things wrong with the way we manage death and those who are grieving, and that we could do it much better. Abigail's pain was obvious through the entire book and I learnt more about grieving than I have in all the research I have done on this topic. I didn't just read her book, I '*felt* it!'

One of the most important aspects for me was that Abigail did not feel capable or able to locate resources or assistance from anyone who understood her grief. She felt that Arron's death was thrown into the mix with all the other victims of the horrendous catastrophe. It was referred to as an event, not the death of individuals. It seemed that their individual deaths were somehow overlooked. Abigail's grief, as is the case in any tragedy of this nature, would not be a private matter: the community, the country, indeed the world, was watching. After her husband's death, life was full of public ceremonies and formalities that acknowledged the attacks but not ones that celebrated individual lives. It is easy to understand how this happened and we can learn from the effect this must have had on so many people. In a similar way, the Black Saturday fires in Victoria, Australia in 2009, resulted in funerals where people grieved over lost communities rather than acknowledging the individual deaths of the victims in a manner that they might have done if only one life had been lost. How much more comforting would it have been for those left behind if there had been a discussion about death before it happened?

Clearly I'm not the first to write or talk about this topic. When the Australian lawyer Robert Larkins' book *Funeral Rights* was published in 2007 there was a huge outcry from the funeral industry. His book aimed to educate the public so they better understood the 'death industry' and, in so doing, enable people to make educated decisions by being fully aware of their choices. He was educating the public on what they needed to hear, but it wasn't a nice picture that he painted. I spoke to Rob about his book and what influence he thinks it had on the industry. Although the book continues to sell well, he thinks the funeral industry probably saw him as someone who would quickly disappear and have little influence on the industry, which regrettably in reality, is probably what has happened. He and I share the same view that the funeral industry continues to deteriorate.

In 1963, Jessica Mitford published her ground-breaking book *The American Way of Death.* This book is still recognised as one of the best about death in the twentieth century. In it Mitford took on the funeral industry. Her book helped bring death out of the shadows and got the public talking about the subject in a way that it hadn't done for decades. She exposed the funeral industry in America for conning Americans into buying expensive funerals that they didn't need and couldn't afford. She called the funeral industry "…a huge, macabre, and expensive practical joke on the American public". In the final chapter, New Hope for the

Dead, she makes mention of FAMSA (the Funeral and Memorial Societies of America) now known as the Funeral Consumers Alliance (FCA), whose task is to monitor funeral laws across the country. The FCA is a non-profit organisation that protects the rights of people across America in regard to planning a meaningful, dignified and affordable funeral.

There was a noticeable increase in the occurrence of discussions and dialogue around death and dying in the media in 2014. Hardly a day goes by when we don't hear of a documentary, a book release, or a radio interview that involves the topic of death and dying. Billy Connelly's *Big Send Off*, a documentary aired in July 2014, followed Billy embarking on a personal and enlightening journey looking at our attitudes towards death. It was heart wrenching at times to watch him have this conversation with 'a cuppa' in hand in front of the camera, but clearly the elements of death he delved into were real and at times confronting for him. The material was fascinating and thought provoking and was interspersed with gently acerbic comments from Connolly.

In a review of the documentary, Jake Wallis Simons said, "This was an intimate portrait of death, from the perspective of a man who is facing it. As, indeed, are we all". Death lends profound equality to us all.

Tender is another documentary which was shown on Australian ABC TV in 2014. It was set against the backdrop of the industrial seaside town of Port Kembla, a feisty and resilient community group (Port Kembla Community Centre) that has determined to take back the responsibility to care for its own dead. Scattered throughout the documentary are stories that cut to the core, revealing why this small band has decided to take on a practice that for many is taboo.

"*Tender* Funerals aim to work with families, the community and area of palliative care, to develop a model of continual care through each stage of the dying process including after death care. The project will seek to realign the care of our dead with the changing values of our culture. There is a desire within the community for a more sustainable, affordable and meaningful funeral practice which builds communities of support and skill while facilitating an authentic experience." http://www.tenderdocumentary.com.au

I am often asked why I seem to be so comfortable around death and I know the answer connects closely to the experiences of my painful childhood. Like many people, I probably have a slanted memory of those years. However, one thing is clear: my mother was an extremely violent and aggressive alcoholic. I recall her frequent suicide threats or actual attempts, as well as her physical and emotional assaults on me or any of my five siblings. Many times I witnessed her graphic attempts at ending her life.

Knowing that my mother might suddenly be gone forever certainly changed my view of life and death. Her suicide attempts taught me that life can change in an instant, suddenly and completely. Living with her was my first experience of the tenuous nature of life. I am sure this is why I developed a sense of detachment and a somewhat nonchalant view of death. In other words, my past experiences prepared me to break through the veil of secrecy that frequently surrounds death.

My past experiences sparked an interest from an early age in wanting to understand why other people seemed so torn apart about death and dying, and also why they feared death.

Research suggests that individuals who experience early-life separation and neglect go on to avoid authentic emotional bonds with others and may adopt a cynical stance about life and death in adulthood. I believe that is probably the case with regard to how I relate to death. My elder brother and my father in later years confirmed that they too, felt life was always hanging by a thread at these times and consequently death was not a distant thought but an ever-present reality.

Introduction

I was certainly much more fearful of my mother's anger and violence than I ever was of her actually dying. I spent many nights lying awake in the early hours, listening, terrified, to her outbursts and wondering what might happen to us. I would wish I were dead or that I might wake from this nightmare, but sadly it was reality and I suffered it for twenty years.

Not surprisingly, one of my younger brothers went on, in many ways, to replicate my mother's life. During his late teens and early twenties he made frequent attempts to take his life until at the age of forty-three he finally succeeded.

I lost my mother, brother and father within a six-year period. The hardest for me was losing my father, who undoubtedly died from a broken heart, two years after the death of my brother. He told me that his biggest regret in life was not being able to 'save Peter'. This is a common reaction among those left behind after a suicide.

Throughout this book I will refer to these losses and how my family coped with the death of my mother, my father and my brother. I recount this history to explain why I am comfortable with the topic of death.

Although most of my childhood memories are negative, frightening and sad, I can finally say that I am thankful for the experiences. They taught me from a very early age to be resilient. I would add, however, that it took me nearly twenty years after my mother's death to find a place of solace, where I understood that she was undeniably afflicted with undiagnosed mental health issues that controlled her daily.

MY NOTES

MY NOTES

MY NOTES

CHAPTER 1

WE KNOW WHEN LIFE BEGINS BUT DEATH CANNOT BE SO EASILY DEFINED

*What we call the beginning is often the end
And to make an end is to make a beginning
The end is where we start from.*
T.S Eliot: Four Quartets – Little Gidding

Determining when a person has died in itself can be much more complicated than one might expect and the reality is that medicine is blurring the lines between life and death. Another element to consider is what happens to our 'soul', if such a thing exists, at the time of death.

No matter what your belief, the reality is that there is a physical beginning and a physical end to life, as we know it. One of life's strange twists is that one tends to live it forward, but only understand it by looking backwards.

In April 2013 I met with Cath McKinney, a pastor at St Martin's in Collingwood, at the Centre for Theology and Ministry in Parkville, Melbourne. As I listened to her refer to "bearing witness at birth and death" I realised the importance of bearing witness to the body right from the very beginning (birth) right through to the end (death). Bearing witness calls us to be present with the suffering and the joy in the world, without judgment or attachment to the outcome. Cath McKinney had recently been involved with the death of a community member and because the family was unable to be with the person at the time of his death, Cath took on that role. It affected her profoundly.

On what basis do we determine death?

When thinking about the question as to 'when is a person dead?', I came to realise that the answer is far from simple. It is an age-old question which has been debated for centuries. If you were to ask at what point does a person actually die, I would suggest that it depends on who you ask. To one person it's the moment the heart stops beating. To another, it's when the brain enters a 'vegetative' state. But a heart can be forced to keep beating; and how dead is a person really, if they can continue to grow, develop and even, in the case of women, give birth after experiencing 'brain death'?

Some patients who have been declared brain dead can begin spontaneous breathing hours later. Medical scientists say that is irrelevant because most brain dead patients do not come back to life. However, a rigorous scientist would say that these cases speak loudly about the flaws in our criteria for death. And, yes, death to a cardiologist means that the heart has stopped and cannot be restarted. But to a neurologist it might mean something else.

◐ DID YOU KNOW?
In 1968, a committee at Harvard Medical School published an article stating that there is a second kind of death: brain death. Even though the heart is still pumping, and one is still able to breathe on a ventilator, the brain stem is not functioning and therefore that person is regarded as brain dead. In 1981 this definition of death was made law in all fifty states of the United States, so now there are two types of legal death in the United

States: real death (cardiopulmonary death) and what some doctors term 'pretty dead', or 'brain death'.

The *Uniform Determination of Death Act* is a State Law that was approved for the United States in 1981. The Act has since been adopted by most US States and is intended to provide a comprehensive and medically sound basis for determining death in all situations.

According to this Act, an individual is dead when he or she 'has sustained either (1) irreversible cessation of circulatory and respiratory functions, or (2) irreversible cessation of all functions of the entire brain, including the brain stem'. This legislation continues to be the subject of debate. Some suggest that it has three primary shortcomings: first, it fails to define the critical term 'irreversible'; second, irreversible absence of circulation is sufficient for death but not necessary; and third, irreversible absence of circulation may be a mechanism of death but is not death itself.

Clearly the core issue of what is the 'appropriate conceptual definition of death' will continue to be debated endlessly.

What is the point of death if someone is suffering from Alzheimer's or dementia?

For a family member who has watched an elderly person lose their mental capacity due to Alzheimer's disease or dementia, their answer might be that they have lost that person already, maybe even years ago, even though the person is still alive physically. The person as they knew them no longer exists.

When someone is in the later stages of Alzheimer's or dementia it is at this point that we can experience what we call an ambiguous loss. It is a tangible sense of loss even though the person is still 'here'. That loss is caused by the fact that the person we once knew no longer exists in that same state. However, the grieving over this may be different than if they had died from a heart attack for example, without the onset of a neurological illness.

Is there a soul? If so, what happens to it at the time of death?

Is there such a thing as a soul and, if so, how is it defined? When we consider whether there is such a thing as the soul I am mindful that the soul is something that can be thought about in religious or spiritual terms and that some people may not believe in the existence of a soul at all.

With my limited religious upbringing, my recollection of what the 'soul' meant to those that believed in one was always couched in biblical terms, that is the soul is an immortal component of human beings; that upon our death, it is released from our bodies to spend eternity in either eternal bliss or eternal torment, depending on our conduct in this life.

From a spiritual point of view, Deepak Chopra describes the soul as "... your core consciousness. It is the ground of your being. The soul is also the co-influence in the meaning context of relationship and archetypal stories. The soul is the source of all our lives. It projects as the mind, as the body and the universe of our experiences."

On the other hand if we were to ask an atheist like Keith Cornish of the Atheist Foundation of Australia, he says; "Atheists maintain that the concept of humankind having a unique supernatural 'soul' is simply a primitive notion which has no basis in fact and that religious organisations are guilty of perpetrating a colossal fraud on ignorant and gullible people, chiefly through the indoctrination of infants".

I acknowledge that everyone will have a different opinion of what the soul is, whether it exists and what, if anything, they believe will happen to it. When working with families assisting them with a dying family member, or with a family organising a funeral, I am careful not to let my personal beliefs and opinions influence how I work with the client.

Differing views of death

Different cultures and religions have their own views on what happens when a person dies, but most of them have one thing in common - the belief in an afterlife. What that afterlife looks like differs according to the religion and culture. If we take a look at other cultures and their ideas and thoughts about death, it is interesting to note both the differences and the similarities.

Ian Brock in his foreword to Joan Halifax's book *Being with Dying* says: "Whilst the dominant orientation of Western culture towards death is avoidance, for over 2,500 years Buddhists have studied the question of how one can best live in the presence of death. In a sense, a life-threatening injury or disease makes Buddhists of us all, waking us from the illusion of immortality, suddenly and from that time forth. From the moment of diagnosis, death becomes the bell that won't stop ringing".

In Hinduism, death is not viewed as abhorrent or the end of existence but simply a step in the existence of the soul, a temporary cessation of physical activity or life on earth. Since Hindus believe in reincarnation and the transmigration of the soul, they approach the subject of death without much fear.

The Mormons believe that someday, like everyone else, your physical body will die but that your spirit does not die. It goes to the spirit world where it continues to learn and progress, where it may be with loved ones who have passed on.

In New Zealand, the Maori believe that those who have died are always with the Marae (the traditional meeting place of Maori people) and that the recently dead are released into the care of those long dead. It is important to Maori people that the dead be brought together to be greeted, respected and farewelled. They believe that the spirit does not leave the vicinity of the body until the time of the burial.

In conclusion, I suggest that the end of life is not as simple to describe or comprehend as one might think. Even the medical fraternity struggles with a definitive answer regarding the moment of death, that will satisfy everyone. It just shows that no one has the definitive answer and the debate is likely to continue for a long time yet.

#POINTS TO CONSIDER

- → The answer to 'when is a person dead?' can be quite complex, especially if considered from a medical perspective.
- → If a person is suffering from dementia, the point when the person no longer recognises anyone and has no involvement with the world around them, may be the 'time of death' emotionally to their loved ones.
- → The 'soul' means different things to different people.
- → Different cultures have their own opinions as to what happens when and after you die.

MY NOTES

MY NOTES

CHAPTER 2

WHY IS IT IMPORTANT TO HAVE AN INFORMED CONVERSATION ABOUT DEATH AND DYING?

Our lives begin to end the day we become silent about things that matter
— Martin Luther King Jr.

As mentioned in the Introduction, one of the primary aims of this book is to ensure we are well informed of all aspects regarding end-of-life care, dying and death. Making irreversible decisions in the absence of all the information is naturally unwise and, in this situation, may have long-term effects. Having a conversation with only partial information is not constructive and in some instances can cause distress and anxiety.

For example, funeral directors may come into a family and only give them the choices they want them to know about, giving them limited choices when there are far more options available to them.

Sadly, the reason that information on death and dying is not readily available and in fact is often difficult to find, is not always honourable. The funeral industry generally does not want this information readily available to the public. This is evident in the number of resources published, providing this invaluable information. These include *Funeral Rights* by Robert Larkins and *The American Way of Death* by Jessica Mitford.

By providing all the information in this book you will be able to find, use, and share highly relevant, easily accessible, and clear information during the decision-making process.

A well-informed person can be an active partner in decision-making about their care or the care of others, with realistic expectations about the likely or potential outcomes of their treatment. The additional level of awareness is a safeguard against potential errors or adverse outcomes.

It is only when you are well informed that you are likely to achieve the best possible outcome.

Reasons why you should have the conversation

Talking about death within a family, or with friends, can have the most amazing effect. When we can sit and chat about death in the context of an inclusive dialogue, regardless of whether a death is imminent or not, and find out each other's beliefs or how they would like their end of life to be, it is extremely healthy. It allows anyone facing death to approach it with as much normality as they can manage.

Here are some of the reasons it is important to have this conversation.

- It enables us to gather general information about the death and dying process.
- It enables us to talk without the sheer emotion that exists when a death occurs.
- We can speak about any fears and anxieties.
- The discussion is had in a comfortable, less hurried manner.
- It empowers people to take charge of their own death.
- We have an opportunity to work out what is important and avoid confusion later.
- We get to work out what is the perceived quality-of-life, or what

- is acceptable.
- We can determine if organ donation is desirable.
- We have a chance to determine preferable basic practical outcomes, e.g. burial or cremation, spreading of ashes, type of coffin or no coffin.
- It enables a discussion that informs choices.
- It gives us an opportunity to be informed of many options we may not normally know about or be aware of.
- We make ourselves aware of our loved one's end-of-life wishes.
- There is clarity around **our** wishes, our fears, and our concerns.
- The dying person's wishes can be followed.
- The information about the dying person's wishes is easy to locate.
- Understanding a person's choices of end-of-life outcomes becomes a great comfort to us and our loved ones.
- It will contribute to us being able to die with dignity.
- It gives us a chance to tell someone how we feel about them.
- We can share the difficult feelings around this topic, e.g. it's easier if you can talk about it together.
- Healthy discussions enhance healthy relationships.
- It can bring people and families together.

The risks of not having a conversation

- It can lead to far more grief than necessary.
- It can make dying and death very frightening.
- We can feel very alone.
- It leads to more guilt because you may wish that you had facilitated the conversation sooner.
- Life can often change in an instant - life is fickle – death even more so. If someone is in a tragic accident or has a stroke and no conversations have been had, we are then left wondering what their wishes might have been. Would they want to be on life support? Were they happy to donate their organs? Etc.

- It can lead to greater stress at the time of death because you have to guess what the person would have wanted. This in itself is painful and distressing to everyone.
- Family connections and interactions can and do change. If a conversation has not occurred and family members are no longer speaking to each other or connections are fractured, it can lead to very uncomfortable, negative discussions where people are struggling with their own needs.

A media release by Palliative Care Australia in May 2014 stated that after surveying 1000 Australians, although 82% said it was important to have plans in place should anything unfortunate happen to them, only 5% had actually made an advance care plan. Only one-third were even aware that such a thing exists. The report also went on to say that this lack of conversation and discussion was likely to affect the choice and quality of end-of-life care for Australians.

If we can value and hold onto an awareness of what arises from the discussions, then it will consolidate relationships on many levels; whether about death and dying or just the feelings such discussions create. This process can be comforting and reassuring.

Death can come in so many different ways and through different circumstances and at any time; indeed sometimes we get very little notice at all. For many reasons and regardless of how a death might occur, it is extremely helpful to have a healthy discussion about end of life, death and dying sooner rather than later. In a world of uncertainty life all too often teaches us there is an inherent danger in postponement.

To those facing death time is of paramount importance, so it is vital to ensure their time is used wisely and is not taken up with negative discussions or a family struggling with its own needs and desires as to outcome.

Can people influence the timing of their death?

Don't think for a moment that people can't influence the timing of their own death – they can! Also, don't be lulled into a false sense of security because someone may seem to have a lot longer to live than might actually be the case. Timing is important – even in death.

This is no more apparent than when we hear of a situation where a person has died the very moment their family or friends have left the room. This can be difficult for family members who often rally around the deathbed, frequently on a rostered basis, only to find that the one time they left the room the person had slipped away.

I know first hand that my father managed to influence his time of death, whilst still fully cognisant, after being told he could no longer live the life he wanted. Given that his mind was far more powerful than his body at that time, he died very soon after absorbing this devastating information. Some family members felt they had not had the conversation with him that they would have liked had they known he would only live a few more days.

Having said all this, it would be remiss of me not to add that I don't see any benefit at all in pressuring a person to have this discussion if they really don't want to and are not ready and willing.

MY NOTES

MY NOTES

MY NOTES

CHAPTER 3

HOW TO MAKE THIS CHALLENGING CONVERSATION EASIER

Where the mind is without fear and the head is held high
Where knowledge is free
Where the world has not been broken up into fragments by
narrow domestic walls
Where words come out from the depth of truth
Where tireless striving stretches its arms towards perfection
Where the clear stream of reason has not lost its way
into the dreary desert sand of dead habit
Where the mind is led forward by thee into ever-widening
thought and action – Into that heaven of freedom, my Father,
let my country awake.

— Rabindranath Tagore

Why is it so hard to have the conversation?

What stops us from having this conversation about death and dying? These days we can openly discuss everything else - our sexual exploits and those of others, children's toilet training and family secrets are all fair game for talk shows and dinner conversation - so why not death?

I am not sure there is a definitive answer as to why this particular conversation is so difficult but two of the key reasons may be that:

- fear and anxiety underpin most conversations about this topic;
- the dynamics between various family members and their respective relationships are naturally all different;

The point at which a conversation will occur in a person's life will vary.

This conversation may occur at anytime but here are some scenarios:

- When those concerned are still in good health and there is no foreseeable or imminent death (the preferred scenario);
- A family with teenage children;
- An elderly couple and their family;
- Two friends having a conversation;
- When a friend or extended family member has died;
- After a funeral when death is top of mind;
- When someone is unwell;
- A young couple with a terminally ill child;
- When a friend's child is unwell;
- When a friend is unwell;
- When any close friend or family member has been diagnosed with a terminal illness;
- When a mother or father of any age has a terminal illness;
- When there is uncertainty around a diagnosis;
- When a death has occurred under any circumstances;
- A family with young children;
- A family with teenage children;
- An older couple, either between themselves or with family;
- Between family members

No matter what the situation is, it is still a hard conversation to have and, for most of us, I expect fear and anxiety rather than a lack of time will be behind the following sorts of excuses:

- It's just too hard;
- It's morbid;
- I'll cry;
- I don't want others to cry;
- I'm not sure who to have the discussion with;
- If I choose to speak with a particular person I'm afraid of upsetting other people;
- I find it too difficult to gather people together;
- How do I know that thinking about it might not make it come true;
- Members of my family have different religious views;
- Some of my family members believe in an afterlife and it would be difficult/impossible to have the discussion;
- I don't think my family will cope with the discussion;
- I am worried I will get upset or I'll upset someone else;
- The thought of terminal illness makes me feel sick;
- I don't want to deal with the reality of a terminal diagnosis; it's too frightening and overwhelming;
- I don't want to think about facing my own mortality;
- The thought of a family member dying makes me feel very sad;
- My family never agrees on anything;
- I may be being selfish but I just don't want to have the conversation!

All of the above excuses may be valid but nevertheless they are still excuses and should not prevent us from having the conversation.

Another reason for not having this conversation might be concern about the reaction it might cause, be it aggression, intimidation, bullying, severe sadness or depression. I suggest that if you find yourself on the receiving end of an aggressive or overly emotional reaction, you cease the conversation immediately and perhaps seek professional assistance.

Unpacking some of the difficulties

Now that we have identified some of the excuses as to 'why it's so hard to have the conversation' it might be helpful to briefly elaborate on each one.

Fear and anxiety

To the best of my knowledge, there are few specific studies devoted directly to examining the reasons for fearing death. However the list of excuses above, compiled over my twenty years' experience in this field, tells me that fear and anxiety underpin just about every excuse offered. It is therefore important to address the subject of fear and anxiety generally.

Confronting death and the anxiety generated by knowledge of its inevitability is a universal psychological quandary. Death is inevitable, regardless of the increasing technologically advances in health systems and medical developments. No matter which way we look at it we are all going to die.

How anxious or accepting are we about the prospect of our own death? Death anxiety means feeling fear, horror, and worry toward death or anything leading to death. In addition, some studies indicate that death anxiety is more prevalent in western rather than eastern culture. (Schumaker et. Al, 1991; McMordie & Kumar, 1984).

Mark Edinberg a psychologist, author and organisational consultant says: 'I think that most families do not talk about death directly. That is, it is not customary at the dinner table to say: "Please pass the vegetables and, by the way, have you all thought about when you are going to die?"

Edinberg continues, "We all know at some level that we will die, but somehow saying this to our parents (or our children) is not easily accomplished. Probably this is due to several factors, including feeling sad (grief) when having the discussion (which can be avoided by not having the discussion at all), being scared about what happens after death, being scared about what happens before you die, or other forms of uneasiness that have been lumped into a technical term, 'death anxiety'. Most research shows that older people have no less death anxiety than young people, by the way."

I believe our basic instinct to survive plays a larger role in our fear than we realise. I am curious to know if the unwillingness to face this fear with proper understanding is due to the emphasis we place upon the physical body. Is it also based upon an innate fear of loneliness due to the loss of those we have been familiar with during our life?

I have come to believe that once the fear of death ceases, in many instances it gives us a certain power over the end of our life journey and the process of dying, and that can bring a great sense of peace. Many people worry about losing control leading up to death and don't like the idea of handing control over to anyone. This is especially so when nearing or facing death. As a person approaches the very end of life there are physical changes that take place as the body begins to shut down its regular functions. There are changes on the emotional and spiritual level as well, in which the dying person lets go of the body and the material world. When someone fears losing control and allowing others to make decisions, often without consultation, this can be very distressing.

When we lose control over the decision making process it often feels as though:

- we can no longer live the life we want to live;
- we have to end our life living in a dreaded nursing home;
- we have to have medical procedures that we simply don't want to have, simply to satisfy the medical staff that they have tried everything. At the same time it conveys to our family that we have tried to hang on for as long as possible even though this may be far longer than we ourself would wish;

- we have to die in a hospital;
- we have to sit this out when others have no understanding of how awful this disease is;
- we can't make decisions for ourselves anymore.

This by no means covers the entire spectrum of fear and anxiety around death and dying, but it gives a brief overview.

If you are afraid to have this conversation you should book a conversation with yourself first, to examine what you are afraid of. If you can do some work on your fears it will definitely help you when you eventually have this conversation with someone close to you. This may even mean having a session with a therapist or counsellor.

This conversation needs to include the end-of-life process, dying and the death itself.

It's just too hard

There is no doubt that for most of us this is a difficult conversation. But we have difficult conversations regularly throughout our lifetime and this is one of the most important we should have. I know from personal experience that once the conversation is started it becomes much more comfortable as it develops and it makes it easier to open the conversation again at a later time, whenever either party might feel the need to talk about it.

It's morbid

Actually this is not a morbid subject at all! Talking openly about death means that we can support each other, our families and ourselves when death has an impact on our life. It makes for a healthier, happier community of family and friends when our beliefs and concerns are out in the open. It is understandable that many people find the topic of death depressing and so shy away from it as much as possible. However, it does not need to be sad or gloomy at all. In fact it can be quite uplifting and empowering.

I'll cry or I don't want others to cry

I want to reassure you that crying is inevitable and I would be very surprised if this didn't happen at some stage during the conversation. Crying is a common response when anyone is thinking or talking about death. It is normal and healthy to express our emotions through tears.

We often worry about crying in front of others and setting someone else off, but it is normal for people to get teary during a conversation of this nature, because clearly we are talking about the inevitability of losing someone dear to us at some point in the future. Talking about some practical elements might assist rather than getting into the more emotional aspect of the conversation too soon. I cannot emphasise enough the importance that humour and laughter play in helping cope with these types of conversations.

I'm not sure who to include in the conversation

This will depend largely on who initiates the conversation – that is the dying person, a family member, a friend, et al. However, from any perspective it is important to think carefully about who is included, who participates in the conversation. Naturally we want a positive outcome, especially as this could well become a precursor for future conversations.

For example:

- If you are trying to gather family members to talk about elderly parents, you may wish to gather all the adults in the immediate family;
- If you are the one who is dying from a terminal illness, I've noticed that initially the smaller the group the more comfortable this

conversation seems to be. So you may wish to gather your children, siblings and/or parents and extended family, after having had a conversation with your next of kin - husband/wife/partner;
- If you are a close friend of someone who is dying you may wish to gather a small group of very close friends together to have this conversation;
- If you are having a general conversation about death and dying when no one is ill it doesn't matter who is in the conversation.

If I choose to speak with a particular person then I may upset others

Yes there is always a possibility that other people may get upset that we didn't confide in them initially, but I must emphasise how important it is to take that risk, because we need to start the conversation with someone. The advantages of taking that risk far outweigh not having the conversation at all. Ultimately others will see that there was a need to start the conversation somewhere.

I find it too difficult to gather people together

We may find gathering family members together difficult because of geographic locations. If this is the case we can avail ourselves of technology such as Skype or conference calls to facilitate this process. It may be difficult because we all lead very busy lives nowadays, or perhaps there is a strained family history or difficult dynamics. However, like any other important situation in life, we have to make time to deal with it. This is, after all, one of the most important conversations we will have.

How do I know that thinking about it might not make it come true?

There are many good reasons for using positive affirmations in your daily life, believing that a *positive* mindset begets *positive* end results. However there is no empirical evidence to suggest that this works in reverse.

Thinking negatively will not result in something awful happening. Having a conversation about death is not going to bring it about.

Members of my family have different religious views

Don't worry this is not an uncommon scenario. There are innumerable *different religions* and philosophical *belief* systems and many families hold different beliefs within the same family. However, regardless of our beliefs we have a responsibility to have this conversation and let others know how we feel. It might be surprising how accommodating others can be if the discussion is approached in a sensitive and open-minded way. We don't all have to agree. This conversation is more about voicing and understanding each other's thoughts and beliefs than coming to an agreement. Certain religions have particular beliefs around the practical elements of timing of the funeral, or whether a person should be buried or cremated. It is especially important to have this discussion when there are different beliefs within a family as it can alleviate any confusion about the dying person's wishes, clarifying their own needs.

Some of my family members believe in an afterlife and therefore there would be no reason to have the discussion

As stated previously, these conversations are about end-of-life care, dying and death, so the views anyone may have about what happens after death is a separate conversation which you may or may not want to have. However the discussion about the end-of-life care, death and dying is still absolutely essential.

People don't cope with 'the conversation'

Although it may be difficult to have a conversation about death and dying, people do cope. 'The conversation' requires everyone to show compassion and care for each other, allowing everyone's voice to be heard. There are times when it will inevitably lead to discussions where our own thoughts about death will get in the way of an honest and open dialogue with a dying or elderly person. Difficult or not, at the end of 'the conversation' we are usually relieved that the discussion took place.

The thought of terminal illness makes me feel sick; I don't want to deal with the reality of a terminal diagnosis - it's too frightening and overwhelming

Whether it is your own diagnosis or some else's, this is a very normal reaction to the very idea of a terminal illness. The reality is that a diagnosis has been made and it is better to talk about it and be honest about the future.

- If you are **the person with the terminal illness** the reality of a terminal diagnosis might be overwhelming initially as it can be a threat to our sense of control, but thankfully most do learn to accept and adapt to the news. Naturally most people are deeply shocked when a terminal diagnosis is initially pronounced. Acceptance or accommodation of the diagnosis might be the most desirable outcome of the conversation you can hope for.
- If you are a person **having a conversation with a terminally ill person**, having a churning stomach for a short time is a small price to pay for the value this conversation offers. It is an opportunity to learn about each other's hopes, of being confided in and of many other feelings. Certain decisions made during the period of diagnosis and death can be quite difficult for some family members or friends to accept, nonetheless this conversation needs to take place.

The thought of a family member dying makes me feel very sad

Such feelings of sadness are very normal when we think of family members or close friends not being around forever. But how much better is it to have a positive conversation and be there for each other, despite the sadness?

My family never agrees on anything

Does any family? This conversation may be no different from many other family discussions where family members often disagree. It may be that we are not asking or expecting everyone to agree, as the conversation might be intended purely to let our wishes be known within a general discussion. Disagreement should not prevent us from having the conversation.

Taking a selfish stand is no excuse either

Some of us might think that it's just too hard to have the discussion and flatly refuse to participate in a conversation around death and dying. As hard as these conversations might be I implore anyone who feels this way not to be selfish. If we don't want to have 'the talk', remember there may be other family members who **need** it. This conversation usually assists family members and is a discussion well worth having. What price do we pay for allowing selfishness to get in the way of one of the most important discussions we will have in our lifetime?

It doesn't matter what the reason is for not having the conversation, it is still an excuse.

#POINTS TO CONSIDER

- → This conversation can be difficult, however once started it gets easier
- → Don't put off what could be done today
- → Your family will thank you – maybe not right now but they will in the future
- → Fear and anxiety can underpin why these conversations are difficult
- → There are plenty of excuses – but none in any way are good reasons not to have the conversation

MY NOTES

MY NOTES

MY NOTES

CHAPTER 4

THE IMPORTANCE OF RELATIONSHIPS AND OTHER CONNECTIONS

*Friendship improves happiness and abates misery
by doubling our joys and dividing our grief*
— Marcus Tullius Cicero

Our lives are built around different relationships. Most people have relationships with family members, close friends, casual acquaintances, co-workers and others. Some relationships are tenuous and some are strong but each of them has the potential to change and grow, which also alters the impact of a death. The depth of these connections inevitably affects our conversations when death is imminent. Naturally they also reflect the intensity of our experience when a death has occurred.

When someone close to us dies, we have a fundamental need to talk to someone about it.

I have noticed that when someone is diagnosed with a terminal illness or when there is a death in the family, relationships are all that matter. Often everything else in life becomes superfluous. We re-evaluate our time commitments and think about what's important. We often rearrange our life to spend more time with the dying person and their extended family. It may also prompt us to look at ways of spending more time with our own family. This is when we often realise that connecting with others is the most important thing we do in our life. It is these relationships that we talk about when someone is facing their own death, or when someone else has died. Some people create their own family which may or may not include blood relatives.

A relationship develops through a genuine conversation, a personal story, eye contact, a listening ear, a laugh, an exchange of a shared feeling or a helping hand.

Stepping beyond the boundaries now and again, to extend an act of kindness, show genuine interest or simply exude positive energy in a sincere smile, can be the building blocks of a great relationship.

Relationships are symbiotic. Both give and both gain. I believe in giving genuinely and generously at the start of a relationship and then giving some more. You can be sure that there is personal reward when you give of yourself to others in a relationship. Giving means offering as little or as much as your comfort level, your time, knowledge, expertise, energy, power or position in life will allow, and watching it come back to you tenfold. This has happened to me in so many ways and still continues to surprise me. I've been a teacher for much of my life, teaching music for twenty-five years, lecturing at University on many business topics, coaching athletics and finally creating my own training college where I could share my skills and teach others around the world. One of the most important lessons has been that sharing a talent brings personal growth and a great sense of fulfilment.

The grief a person feels on a death is usually directly related to their connection with the deceased. I see this on many levels: often the closer the relationship the greater the grief, conversely, the greater the sense of guilt the harder the person may feel the grief. The closer your emotional attachment to the person, the greater the likelihood of having a strong grief reaction.

I have also observed that the death of people we don't know can often have a big impact on our life and trigger a strong grief reaction.

Why do large-scale tragedies affect us?

We usually feel shock and grief when a major disaster occurs, even one that may be a long way from us, or has no actual direct link to us. Tragedies such as the 2001 World Trade Center terrorist attacks or the Malaysian Airlines disasters in 2014 or the 2015 earthquakes that rocked and destroyed much of Nepal or, closer to home the 2009 Black Saturday bushfires. One wonders why we would be so emotionally connected to a death with which we are not directly involved and that is not directly connected to us? One reason I believe is that in this technically advanced world this sort of information is so instantly accessible; we see the terrible pictures of destruction and death, hear victims' stories in graphic detail. It all seems very real and close. We cannot ignore these images and stories and they trigger our own unexpressed grief, our unspoken fears. Also, we may feel deep empathy with the families of those closely related to these tragedies.

Worldwide traumas can leave us with a real sense of confusion and fear and *can* have a significant *impact* on our emotional health and daily functioning. It is not surprising that people not directly related to these tragedies may have difficulty in understanding why they grieve so deeply over these events.

It is not just close relatives or friends whose deaths create a sense of shock. We can also get this same feeling of grief and shock when someone more emotionally distant dies suddenly or in a tragic way. Sometimes it is only when someone has gone that we realise that they were in fact important to us in some way. In 2012 Lyndon Shea, a fellow celebrant and past student at my college, died. At that time I was not aware that he had been unwell, even though I'd known him for a few years and had spoken to his wife just weeks before his death when she was looking for assistance with her best friend's funeral. I struggled after finding out that he had passed away, because although he was a colleague I hadn't been personally close to him. I asked myself why I was so upset and I realised that he and his wife were people I admired greatly and I felt a real sense of loss. I also felt a strong sense of loss for his wife, as they seemed such a great team. I was fortunate to be able to attend Lyndon's funeral, which was held in a hall within a local park and conducted by a personal friend of his. The gentleman who conducted the ceremony did a wonderful job and I found it an immensely uplifting experience, where we all laughed and cried and shared our thoughts about Lyndon.

Lyndon's death came as a shock and I found myself thinking about him constantly for many weeks after, thinking about the enormous contribution he had made during his life. I felt very fortunate to have known him and grateful for the time I had shared with him and his family.

Recent events in Australia such as the death of Phillip Hughes, the Australian International cricketer, and the death of the two hostages in the tragic event in central Sydney in December 2014, are two prime examples of deaths that affected people all over the world. Most of those people had no direct link to any of the fatalities, yet many individuals felt a terrible sense of loss and grief associated with these three deaths.

One reason I believe these 'distant' or unrelated deaths affect us in such a visceral and tangible way is because they tap into deeper grief of previous losses, a grief perhaps unexpressed before and which often sits just below the surface. Naturally any death also tends to bring our own mortality to the fore.

It seems relationships suddenly seem to matter so much more when you know you are dying. It is not uncommon for a terminally ill person to be told by a doctor to 'put things in order at home'. The implication here is 'make sure you don't die with regrets about things left unsaid' as well as 'sorting your practical affairs'. One wonders why it takes the 'stark reality of death' for us to see the importance of relationships? I hear people with who I work say they "wish they had said this or that", and "*if only* they'd had time to say what they wanted to the person". I wonder if this is the result of denial, denying you will die or is it simply our nature to take things and people for granted?

Impending death has a way of unexpectedly unearthing the past so that it comes together with the present, sometimes in an unpleasant and difficult way. This can be the reason people hesitate in having those difficult conversations.

Ginny

Whilst writing this book close friend and work colleague Ginny Bydder was diagnosed with a terminal illness. Initially she was given 3-6 months to live. It came as a shock because up until that point she had seemed quite healthy and was leading a very normal life. After a few tests Gynny was initially diagnosed with stomach cancer. However the doctors soon realised that her situation was worse than first thought and subsequently she was diagnosed with 8 brain tumours.

Ginny in her usual no-fuss style decided to put her affairs in order to ensure that her husband Michael was looked after and that her wishes were complied with. I assisted her in obtaining some necessary paperwork and organised a discussion with Dr Rodney Syme of Dying with Dignity Victoria. She wanted to plan all that she could to ensure as much as was possible that she had a 'good death' and that she was able to stay in control of her treatment and medication.

Two months down the track Ginny's life had changed completely from the life she previously led. She had worked for me for a few years and, as my right hand person, had been instrumental in co-creating a training course for new celebrants. During these years we spent a lot of time together and talked every day about student' assessment and the course in general. She had completed the funeral celebrant course with me, but clearly found her passion was in weddings, not funerals. Within two months of her diagnosis she found it difficult to do the simplest tasks and her days were now spent sleeping and trying to manage her energy and pain levels as best she could.

She was quite happy with her lot in life and seemed to accept the difficult blow she had been dealt. Thankfully she had not lost her sense of humour and we laughed when she realised she would never have to experience Alzheimer's or dementia, which was a huge relief for her. She was more than happy to let go and not have treatment that could easily have left her in a painful state for the remainder of her days. She wanted to live out the four to six weeks she had left in a pain-free way and enjoy the time she could spend with her husband and chosen family and friends.

What effect does not seeing eye to eye have on a conversation?

I didn't always see eye to eye with my dying friend Ginny, especially the discussions we shared about the fact that she did not want a funeral. Her husband Michael and others were not keen on this decision and would rather have had some way of celebrating her life and being able to grieve as a group. I did continue to talk with Michael and Ginny about what if anything, might be acceptable to them both. However Ginny was adamant that she did not want a funeral and we were not able to change her mind.

Ginny was so well organised and adamant that her instructions were blatantly clear. Whether we liked it or not, we followed her instructions out of respect for her, but undoubtedly it was difficult at times when we didn't agree with her decisions. She was particular about who she chose to surround herself with and that was only a handful of people. There is no right or wrong in this situation. Ginny had the right to make decisions for herself and we had a duty to follow them through for her sake.

Ginny's husband was very supportive in her decision not to

undergo further treatment than she absolutely had to, which is often an extremely difficult decision for those involved. On the one hand you want the person not to have any unnecessary treatment that might just delay the inevitable and possibly reduce the quality of life they have left, but on the other hand there is always the thought that a miracle cure may be found. For Ginny her prognosis was clear and her oncologist agreed that any further treatment would not be in her interests. At least she could spend the rest of the life she had left living the best she could without having to undergo any painful or unnecessary treatment.

Ginny planned how she would die, she was not afraid of death. She wanted no fanfare and she was to be cremated immediately. And so she was.

I am proud to say that my friend and colleague died a very dignified death. Soon after Ginny's death Michael, her sister Jackie, her cousin Linda and friend Margi and I said our farewells and spread Ginny's ashes in her backyard whilst her two dogs played around us. It was a sad day but we enjoyed spending the precious time together sharing stories and anecdotes about Ginny's life and allowing the healing process to begin.

The benefits of strong, close relationships

Most pull away from sharing their innermost thoughts and feelings. It is not in everyone's nature to express their feelings easily. I admire people for their ability to speak about how they feel without fearing how others might react. Our feelings are important because they help us to know ourselves, to be real, and to connect more deeply with other people. It is refreshing when a person is able to communicate easily, but not many people in life have that facility.

As the Dalai Lama has written in his book *Compassion*, "...ultimately, the reason why love and compassion bring the greatest happiness is simply that our nature cherishes them above all else". The need for love lies at the very foundation of human existence. This is part of the profound interdependence we all share. However capable and skilful an individual may be, left alone, he or she will not survive. However vigorous and independent one may feel when life is going well, when one is sick or very young or very old, one must depend on the support of others.

Connections to others satisfy a basic human need in us to be close to and supported by others. We are happier, healthier and live longer when we have strong, close relationships in our life. If we think about the role social media has in life one could conclude that it is easier to forge relationships because it is easier to stay connected via the internet. I would suggest this is not the case, because although social media allows us to stay in touch, it does not really foster relationships that create solid foundations. Maintaining a strong relationship over a period takes time takes effort.

How do people react when informed of a terminal illness?

When faced with the terminal illness of a loved one, each person's journey is individual. I have noticed that relationships do not usually change when people are faced with bad news. Similarly, family dynamics in the hospital often remain consistent with the dynamics experienced throughout life. It is important to build on relationship strengths that were in place before the terminal illness was diagnosed. It is also important to be open to the possibility of healing a broken relationship during this time of flux. As a result, many find this time to be among the richest of their life.

Naturally, there are those who do struggle to cope with this type of life-changing news and some very close friends just might find it too difficult and withdraw. Raising the topic of death and dying can be difficult, but once the discussion is out in the open it is much easier for all involved.

People often worry about what they can say to someone who is dying but I would encourage you to talk about the situation with them. It is quite usual that once someone is given a terminal diagnosis and has reached the stage of acceptance they are very likely to want to talk. It is at such a time that one often hears wonderful stories of their life that may never have been recounted otherwise.

Listening to someone talk about the fact that they know they don't have long to live, and being able to sit with them as they discuss their medical treatment can be very beneficial. It is a good opportunity for you to have a conversation with them about 'where to from here?' and to find out what would assist them most - a call every few days - a hand with the housework - cooking some food - assisting with a roster for transport to and from treatment or anything they feel might be helpful. Let the person decide and don't be disappointed with their answer, as hard as that might be. Continue to offer that assistance whenever possible, because things change and what was rejected once might not be rejected on another occasion.

You need to be aware and understand that this is a difficult time and the person themselves may not know what they want done from one day to the next. But it is important to always be there for them, in whatever capacity you can manage. Remember that this is a situation that changes from day to day and that it can change in an instant. When patients are going through treatment it can be very onerous for all family members. Patience can be stretched, finances can be stretched and tolerance can be stretched.

◐ **DID YOU KNOW?**

People with a life-limiting illness want to feel they are living with the disease, not dying from it. But that can be difficult unless they have the right team, and right support network around them.

Who are we after a death?

Where there is a strong relationship and an impending death, we then start to wonder what happens to the relationship when they're gone. Who are you? What will your role be now?

Petrea King of the Quest For Life Foundation says, "We often identify who we are through our relationships and so when a person dies we are confronted by those deep existential questions of ... well who am I, what is my role in life, is there any role for me now in my life, given I knew who I was when that person was here, but now I don't know who I am?"

After the death of someone close, our life will never be the same without them. However, grief can help bring maturity. Sometimes, the death of someone close leads those left behind to find a new inner strength which was not evident before. Sometimes we can care for an elderly or sick person for a very long time and during that time we can neglect our own needs. So when death occurs we have a chance to reconnect to others, find ourself again or reinvent ourself.

Anthony Robbins, life coach, self-help author and motivational speaker said, "The quality of your life is the quality of your relationships".

#POINTS TO CONSIDER

→ Good relationships are symbiotic; they assist and support both parties.
→ Often the closer the relationship the greater the grief.
→ Many people are not able to express their feelings easily.
→ We often identify who we are through our relationships.
→ Lives are changed as a result of a death.

MY NOTES

MY NOTES

MY NOTES

CHAPTER 5

RIGHTS, CHOICES AND THE LAW: WHAT WE NEED TO KNOW

Almost everything - all external expectations, all pride, all fear of embarrassment or failure - these things just fall away in the face of death, leaving only what is truly important. Remembering that you are going to die is the best way I know to avoid the trap of thinking you have something to lose. You are already naked.
There is no reason not to follow your heart.

– Steve Jobs

The next few sections will deal with the issues around end of life, dying and death. From palliative care, to advance care planning, The Medical Treatment Act, the Baby Boomers' approach to death and dying (baby boomers are those people born between the years 1946 and 1964) and the options or choices we have when a death is imminent or when a death has occurred. There are many decisions to be made at such a time, for example whether or not to use a funeral company when the time comes to arrange the funeral.

> Please remember that the law is dynamic and while every attempt is made to ensure the content in this book is accurate, complete and up-to-date, some laws may be subject to change. If you have a legal query, it is recommended that you seek legal advice from a relevant authority.

PART 1

WHEN A DEATH IS IMMINENT

As mentioned, one of the aims of this book is to provide information on choices, rights and the laws surrounding end of life, dying and death. Because this topic is not widely discussed the public, generally speaking, is often unaware that they do have choices. Perhaps there is also an element of the funeral industry not wanting people to know they have choices because they fear they will lose the business to a competitor, or they think that what you are asking is too hard to facilitate, or perhaps it just doesn't work within their business model.

I am a keen advocate of people's right to choose their own way of living and dying. I want you to know about the choices you have, so that you are well informed to make educated decisions.

Let's have a look at the end-of-life topics covered in this chapter:

- palliative care;
- advance care planning;
- physician assisted dying (PAD);
- the Medical Treatment Act;
- euthanasia;
- dying at home;
- end-of-life care generally;
- end-of-life decisions on treatment;
- legal documents including Enduring Power Of Attorney (if required);
- location/place of death.

Choices regarding the above issues need to be considered from the perspective of the dying person and from the perspective of family and friends. They need to concentrate on how they can get involved in the discussion, assist the dying person with making end-of-life decisions and ensuring that their wishes are followed through.

Let's first look at the nature and scope of end-of-life concerns for people with a life-limiting illness.

Concerns around quality of life

Clearly the only person able to decide on his or her own quality of life should be the dying person. Not the doctors, not their family or (their) friends. There are, of course, some exceptions, such as in cases of dementia or Alzheimer's or other mental incapacity, or in such instances as when a patient is in a coma and therefore unable to make end-of-life decisions.

The concerns will often centre on how your own quality of life is affected:

- physically;
- socially;
- emotionally and psychologically;
- spiritually and existentially.

I attended a conference run by the Australian Psychological Society in Melbourne in August 2013, where a group of psychologists discussed the topic: *When a cure is not possible: end-of-life issues*. We, the participants, spent the day discussing what a person might encounter as they approach death, relating to quality of life.

It is likely that a dying person will undergo pain, confusion, loss of function, reduction in activity, increased psychological distress and disruption to social activities. Some of the physical difficulties may be related to the condition or treatment and could include fatigue, pain, vomiting and constipation. If we have a life-limiting illness we may not be able to care for ourself, we might have problems with mobility and may have gone from being independent to being dependent, often in a very short period of time. Those who find this transition difficult may become quite defensive about needing help and may have difficulty accepting support from others, to the extent that they become angry with those trying to help.

Societal changes could mean a change in the dying person's role in life. There may be separation from family, after which there will be new dependencies. We may have to give up work, which often creates a financial strain. We might find ourselves becoming socially isolated, which can strain close relationships.

Some of the emotional and psychological issues are frequently unrecognised and under-treated at the end of life. Some of the emotional issues that can come into play are anger, loss of control, fear, hopelessness and helplessness, uncertainty, loss of dignity, anxiety and depression, grief and loss (anticipatory and actual) and guilt. This is especially so when someone is dying from what one might term a self-inflicted disease such as alcoholism or smoking, or when a symptom has been left unchecked and undiagnosed until it is too late.

There is often an increase in 'death anxiety' when treatment becomes ineffective, which often presents as depression. This anxiety however can be reduced when patients obtain accurate information and are able to take control of what they can.

It is important to mention that grief has often been incorrectly diagnosed as depression. As Andrew Solomon suggests in his TED Talk, *Depression, the secret we share* (October 2013), "...people often tend to confuse depression, sadness and grief. Grief is explicitly reactive. If you have a loss and you feel incredibly unhappy and then six months later you are deeply sad but you are functioning a little better then it's probably grief, and it will ultimately resolve itself in some measure. But if you experience a catastrophic loss and you feel terrible and six months later you can barely function at all then it's probably a depression that was triggered by the catastrophic circumstance. The trajectory tells us a great deal. People think of depression as just being sadness, however it is actually much too much sadness, much too much grief and far too slight a cause."

Spirituality and existential issues centre on post-trauma personal growth, searching for meaning and purpose, finding a philosophical explanation for illness and the sense of loss of hope and confrontation with mortality.

Ernest Becker in his book *The Denial of Death* says "…death anxiety tends to become an issue when death is no longer a distant prospect and this is when accurate and reassuring information can reduce the level of anxiety. We do know that caregivers who are comfortable with death are more likely to interact positively with the terminally ill."

The Debate of the Age Health and Care Study Group identified these 'principles of a good death'.

- To know when death is coming, and to understand what can be expected.
- To be able to retain control of what happens.
- To be afforded dignity and privacy.
- To have control over pain relief and other symptom control.
- To have choice and control over where death occurs (at home or elsewhere).
- To have access to information and expertise of whatever kind is necessary.
- To have access to any spiritual or emotional support required.
- To have access to hospice care in any location, not only in hospital.
- To have control over who is present and who shares the end.
- To be able to use advanced health care directives that ensure wishes are respected.

- To have time to say goodbye, and control over other aspects of timing.
- To be able to leave when it is time to go, and not to have life prolonged pointlessly.

When we or a loved one are unwell and nearing death there are quite a lot of choices to consider about how care is managed and even, in many situations, where we die. When people are concerned about end-of-life care their wishes should be written down and the necessary paperwork put in place to ensure their wishes are followed.

This is discussed later in this chapter, under 'Advance care planning'.

Palliative Care

It is worth looking at the current system that most families would be familiar with, regarding palliative care.

Palliative care is care provided by health professionals to patients with an advancing disease or terminal illness, regardless of age. Traditionally, palliative care towards the end of life has been offered mainly to cancer patients. However, it must now be offered for a wider range of serious illnesses and integrated more broadly across health care services. Specialised palliative care services at end of life can be offered either in a hospice, in a hospital or at home.

The goal of palliative care is to improve the quality of life for patients, their families and carers by addressing the many needs they may have. In Australia about 60% of patients have symptom management in a Palliative Care Unit then return home. The other 40% die in palliative care within institutions such as hospital. Patients themselves should be important partners in planning their care and managing their illness. When people are well informed, participate in treatment decisions and communicate openly with their doctors and other health professionals, they help to make their care as effective as possible.

It is natural to expect communications to be challenging when discussing the end of life with the person and their family members. The key component to this discussion being effective is the ability to always convey the seriousness of the illness. This point may need to be reiterated several times in different ways for the patient and their family to fully understand the prognosis. So making it simple and clear, using language at the appropriate level of understanding is imperative.

A complaint often heard from families and from the patient themself is that, in their mind, they were told something which did not eventuate or was not true; such as 'we will get you better'. It is imperative that all health care professionals and all family members are careful with the language they use and ensure they gain confirmation from the patient and their family that they have understood what they have been told. 'Getting you better' might just mean they'll give you pain relief; it may not mean you will be cured fully.

What is the role of the palliative care worker in their end-of-life care of a patient?

In the Royal College of Nursing, Australia statement on this subject, palliative care is defined as "... a concept of care which provides a coordinated medical, nursing and allied health service for people with progressive incurable illnesses, delivered where possible in the environment of the person's choice, and which provides physical, emotional and spiritual support for patients, for families and for friends. The provision of palliative care service includes grief and bereavement support for the family and other carers during the life of the patient and continuing after death."

I interviewed Michelle Hooke, who at the time was Nurse Unit Manager of the Palliative Care Unit at the Olivia Newton-John Cancer and Wellness Centre of the Austin Hospital, Melbourne. Michelle is currently the Nurse Unit Manager of Cabrini Health Palliative Homecare and Consult Services, Melbourne. Michelle has a long and varied involvement with end-of-life management, working with patients and their families for some twenty years. She talked at length about her experiences and the thoughts that she has developed from them. Michelle's story is for those who are dying, for their families and for friends who are caring for them. It may help you become aware of some of the issues that medical staff deal with, and to enable you see how you might need to get more directly involved in making decisions, in order to get the sort of management that suits you.

> ## The Hippocratic Oath
>
> The **Hippocratic Oath** is an oath historically taken by physicians. It is one of the most widely known of Greek medical texts. In its original form, it requires a new physician to swear, by a number of healing gods, to uphold specific ethical standards. Of historic and traditional value, the oath is considered a rite of passage for practitioners of medicine in many countries, although nowadays various modernized versions are often used.
>
> In swearing by the Hippocratic Oath a doctor undertakes to:
>
> Fulfill, to the best of my ability and judgment, the covenant:
>
> Respect the hard-won scientific gains of those physicians in whose steps I walk, and gladly share such knowledge as is mine with those who are to follow.
>
> Apply, for the benefit of the sick, all measures which are required, avoiding those twin traps of overtreatment and therapeutic nihilism.

> Remember that there is art to medicine as well as science, and that warmth, sympathy, and understanding may outweigh the surgeon's knife or the chemist's drug.
>
> Not be ashamed to say "I know not," nor will I fail to call in my colleagues when the skills of another are needed for a patient's recovery.
>
> **Note:** These are just some of the commitments made under the Hippocratic Oath.

A nurse's story

Michelle Hooke has been involved in oncology in the private sector since 1996. Her work has focused around the end of life. In 2002 she became a discharge palliative care consultant of a seventy-bed ward in a major hospital.

In earlier times doctors tended to focus solely on the immediate medical issue and generally didn't look at an individual's overall wellbeing. Michelle wanted the doctors to be much clearer to her, her staff and the families in honestly outlining the true condition and prognosis of the patient. Instead, there was a great deal of ambiguity in communications with the medical professionals, which helped no one.

In 2004 Michelle attended a conference on palliative care which was to have a life-changing impact on her. Most, if not all, of those attending the conference followed the World Health Organisation definition of palliative care from the time of diagnosis. The 'take home message' from the conference was, "We can treat to any degree, but it's not about just about the disease, it's about the individual person."

As she puts it Michelle learnt about the 3 Ds – Death, Dying and Dead. She does not subscribe to using the clichés such as 'going to God', 'passing away', 'going to a better place', because to her these remove honest attention away from death itself. She realised that we have 'anesthetised' death so much that it has become alien to the most people. Fifty years ago or less, death was an integral part of life. Dying doesn't mean that you are already dead: It does mean that you still have time to live. That is what had such a profound effect on Michelle, "That point of view got me thinking and I came back from the conference with a different view of what palliative care should be".

On her return, Michelle tried to implement a number of the things she had learnt at the conference, all of which failed. She felt broken. She was trying to change a culture when she had not been taught how to implement such change. Being in the private sector, she was governed by what the health funds allocated. On a personal level she found that if she was honest and straightforward with her patients and did not shy away from the subject of death, they welcomed that kind of transparency. To her great disappointment she was not able to implement this change across a whole of department.

There were many reasons why Michelle was unable to implement change:

- Culture
- Business structure / lack of money
- Communication issues
- Doctors difficulty with expressing issues around death

Michelle saw many instances of miscommunication. Doctors don't always have good communication skills. In addition, most doctors do not like to talk about death. In Michelle's broad experience they often leave those discussions to other members of staff.

Working alongside the doctors she would hear them say such things as, "Well you can't ever give up hope", and the doctor would continue to treat the patient with blood transfusions and chemotherapy up until the day they died. These people were never given a good death and consequently they did not always have time, or were not well enough, to put their affairs in order or to resolve any personal issues they have may wished to before they died.

Michelle says doctors can lose sight of the right of patients to have a dignified death. It is easy to understand there may be a conflict between 'giving life-prolonging treatment' and 'doing no harm to the patient'. To treat or not to treat: that is the question. Michelle believes that doctors can lose this balance. No doctor wants to see patients enduring unnecessary suffering, but this can happen all too easily if they become so absorbed in diagnostic and treatment options that they lose sight of the individual.

Fortunately Michelle worked with many wonderful doctors who understand quality of life considerations and go to great lengths to explain the treatment and the prognosis and do their all to give a patient the best possible chance, as well as enabling patients to make their own decisions as to how they would like to proceed when treatment is no longer working.

In Michelle's experience, most people do not want to hear all the medical terminology as it means nothing to them. If they are dealing with an end-of-life situation their head and emotions are really completely taken up with that and usually they can't retain anything technical.

Michelle's personal experience casts light on her deeply held beliefs. She says, "My mother's death was a very difficult experience for me and may explain why ever since becoming a nurse it has been important to me to give all patients the benefit of knowing the truth…"

When Michelle was eleven her mother died as a result of an accident. "As my parents were divorced, my grandmother took us to see our mother in the intensive care unit. As the nurses told us that our mother was "doing such a remarkable job", we went away one long weekend. When we came back we were told that our mother was dead. To compound the loss, we were not even allowed to go to the funeral."

"As you can imagine I still have unresolved issues. I still think about going to school the day of her funeral and coming home to find everyone in my house drinking and eating. I was very upset that they were all laughing and my mother was dead, and I didn't understand because I had missed a big part of what I needed to be able to understand what was happening. Effectively, I was not allowed to grieve. 'You're too young. What would you understand?' they said to me."

When Michelle's grandmother died the situation was very different. The grandchildren were involved and were included in everything. They were allowed to see their Great-Grandmother's body. It was a positive, healthy experience.

"My family life was obviously quite difficult but with the benefit of my work I have resolved many personal issues. Still, I never anticipated ending up in palliative care."

Palliative Care under the World Health Organisation model has been around for over twenty years. But this model has only really been accepted in the last five years, as a result of the resistance inherent in the medicalised approach to death. The WHO protocols have strongly promoted the importance of family involvement. As an educator to palliative care workers, Michelle emphasises that they are dealing with ordinary people who are faced with one of the most difficult times of their life. The palliative care workers, doctors and nurses are only involved for a very brief moment in the dying person's life. The patient's family obviously has a much greater involvement. Michelle would like to see families more involved, but the fact is that for quite some time now hospitals have been run as businesses and, sadly, excessive family presence is in conflict with their required efficiency...

Although there have been many changes in palliative care it appears that many patients still want the 'hospice model', where you can stay until you die. The reality is that most palliative care units are short-term units of two to four weeks – they only take patients who have a treatable condition, such as ulcerative and inflammatory conditions.

Michelle cites instances when she has had to make a decision to send someone home because they had no symptoms that she could assist with. These decisions were made purely because the hospital had a business to run. The family does not always readily accept these decisions. Residential care facilities may be the only option for some families.

Michelle has observed that there is a distinct change when a patient who has been receiving palliative care at home moves to an institution like a hospital. There is often a shift in the way a patient's wishes are adhered to – and she believes this is mainly because of the *bureaucracy* in the administrative system governing any large institution. Often what was possible at home may now not be possible within the hospital – and this then leads to patient's wishes not being observed.

"While the consultants are usually very experienced they often make end-of-life treatment decisions that don't accord with the patient's known wishes. This is not really difficult to understand: their focus is on keeping the patient alive where the family may wish to 'let nature take its course'. It all comes back to a doctor's interpretation of the Hippocratic Oath, fundamentally to preserve life. Keeping in mind that sometimes the desperation of a family for life to be maintained at all costs adds to this pressure.

Whatever the case, the family often is not consulted. Families can be difficult, they can be aggressive towards medical staff and they can challenge doctors, but that is their prerogative and we must talk to them, clarify the situation and discuss options."

Michelle also likes to include family members in the preparation or cleaning of the body after death, should they wish, rather than asking them to leave the room for the nurses to 'conduct secret nurses business'. She stresses that it is not 'secret nurses business'; it is a family affair. The reality is that the body may not look great but the family should have a right to make the decision as to what it does or does not want to view or touch or participate in.

Michelle and I discussed the work of Professor Bill Silvester of the Respecting Patient Choices Program at the Austin Hospital. Michelle commented that as far as she is aware death is not taught in medicine. Cure is taught in medicine, but not death. The Hippocratic Oath states "do no harm", but if you constantly deny people you are in fact doing them harm. Bill Silvester's role at Austin is to change the way the doctors approach death with their patients.

A young medical student shared with Michelle her take on doctors and death – she said "...from an early age there are those of us who don't know how to fail. We are not taught to fail. The high achievers - and doctors usually are - don't fail. They've never failed anything in their life. And to many of the doctors losing a patient is failing....!"

Michelle commented that an important part of her role as a senior nurse is to encourage doctors to be real with their patients and talk to them in plain English! However she is constrained by the politics of the hospital where most doctors will not take advice from a nurse on how to talk to a patient. As for the public at large, doctors are increasingly likely to be challenged and questioned.

Michelle worked with Dr Rodney Syme at the Freemasons Hospital, Melbourne, many years ago. She remembers that he always gave his patients options and was very inclusive of families. She witnessed his patients "die beautifully". Elsewhere, many patients experience a traumatic death because doctors cannot stop treating them past the point where it is beneficial. Michelle says she and many nurses worry about this and are sometimes deeply affected, to the point of needing counselling. She says Dr Syme left the timing of ending treatment largely with the patient, after preparing them well to make an informed decision.

Michelle explains "what has changed in this field is that there are now people within palliative care who are prepared to speak up and know how to talk to families and include them in the decision making process. By speaking openly we can often reduce fear. For us it's all about demystifying death. In our organisation it is documented in our strategic planning that this is a must."

She goes on to explain that she doesn't even tolerate the staff using words that try to smooth things over. "When staff use words or phrases such as 'they are resting in peace', what would we know if the deceased is resting in peace. I want them to just say they died! When we are real. Then people thank us".

Michelle's goal is "to bring palliative care back to where it started: let's humanise it and bring it back to the family" she says. "We see death on the television everyday. Death is everywhere. And yet we can hardly even say the word. Isn't that rather ironic?"

"Some patients have their own documented end-of-life plan. Whenever possible I like to follow it, although, under some circumstances the patient may wish to change things – after all it is a fluid document. I would never make this decision for them by myself. Staff from the Respecting Patients Choices Program might become involved and re-write the plan together with the patient." Michelle continues, "If the patient chooses not to have treatment, then that decision should be respected".

This then brings up another dilemma about who determines quality of life. Doctors and their patients don't always agree on what defines quality of life. If a patient wants life-prolonging treatment and the medical team does not agree, it is the medical team that will make the decision to stop treatment.

"There was a patient with a tracheostomy who accepted her situation and believed that her quality of life was of an acceptable level. According to her wishes we resuscitated this patient after a respiratory arrest and she was taken to the ICU. Members of the Intensive Care team were unhappy that she had been resuscitated. I responded that it was her wish. They were adamant that she should not have been revived and refused to treat her. This decision was made because of money and the medical team having a different view regarding quality of life."

Michelle goes on to say, "If an end-of-life plan is made when a patient is still relatively young, then a medical team may choose to disregard it. I myself have an end-of-life plan, but if I had a stroke today the doctors would not consider my plan at all and would resuscitate me because I am forty-eight years old. However, when discussing this with the doctors I spoke of the risk and potential prognosis after a stroke, explaining that in such an instance I would prefer to die. However the doctors totally disagreed. The Doctors could not understand my decision and proceeded to tell me that I would be resuscitated regardless."

"On the other hand, a patient who subsequently died had talked to me about palliative care and how she thought it should be 'rebranded'. She was sick and tired of it being about death, when it's actually about dying, especially when she wanted to live." Michelle agrees completely. "We need to humanise our treatment of patients: treat them with compassion and love and speak to them as individuals. As long as a person is still alive we need to treat them as still living."

Michelle continued, "Looking at the larger picture, with the rising population and so many baby boomers heading towards their senior years, I think we need to run outpatients carers' training clinics. Research tells us that over 85% of people want to die at home and we do not have people (families and friends) trained to assist them. I would envisage home carer training designed to help patients stay in their own home wherever possible if that is what they want. One of the problems today is that everyone is working because they have to. Many people who previously were able to assist as home carers could perhaps become volunteers, if practical entitlements existed."

Another person who has worked a great deal with this topic is Molly Carlile AM, a palliative care activist, author and speaker and General Manager of Innovation and Integrated Cancer Services at the Olivia Newton-John Cancer and Wellness Centre, Austin Health. She calls herself the 'Deathtalker™' and encourages people to become better informed about death and become empowered to have meaningful conversations both within the family and in the wider community.

Molly considers that nursing is in a state of crisis, mainly on account of reduced funding, employment cutbacks and increasingly bureaucratic demands of nurses. As hospitals today are run as businesses, nurses and medical staff are required to complete a lot of extra paperwork, much of it for statistical reasons. Molly suggests much of this could be done while nurses are with the patient. "The patient loves it when a nurse spends that little bit more time and engages with them."

Michelle suggests the following as an ideal model of palliative care:

- offer carer training and run clinics to teach families to care for their loved ones;
- have family more involved throughout the entire process;
- make the dying process real;
- have a transparent approach;
- speak the truth'
- focus on patient-centred care.

"Many doctors and nurses consider knowledge as power and tend to keep it to themselves. On the other hand, if I pass it on I see that as manifestation ten-fold."

Michelle sees herself as an advocate for the patient and their family and likes people to be treated as she herself would want. She believes they should be accorded the dignity they deserve.

Another point Michelle makes is that some nurses talk in code while at the patient's bedside. "This is not respectful. Nurses should not treat patients as though they are not in the room. We speak about our patients being institutionalised, when in fact it's the medical staff who are institutionalised."

This idea should form the basis of future reforms on the institutional level. At the moment this is happening on a personal level, with brilliant and sensitive professionals scattered through the system. However, the change that needs to happen is ultimately a systemic change. So, are we waiting for the hundredth monkey effect or is it possible now to introduce reforms from the top?

I am extremely grateful to Michelle Hooke who is an inspirational pioneer of palliative care.

The World Health Organisation (WHO) definition of Palliative Care

WHO promotes palliative care as an approach that improves the quality of life of patients and their families facing the problem associated with life-threatening illness. It advocates the prevention and relief of suffering by means of early identification and impeccable assessment and treatment of pain and other problems, physical, psychosocial and spiritual. WHO considers palliative care needs to:

- provide relief from pain and other distressing symptoms;
- affirm life and regard dying as a normal process;
- intend neither to hasten nor postpone death;
- integrate the psychological and spiritual aspects of patient care;
- offer a support system to help patients live as actively as possible until death;
- offer a support system to help the family cope during the patient's illness and during their own bereavement;
- use a team approach to address the needs of patients and their families, including bereavement counselling if indicated;
- improve the quality of life and also positively influence the course of illness;
- apply early in the course of illness, in conjunction with other therapies that are intended to prolong life, such as chemotherapy or radiation therapy;
- include those investigations needed to better understand and manage distressing clinical complications.

World Health Organisation Definition of Palliative Care for children

Palliative care for children is a special field. The World Health Organisation defines palliative care appropriate for children and their families as follows:

- Palliative care for children is the active total care of the child's body, mind and spirit, and also involves giving support to the family;
- It begins when illness is diagnosed and continues regardless of whether or not a child receives treatment directed at the disease;
- Health providers must evaluate and alleviate a child's physical, psychological, and social distress;
- Effective palliative care requires a broad multidisciplinary approach that includes the family and makes use of available

community resources; it can be successfully implemented even if resources are limited;
- It can be provided in tertiary care facilities, in community health centres and even in private homes.

These principles also apply to other paediatric chronic disorders (WHO, 1998a).

~~

In an article by Jessica Nutik Zitter, an intensive care doctor at Alameda County Medical Centre in Oakland, California, *A 'Code Death' for Dying Patients*, published in *The New York Times* on 10 April 2014, she says, *"I am trained to save lives. Yet the reality is that some of my patients are beyond saving. And while I can use the tricks of my trade to keep their bodies going, many will never return to a quality of life that they, or anyone else, would be willing to accept. I was trained to use highly sophisticated tools to rescue those even beyond the brink of death. But I was never trained how to unhook these tools. I never learned how to help my patients die. I committed the protocols of lifesaving to memory and get re-certified every two years to handle a Code Blue, which alerts us to the need for immediate resuscitation. Yet a Code Blue is rarely successful. Very few patients ever leave the hospital afterwards. Those who do rarely wake up again."*

Dr Zitter openly suggests that doctors need to relearn what she terms 'the ancient art of dying', and support the introduction of what she calls a 'Code Death'. She draws the analogy of midwives who plan with their new mothers how their baby will enter the world, a plan that prepares for the best and accommodates the worst, often in fine detail. She explains that doctors must learn something about 'midwifing death'; a midwife is a facilitator of transition into life. She advocates that it is possible to prepare for death in the same way that we do at the birth of a child. Dr Zitter continues, *"We need to teach it, practice it, and certify doctors every two years for it. Because helping patients die takes as much technique and expertise as saving lives."*

The key point she makes in her article is that *"Until the early twentieth century, death was as natural a part of life as birth. It was expected, accepted and filled with ritual. No surprises, no denial, no panic. When death's time came, the steps unfolded in a familiar pattern, with everyone playing their part. The patients were kept clean and as comfortable as possible until they drew their last breath. But in this age of technological wizardry, doctors have been taught that they must do everything possible to stave off death. We refuse to wait passively for a last breath, and instead pump air into dying bodies in our own ritual of life-prolongation. Like a midwife slapping life into a newborn baby, doctors now try to punch death out of a dying patient. There is neither acknowledgement of nor preparation for this vital existential moment, which arrives, often unexpected, always unaccepted, in a flurry of panicked activity and distress".*

In my experience palliative care has encouraged medicine to be gentler in its acceptance of death, yet medical services in general continue to regard death as something to be resisted, postponed, or avoided. If the patient is terminally ill and there is a safe transparent process then they should be able to have full control to decide when the end of their life occurs and how that happens.

Even with its limitations there is much to applaud about the introduction and expansion of palliative care. I need to add here though that there is often a big disparity between home palliative care and institutional palliative care. By this I mean that if the patient goes into some type of institution for their last days, often the excessive bureaucracy or adherence to rules and formalities associated with these institutions makes it impossible to follow through on previously agreed upon end-of-life decisions. The red tape is often in place to protect the doctors and staff and nothing more. And the regret and tragedy of this is that the patient's wishes might be disregarded.

Dr Rodney Syme, author of *A Good Death*, gave an example of palliative care actually letting a patient down. Dr Syme had a patient with an incurable disease of the lungs and while under home palliative care everything was going along smoothly and the patient felt very positive about his care. As death got closer he had to make the decision whether to die at home or in hospital. His medical support team suggested that as he only had a week or two to live he would be better in hospital where pain management would be easier. Consequently, he was taken to hospital where they kept him alive for seven terrible weeks, much to the horror of the patient and his family. The doctors kept him alive unnecessarily, against his express wishes, and he died a very painful, protracted death. Dr Syme assured me this is not an isolated case and it cries out to me that something is seriously wrong with this model.

Dr Atul Gawande in his documentary about his book "Being Mortal – illness, medicine and what matters in the end" says that "…medicine (medicating and operating) is the easy part – the other stuff is much harder to deal with. In medicine when we're up against unfixable problems we are often unready to accept that they are unfixable. You can't always count on the doctor to lead the way – sometimes the patient has to do it."

Advance Care Planning

Professor Silvester is the director of the Respecting Patient Choices Program at the Austin Hospital, Melbourne. I met him at a workshop in Melbourne in 2012 called 'The Art of Living and Dying', where he presented his paper *Do we really know what our patients want and do we respect it?* His presentation was inspiring and also challenging on so many levels. He was compassionate and vocal in his desire to understand and respect the wishes of the dying. He challenged us to question whether we should interrupt the end-of-life process. He posed the question, "Should we as doctors intervene?"

He stressed that the decisions made at the end of life should be shared. He stated that most people die from a chronic illness and not sudden death, so we should make the time to make these decisions and make them known to our loved ones and our medical advisors. Sadly over 50% of people are not in a position to make their own decisions when nearing death. Professor Silvester spoke about the Hippocratic Oath doctors have to take and how the doctor's default is always to 'treat'. He explained that under Australian common law that final decision is made by the doctor, who will often treat aggressively.

This attitude means that many of us will be kept alive under circumstances that are not dignified, frequently suffering in a way that we would not wish.

Some of the research presented at this workshop showed that during end-of-life medical treatment patients' responses to how they felt during this time were that:

- the doctors didn't listen;
- the patients felt ignored and in the way;
- they weren't wanted because they were too old;
- doctors wouldn't speak to them and kept discussing things with the patient's family.

Professor Silvester made an extremely relevant and poignant point; that families often think they are protecting the ill person by not talking to them about death, when it is actually the 'elephant in the room' that most patients will talk about if asked. Many will welcome the opportunity to express their own fears, apprehensions or positivity about the future.

Documents

There are three important documents we need to think about and discuss with our family early on if we want to have a say in our end-of-life treatment. The three documents each have a different purpose.

- Enduring Power of Attorney (Medical Treatment).
- Advance Healthcare Directive, Living Will, End of life Directive.
- Refusal of Medical Treatment Certificate.

Enduring Power of Attorney (Medical Treatment)

A Power of Attorney is a legal document that lets you choose someone who can make decisions for you, on your behalf. Having one in place ensures that your requests are known by someone who you trust to follow through and act on your behalf, should you become unable to do so yourself.

An Enduring Power of Attorney (Medical Treatment) is a legal document that allows you to appoint someone to make **medical** decisions for you. These may include agreeing to certain medication, surgery and other medical procedures, or not.

An Enduring Power of Attorney (Medical Treatment) gives your appointed decision maker the authority to act when you can no longer make your own choices. It does not come into effect until you are no longer able to make your own decisions.

It is worth noting that an Enduring Power of Attorney (Financial) cannot be used to make medical treatment or lifestyle decisions.

Advance Healthcare Directive – Living Will – End of Life Directive

These three terms all mean the same thing. They are documents created while a person is legally competent, that define the treatment that person wishes to receive or refuse should they become incapable in the defined circumstances.

'Medical treatment' means:

- an operation; or
- the administration of a drug or other like substance; or
- any other medical procedure, but does not include palliative care.

Refusal of Medical Treatment Certificate

This document enables you, or someone appointed to represent you, to refuse medical treatment for a current medical condition by signing a Refusal of Medical Treatment Certificate.

It is illegal for medical practitioners to continue to treat you if they know that there is a valid Refusal of Medical Treatment Certificate in force. As the certificate applies only to a current condition and not to an illness or condition that may occur in the future, it may not be used as an 'advanced directive'. The certificate ceases to operate once the circumstances that gave rise to it are no longer relevant. Also, the certificate does not cover medical procedures or other procedures that would be considered as warranting palliative care.

Physician Assisted Dying (PAD)

Physician assisted dying occurs when a physician facilitates a patient's death by providing the necessary information and/or means to enable the patient to perform the life-ending act.

In physician assisted dying:

- The physician provides the information and/or means;
- The patient performs the act.

This is in contrast to euthanasia where the physician performs the intervention.

Some of you may, as I did, have preconceived ideas about physician-assisted dying, but when researching it and understanding it more fully I came to realise that none of us can pass judgment without really 'walking in the other person's shoes.' Of course, there are many people who have chosen to end their life, or have asked others to do it for them due to a chronic illness that rendered their quality of life hopeless. It is not just cancer where this occurs. A person who has an incurable disease such as Motor Neuron Disease (MND), which is a chronic and inexorable disease, often faces far greater suffering than a person with a life-limiting cancer. These people have what is commonly referred to as a 'hopeless illness', incurable and with no apparent ending. While the disease is ravaging their body, their mind remains as sharp as ever. The disease is incredibly disabling physically and the psychological and existential distress can be enormous. Many a doctor has had his/her mind changed about PAD when they are caring for a patient with MND.

Professor Michael Ashby, a noted Australian expert on palliative care and Professor of Palliative Care at Monash University said: *"For many people who are dying it is not just a question of comfort or absence of physical suffering but a loss of function, independence, and role,* which are hardest to bear. However, the idea that modern palliative care can relieve all the suffering associated with death and dying is a flawed approach." He also went on to say that: 'Palliative care is a model of care, not a moral crusade, and should not be used as a strategic weapon in social debates."

After learning more about the differences between euthanasia and physician assisted dying I decided to contact Dr Rodney Syme, one of Australia's most vocal supporters and activists for PAD and author of A Good Death

During my research I listened to a recording of 58-year-old Victorian journalist Steve Guest, who was suffering from cancer of the oesophagus which prevented him from swallowing. In 2005 Steve consulted Dr Syme and Dr Philip Nitschke of Exit International, both of whom supported Steve by giving him advice that gave him control over the end of his life.

I believe Dr Syme's primary agenda was to assist Steve in his request, but I also appreciate that he additionally wanted to challenge the legal system by using this example to further his quest for a change in legislation. Dr Syme spoke with many journalists during this time, and in many ways provoked the law, but many years later an inquest still has not been held over Steve's death.

Steve Guest spoke several times with Australian talk back radio host Jon Faine on the morning programme on 774 ABC in Melbourne, and he left a recording thanking Dr Syme for his contribution to his end of life, to be played on talkback radio. On the recording he said how much his connection with Dr Syme mattered to him.

More information about Steve Guest can be found at http://www.dwdv.org.au/about-us/history/dwdv-history

As part of the research for this book, I was fortunate to have an opportunity to interview Dr Syme, Vice President of 'Dying With Dignity Victoria' at his home in Melbourne. It was interesting to hear him talk about his work with terminally ill patients and their families. He suggested that one of the most difficult things for the terminally ill is that no one wants to listen to them. Their family does not want to have a discussion about their death and many doctors will avoid any talk about the challenges that a person who is suffering faces. Naturally, there is a fear of serious professional consequences. It is a difficult balancing act.

Dr Syme says that the aim of the Dying With Dignity organisation is to change the law so that medically assisted dying is permitted at the request of competent, incurably ill people who wish to avoid pointless suffering and degeneration. The dying like all of us, find it painful to be a helpless victim. They often feel that no one wants to hear what they really want: to retain some element of control over their own dying. Once these patients are given approval for this assistance, one of the most profound outcomes is that their mental state is improved dramatically. The key point in this discussion is that regardless of whether the person actually decides to take the medication or not, they are comforted greatly simply by knowing they can be in control of their end of life. Research shows that most people in this position who do obtain this type of medication never actually use it.

Dr Syme strongly believes that for change to occur there needs to be a greater level of communication about death with family members, to find out their views, as well as doctors to work out what can be done.

There is much evidence to support that if a patient had a 'good death' then the grief of the bereaved is diminished. I personally believe this is true. In this type of situation, if a person has a death which they consider is a 'good death', one where they choose the time, the place and the manner where they feel secure and in control, and they get the chance to say goodbye on their terms, it can be a peaceful and serene occasion.

Dr Syme is a well-known advocate of terminally ill people preparing an advance healthcare directive that will stand regardless of their mental health in the future. He is very clear that his organisation (DWDV) does not assist or support death for competent individuals who are **not** suffering a terminal or an advanced incurable illness where there is profound suffering.

Dr Syme says he went into medicine to stop people from suffering. However, when you consider that doctors save lives, just how far does that go? To what lengths should a doctor go in order to give a temporary reprieve to a patient who doesn't want to live?

Considering that the Hippocratic Oath is a document that has survived and remained relevant for more than 2,500 years, common criticisms of the classical oath include its invocation of the ancient Greek gods and its prohibitions against abortion, euthanasia and any form of surgery.

The Australian Medical Association has adopted the World Medical Association's *Declaration of Geneva* as a contemporary companion to the 2,500-year-old Hippocratic Oath, for doctors to declare their commitment to their profession, their patients and humanity.

The Declaration of Geneva states:

At the time of being admitted as a member of the medical profession:

- I solemnly pledge to consecrate my life to the service of humanity.
- I will give to my teachers the respect and gratitude that is their due.
- I will practise my profession with conscience and dignity.

- The health of my patient will be my first consideration.
- I will respect the secrets that are confided in me, even after the patient has died.
- I will maintain, by all the means in my power, the honour and the noble traditions of the medical profession.
- My colleagues will be my sisters and brothers.
- I will not permit considerations of age, disease or disability, creed, ethnic origin, gender, nationality, political affiliation, race, sexual orientation, social standing or any other factor to intervene between my duty and my patient.
- I will maintain the utmost respect for human life.
- I will not use my medical knowledge to violate human rights and civil liberties, even under threat.
- I make these promises solemnly, freely and upon my honour.

The Australian Medical Association *Code of Ethics,* under section 1.4, The Dying Patient states:

- Remember the obligation to preserve life, but where death is deemed to be imminent and where curative or life-prolonging treatment appears to be futile, try to ensure that death occurs with dignity and comfort.
- Respect the patient's autonomy regarding the management of their medical condition, including the refusal of treatment.
- Respect the right of a severely and terminally ill patient to receive treatment for pain and suffering, even when such therapy may shorten a patient's life.
- Recognise the need for physical, psychological, emotional, and spiritual support for the patient, the family and other carers, not only during the life of the patient but also after their death.

However, the American Medical Association clearly has a firm view that physician assisted dying is not acceptable. I wonder how long it will be before they have a change of heart. They say:

> It is understandable, though tragic, that some patients in extreme duress, such as those suffering from a terminal, painful, debilitating illness, may come to decide that death is preferable to life. However, allowing physicians to participate in assisted suicide would cause more harm than good. Physician-assisted suicide is fundamentally incompatible with the physician's role as healer, would be difficult or impossible to control, and would pose serious societal risks. Instead of participating in assisted suicide, physicians must aggressively respond to the needs of patients at the end of life.

Over the last few years doctors have become much better at ceasing treatment when a person is getting closer to death. However, we are still a long way from giving the suffering patient full control. We see staff practising euthanasia, under medical direction, even if no one calls it that, but it is not enough and still leaves the doctor in charge, not the patient.

◐ DID YOU KNOW?
Following a parliamentary inquiry into issues related to the treatment of dying patients, the Victorian Government enacted the Medical Treatment Act in 1988. This Act reflects the strong community and professional consensus that individuals, their families, their friends and medical staff should be assisted in law in making informed decisions about whether medical treatment should be continued, particularly at the end of life.

The Act encourages community and professional understanding of the changing focus of treatment from cure to pain relief for terminally ill patients.

The Medical Treatment Act

The Medical Treatment Act, 1988 established the following:

- the right existing under common law to refuse medical treatment.
- an offence of medical trespass where a medical practitioner carries out, or continues any procedure or treatment, that a competent person refuses.
- protection from criminal or civil liability to the medical practitioner who acts in good faith and in accordance with the expressed wish of the fully informed, competent person refusing medical treatment.

In addition, the Act establishes the right of a competent individual to appoint an agent to make medical decisions on their behalf, in the event that they are unable to make these decisions for themselves. The power given an agent is called an Enduring Power of Attorney (Medical Treatment) and with it the agent has the power to determine whether medical treatment should be given or refused.

As Dr Rodney Syme says: "It is unfortunate that the Medical Treatment Act is little known or understood by the public, although it should be well known to the medical profession. To enable physician assisted dying to be lawful there would have to be a clear process put in place to protect the dying person at all costs."

The criteria might be something like the following:

- The process would have to be transparent.
- There would have to be a careful assessment of the diagnosis.
- A second doctor's opinion would be necessary.
- There would have to be a careful assessment of the dying person's state of mind, to be able to understand the nature and effect of their decision, and not just a decision made due to depression

which might be reduced with proper medication and support.
- The requests for physician assisted dying would have to be submitted a number of times. This should not be just a spontaneous request.
- The patient themselves must be the one to administer the drug, not the doctor (this ensures that the patient has control).

The doctor's role would be to:

- establish that a serious life limiting illness exists;
- establish that the patient is aware of the treatment available to them;
- organise a second opinion if required;
- make a considered opinion;
- not charge a fee higher than the standard consultation fees;
- include family members in the process, if the patient approved;
- report to the appropriate authorities (Coroner) after the death if necessary. For example, sometimes it can be the refusal of treatment, including refusal to eat and drink, that can bring on death so in this instance it is the refusal of treatment that is the cause, and consequently not a reportable situation.

Former Northern Territory (Australia) chief minister Marshall Perrin says euthanasia will one day be legal in Australia. He says:

> "The Western world will, in time to come, look upon this period when we compelled people to suffer horrifically in death against their will as almost barbaric. It is a social change. We are in the process of it now, the early stages of it. It is happening elsewhere in the world, of course satisfactorily. It is absolutely inevitable that it will happen in Australia.
>
> The Australian judiciary has been sending a persistent signal to our parliaments on the issue of 'mercy killing', by not putting

any single doctor in jail as a result of the numerous court cases or enquiries into deaths where physician assisted dying was evident, but our politicians have been deaf to this signal."

As Steve Guest said: "The best palliative treatment ever is to give the terminally ill patient peace of mind, by giving them control".

There is much evidence to suggest that a good and dignified death can assist the family after the death. Much of the grief can be softened by the acceptance of dying, and with excellent communication that can flow from that acceptance. Physician assisted dying will open the door to communication and allow the time remaining to be used positively, which is impossible when the person continues to suffer greatly, or worse still, when the patient is being treated non-stop and there is no time for them to resolve anything prior to their death.

As Dr Rodney Syme says in his book *The Good Death,* "A right to live does not include an obligation to do so, under any or every circumstance. It is surely true that we can waive such a right, and this is the basis of our autonomy in end-of-life decisions."

Timothy Quill, an American physician, says, "Although I know we have measures to help control pain and lessen suffering, to think that people do not suffer in the process of dying is an illusion."

In a legal first, Lecretia Seales, a 42 year old terminally ill Wellington lawyer is asking the High Court of New Zealand to uphold her right to die at the time of her choosing. Lecretia is seeking the right for a doctor to help her die without criminal prosecution. Assisting suicide is a crime punishable by up to 14 years in prison but Ms Seales' case relies on the provisions in the New Zealand Bill of Rights Act which protect the rights to not be deprived of life or subjected to cruel treatment.

Lecretia Seales, 42, is dying from an untreatable brain cancer and believes it's a "fundamental human right" to be able to choose to end her life with medical assistance, if she wants to, before her suffering becomes intolerable.

In a March 2015 article written by Jared Savage Investigations Editor of the New Zealand Herald - http://www.nzherald.co.nz – he states – "her challenge closely mirrors a recent Carter v Canada case where the Supreme Court of Canada overturned a criminal ban on medically assisted deaths and gave politicians 12 months to rework the legislation. The case was originally brought on behalf of two women with degenerative diseases, Kay Carter and Gloria Taylor. The unanimous 9-0 decision by the judges found the criminal charge of assisting suicide - which like New Zealand had a maximum sentence of 14 years in prison - infringed on the rights protected in the Canadian equivalent of the Bill of Rights. A key part of the judgment was the finding that the ban deprived some patients of the right to life".

To read more about Lecretia and her battle please go to a blog, Lecretia's Choice. On 5th June 2015, Lecretia who battled heroically for the right to die, passed away naturally in her own home on the same day as the landmark judgement in her case was made, denying her the right to end her life. Her work has paved the way for a wider debate about this important topic.

Around the world there are many countries/states that have adopted some form of medically assisted dying and/or assisted suicide for terminally or hopelessly ill competent adults. All but Switzerland forbids foreigners coming for this type of help.

- Switzerland (1940)
- Oregon (1994)
- Colombia (1997)
- Albania (1999)

- The Netherlands (2002)
- Belgium (2003)
- Luxembourg (2008)
- Washington (2008)
- Montana (2009)
- Vermont (2013)
- New Mexico (2014)
- Canada (2015)

If some accident or medical condition deprives me of my dignity or quality of life, I would not want to linger in that condition. I should have the right to determine in advance what quality of life is acceptable to me and also have the right to choose when to die should that quality irredeemably be lost.

I believe that terminally ill people and those approaching the end of their life generally should be able to decide how, when and where they will die, if they so choose. I know I want the same control over the way I die as I have had over the way I've lived my life. I know there are many people who have been deprived of a decent parting because of our out-dated laws. I sincerely hope that one day soon the laws here in Australia are changed to accommodate the individual's right to die a dignified death.

I urge everyone to think about the documents mentioned earlier in this chapter.

- Medical power of attorney.
- End-of-life directive: advance healthcare directive; living will.
- Refusal of Medical Treatment Certificate.

To keep abreast of changes in this field I recommend the Dying With Dignity website, <www.dwdv.org.au> or the Victorian Office of the Public Advocate, <www.publicadvocate.vic.gov.au>. This website has up-to-the-minute information on new developments, proposed law changes and actual changes in the law regarding this topic.

PAD is debated the world over. In July 2014 the UK Lord Falconer's Assisted Dying Bill received its second reading in the UK House of Lords. According to the *British Medical Journal*, the bill would allow adults who are expected to live six months or less to be provided with assistance to end their lives should they choose. The BMJ summarises the proposed safeguards: two doctors must be satisfied that the person is terminally ill, has the capacity to make the decision to end his or her life, and has a clear and settled intention to do so. This decision must have been reached voluntarily, on an informed basis, and without coercion or duress. Both doctors must be satisfied that the person has been fully informed of the palliative, hospice, and other available care options. Once both doctors have countersigned the declaration that the person wants to end his or her life, the attending doctor can prescribe the life ending medication, which would be dispensed only after a 'cooling off' period of 14 days (or six days if prognosis is less than a month). The person would administer the medication themself. This is what differentiates 'assisted dying' from 'voluntary euthanasia', where the doctor administers the lethal drug(s).

We follow this vigorous debate with great interest.

Euthanasia

Years ago, when visiting Canberra for a meeting, I found that an Exit International conference was being held in the hotel where I was staying. I had the chance to speak briefly with Exit's founder Dr Philip Nitschke, about his organisation.

Exit International is a leading organisation providing information and advocacy on voluntary euthanasia and assisted suicide. It was founded by Dr Nitschke in 1997 after the world's first voluntary euthanasia law – the Northern Territory *Rights of the Terminally Ill Act* - had been overturned by the Australian federal government. Acting in accordance with this Act, Dr Nitschke became the first doctor to administer a legal, voluntary, lethal injection. Exit International and Dr Nitschke have been very vocal in Australia.

The Northern Territory Legislative Assembly passed the Act on 25 May 1995. It explicitly legalised euthanasia under the stewardship of the Northern Territory's Chief Minister, Marshall Perron. Perron says "*The Northern Territory likes to think of itself as frontier country - it is certainly at the forefront of the international debate over euthanasia. On 25 May 1995 it became the first jurisdiction in the world to pass laws allowing a doctor to end the life of a terminally ill patient at the patient's request. In doing so, the law permits both physician-assisted suicide and active voluntary euthanasia in some circumstances. However, under the Rights of the Terminally Ill Act 1995 (NT) strict conditions apply: it is neither an unqualified 'licence to kill' nor an unqualified affirmation of a competent adult patient's right to assistance in dying.*"

The Act entered into law on 1 July 1996. It allowed terminally ill patients to commit medically assisted suicide, either by the direct involvement of a physician or by procurement of drugs. It required a somewhat lengthy application process, designed to ensure that the patients were both mentally competent to make the decision and were genuinely terminally ill.

Under the Act,

- A patient had to be over eighteen and be mentally and physically competent to request his or her own death.
- The request had to be supported by three doctors, including a specialist who confirmed that the patient was terminally ill and a psychiatrist who certified that the patient was not suffering from treatable depression.
- Once the paperwork was complete, a nine-day cooling-off period was required before the death could proceed.

Four people used the law to legally end their lives before the federal parliament in 1997 made the Act inoperative by amending the federal *Northern Territory (Self-Government) Act 1978*.

A discussion paper that guided the latest attempt at voluntary euthanasia laws in Tasmania was developed. Greens leader, Nick McKim, has co-sponsored legislation with Premier Lara Giddings, to get parliamentary support for the legal right to die with dignity. In November 2013 Premier Lara Giddings and Nick McKim lost their bid to give terminally ill people the right to take their own lives in that state. Debate on the contentious private member's bill lasted almost ten hours over two parliamentary sessions before it was put to the vote. The outcome was that the euthanasia law was defeated by two votes. The legislation would have allowed terminally ill Tasmanians to end their lives ten days after making three requests to their doctor.

Several other legislative attempts have been made to legalise euthanasia in parts of Australia. However, at present, it remains unlawful throughout Australia.

Although there are many supporters for euthanasia I believe that there is still a serious lack of rigorous safeguards to ensure people do not die prematurely without any life limiting illness or from any other type of 'hopeless illness' with no cure. When there is no doctor involved there is the potential danger of people being easily able to purchase medication that will end their life, without the due process of a professional assessment.

Dying at home

For many reasons some families will prefer that their loved one die in hospital, surrounded by a medical team who can monitor and treat them.

However, other families are opting for a different type of assistance and prefer to have the person at home as much as possible during this time. Of course, there are a multitude of different scenarios but as long as the person has adequate pain management, little or no other intervention may need to occur. If the family is prepared to handle this at home, it can surround itself with the appropriate support team. Pre-arranged palliative care workers can assist up until the time of death. Speaking with palliative care workers in advance of when they might be required is the ideal. This then means the dying person and the family have met the nurses and have discussed their needs, so it is not a stranger who walks in the door at the eleventh hour.

In Australia there are people like Zenith Virago who started The Natural Death Care Centre Inc., a charity and a non-profit incorporated association located in the Byron Shire, northern New South Wales.

Their website states that "they are currently a small, passionate organisation and a beautiful work in progress". The organisation is modelled on the United Kingdom Natural Death Centre and is part of the great global wave of demystifying and reclaiming death. I really admire what Zenith and her organisation are doing in Australia.

The organisation lists its aims as:

- assisting people to take a more natural approach to dying and death;
- exposing and dispelling myths;
- encouraging people who want more involvement;
- providing clear and useful information, advice and referral;
- offering options, education and preparation;
- opening dialogue and offering assistance to achieve a more beneficial experience;
- support for those who wish to conduct a more meaningful, personalised and appropriate ceremony.

Just as many people have chosen a more natural lifestyle, they often choose to have a more 'natural style' of death.

Victoria Spence in Sydney is another advocate of bringing the process of dying back into the family home. For information on her 'death literacy' practice and end of life, please see <www.liferites.com.au>.

On Victoria's website she states, "My practice as a consultant and celebrant, integrating end-of-life and after death care, is built on supporting you to have the information and resources and to know how to be fully present and involved in creating the most reflective and authentic ceremony possible."

Both Victoria and Zenith are celebrants who facilitate the end-of-life process with the family's wishes at the heart of the 'dying at home process'.

When my friend Lyndon Shea, mentioned in Chapter 4, was losing his battle it was important to his wife Sherinda to look after him and to care for him at home until his death. I remember talking to her about this months after Lyndon had died. When he died in their home he was surrounded by calmness and love. No one was rushing around, lost in busy-ness and trying to avoid what had just happened. They were, in a very quiet way, connected with each other and Lyndon, just being with the dying process.

This did not stop at the moment of death; his family and close friends had the privilege of attending to his body after death. Many of us today have lost a vital connection to the life cycle of birth and death. Years ago it would be common for all family members to attend a dying person, to bear witness as death approached and to be there together as a community of family and friends to tend to the body after death. Sadly this practice has been lost over the years.

Since *rigor mortis* takes at least three to four hours to set in, a family can have a lot of time to sit and be with the person, to bathe and dress them if desired. There is no hurry, no need to rush at this time.

If you want to keep the body at home after the death then there will be certain practical things that you may need assistance with.

- Fluids can leak from the body, so orifices might need to be plugged.
- Bodies continue to move, so it is quite possible that facial muscles or limbs may continue to move. This is very normal.
- Don't take dentures out because you will find it hard to put them back in.
- Gently close the lids if the eyes have remained open after death. Soft masking tape may be required to close the lids if they continue to open.
- Use a scarf to hold the mouth shut if the mouth has remained opened. Some people use a rolled up towel under the chin for this purpose also.
- The body will continue to cool so don't be surprised if it is quite cold, and remember to warn family members of this because it can be quite a shock if they go to touch the body and realise just how cold it is.

What is important to consider when you are planning to have someone die at home?

- Surround yourself with the people who will support and assist you. Don't feel obliged to have others around you who you do not want there.
- Obtain the information you need or want by asking questions until you get the answers.
- Don't be rushed. Take your time. Be comforted in that you can continue to treat the body during this time just as before the death.

- Don't be rushed into making decisions that can wait.
- Do what you think is right.

Preparing a body for burial is a ritual that is both ageless and tribal. If you are interested in handling everything at home after the death, including washing and cleaning the body, then might I suggest you read the following remarkable article about a community of family and friends who, with the assistance of a home-funeral advocate, care for the body of their twenty-two-year-old who died as a result of a car accident.

<www.thedailybeast.com/articles/2013/02/05/inside-a-home-funeral.html>.

Even though a dying person themselves may choose to die at home surrounded by loved ones, some family members may not be able to handle a death occurring in the home that they have to continue to live in. So these discussions need to happen early on to ensure everyone's needs and wishes are addressed.

The baby boomer approach to death and dying

I am wondering what this discussion might sound like in 2020 when the 'baby boomers' have had a more active voice in this debate. Baby boomers are those born between approximately 1946 and 1964. Presently the people who could most advocate for this legislative change are too sick to rally. The baby boomers will make it known what they want and they will push for laws to change. I collected over 1200 completed questionnaires from people all over Australia and New Zealand and found that the majority of them believed that baby boomers would make a difference to the outcome of end-of-life issues.

In 2012 Monica Williams-Murphy MD, an emergency physician and author of *It's OK to Die*, said that baby boomers will change end-of-life care. In this article she predicts the baby boomers will:

- expect to live longer and will seek out technologies to do so;
- author and create the 'natural death' movement;
- be responsible for death becoming 'de-medicalised' so it will again be viewed as a natural event that can be managed in natural settings such as the home;
- change the experience of dying in medical institutions and because of their involvement more efforts will be made to humanise the experience and to make it more intimate;
- seek more control over the dying process, especially those who like to be in charge;
- gradually increase the dialogue about assisted suicide and other new and different pathways for obtaining control over the dying process.;
- expect more non-traditional, cost-conscious funeral preparations.

#POINTS TO CONSIDER

- → You have rights and you have choices concerning death.
- → It is best that you know these before a death occurs so that you are not suddenly faced with finding out those rights when you are under stress.
- → Some of these choices are about putting legal documents in place.
- → Some of the choices are about the care you wish to have.
- → There is such a thing as 'a good death' and a dignified death.
- → Dying at home is a choice for many.
- → People react differently when a death occurs and this is okay.
- → You cannot predict how you will cope with the death.
- → Create a sense of calmness if possible, surrounding yourself with loving and supportive family and friends.
- → Don't be rushed into making decisions.

- → Palliative care can be a very good ally.
- → Doctors should not overrule a decision made by a dying patient.
- → Doctors are not trained in death; death is not taught in medicine. They learn at lot of things in medical school, but mortality isn't one of them.
- → Patients should be well informed of their choices while they are still compos mentis.
- → The patient is the best person to determine his or her own quality of life.
- → Advance care planning is imperative.
- → Physician assisted dying is a choice.
- → Where euthanasia is legal it is an option for some people.
- → We are seeing changes now that baby boomers are getting to an age where they are thinking about their mortality. This group is far more likely to start thinking about this topic earlier than its predecessors.

PART 2
WHEN A DEATH HAS OCCURRED

Oh heart, if one should say to you that
the soul perishes like the body,
answer that the flower withers, but the seed remains.
— Kahlil Gibran

In this chapter we will look at what is important when a death occurs, how we can best support those closest to the dying person during this time and what choices, rights and law exist at this time. It is important to understand that there is no right or wrong in this situation. We have choices as to how the process unfolds. How we are supported matters greatly at this time. The needs of a bereaved person will depend on the circumstances of the death, where they are at the time and whom they are with when death occurs.

Everybody reacts differently to the death of a loved one or a friend or acquaintance. I remember vividly the deaths of those closest to me. My father-in-law died in a tragic sailing accident when I was about twenty-four-years old. However the death of my brother who took his own life, and the death of my father just a short time later were probably the two that affected me the most. The death of my grandmother and my grandfather, with whom I was very close, also affected me deeply. Because I was close to all of these people I had a very tangible sense of shock and disbelief when each of them died. Even after all these years I think of them often and it is strange to realise that they are no longer with us. It is as though that initial shocking realisation that you will never see them again is experienced over and over again. Personally, it was important for me to be with family at the time of these deaths, one of the reason being that we had a shared sense of loss.

At the end of this chapter Amanda Pryce, who lost her son when he was a young adult, speaks about the profound impact of her loss.

Many different circumstances and influences that affect the way we react when first told about a death. Our reaction depends on:

- Where we are at the time;
- How we are feeling before we hear the news;
- Who we are with at the time we hear the news;
- The circumstances of the death itself;
- Whether we knew the person was unwell;
- What contact we had had before the death;
- How close the relationship was;
- How close we are to those who loved that person the most;
- How supported we feel at the time.

With most deaths, the feeling of grief has a great deal to do with our feelings, emotions and thoughts towards the deceased, their family, and the connections between you all. However, if the death is part of a larger tragedy then the shock may be heightened, because we are concerned not only about the person or people lost, but also about all those connected to them and to the catastrophe. In such circumstances our own personal grief can get lost amid the communal grief.

What is important at a time like this is that people are supported, listened to and assisted in a way that suits each individual.

After death choices

It is perhaps surprising how many choices one is faced with and the number of decisions that need to be made once a person has died. Some of them may be familiar to you, there are others you may not be aware of. Some of the choices that need to be made include:

- how to transport the body, if desired or necessary, to a place where it can be kept until the funeral or its final resting place;
- deciding whether to appoint a funeral director or not;
- where the body is kept while awaiting a funeral, or whether to keep the body at home;
- how to obtain a death certificate and how to register the death (if a funeral director is not appointed);
- organising the funeral arrangements;
- preparing the body for burial or cremation and deciding what, if any, mortuary service is wanted for this. Would you prefer the mortuary to embalm and present the body or would you like to be involved in clothing* and preparing the body, such as doing the hair and makeup?
- preparing and placing death notices;
- organising the appropriate paperwork for the final disposal of the body, that is for burial or cremation;
- purchasing a coffin, a casket or shroud, or other garment
- purchasing an urn for the remains if required.

*You might consider a special 'garment for the grave'. Graduate celebrant Pia Interlandi is a fashion designer making biodegradable burial garments, with client family participation. Her work often incorporates scientific and psychological concepts of death. <http://www.piainterlandi.com/>

Pia says *"My role, which began as designer, transformed into maker, sculptor, scientist, celebrant, dresser and death-wear facilitator. Garments for the Grave is a practice that has emerged from previous project work, and uses skills from the fashion realm whilst incorporating elements of funeral celebrancy. It is a practice that functions as ritual engaged through the creation or fashioning of a burial garment. It neither denies nor flirts with death, but presents it in a way that invites observers to view it as natural, undeniable, inevitable and at times, beautiful. The garments are designed for easy inclusion of dressing rituals performed by the family. There has been significant attention from the press regarding this work, which is an indication that it is a 'fashionable' topic, and a realisation that there is a need and demand for this type of engagement."*

Pia has travelled extensively to research death practices, especially in the UK, and is also the inaugural President of NDAN Natural Death Advocacy Network.

In Victoria Libby Moloney set up Natural Grace funerals <www.naturalgrace.com.au>, a Holistic Funeral Company able to assist families with family led funerals. Natural Grace is passionately and actively committed to social and environmental sustainability and is one of a handful of funeral companies that has a Sustainability Policy. Their mission is to provide natural, environmentally sustainable choices in after death and funeral care.

◐ DID YOU KNOW?
The law does not require the family to engage the services of a funeral director, nor does it require a formal ceremony.

Who needs to be contacted when a person dies?

When someone dies at home:

There may be local laws that relate to your situation but an example of the process is:

If the death was expected, as in the case of a life-limiting illness or disease, and you wish to spend time with the person after they have died, you are entitled and it is a good idea to do so. You may invite others, family and friends, to do likewise. There is no hurry to call an ambulance or meet any legal requirements. Many people think that the moment a person dies the law requires them to call the police, or an ambulance. This is not the case. If the person is elderly or terminally ill and the death was expected there is usually no rush to remove the body.

If death is sudden and unexpected, the doctor should be notified at once. Unless the coroner is involved, the doctor will issue a certificate stating the cause of death. This is required by the Registry of Births, Deaths and Marriages. There is a separate section below which discusses the role of the Coroner's Court.

If the body is to be cremated, the doctor will arrange for the signature of a second doctor, required to complete the cremation certificate.

If we look at the law in Victoria (Australia) as an example. In Victoria, two documents must be issued for a cremation: 1. Medical Certificate of Cause of Death and 2. Certificate of Registered Medical Practitioner Authorising Cremation

Medical Certificate of Cause of Death

The doctor who was responsible for a person's medical care immediately before death, or who examines the body of a deceased person after death, must notify the Registrar of Births, Deaths and Marriages. The report to the Registrar must be made within 48 hours after the death and must be in the prescribed form.

The doctor who completed the Medical Certificate of Cause of Death is also required to give the Certificate to the funeral director or other person who will be arranging for the disposal of the human remains.

Certificate of Registered Medical Practitioner Authorising Cremation

A Certificate of a Registered Medical Practitioner Authorising Cremation must be signed by a registered medical practitioner who did not complete the death certificate.

If the practitioner refuses to sign this certificate, he or she must endorse that fact on the Certificate.

A Certificate of a Registered Medical Practitioner Authorising Cremation requires the practitioner to certify that:

- They are registered under the National Law;
- They have read the statements contained in the Application for Cremation Authorisation;
- They have examined the body of the deceased; and
- Have sighted:
    – Completed death certificate; or
    – Completed Medical Certificate of Cause of Perinatal Death
- Has made careful and independent inquiry into the circumstances surrounding the death;
- Agrees with the cause of death as listed on the death certificate;
- Doesn't consider the death to be a reportable death pursuant to Coroners Act 2008;
- Doesn't believe there are circumstances that might necessitate further examination of the body before it is cremated or which could make exhumation of the body necessary at any time in the future;
- Doesn't consider there is any reason cremation should not proceed;

> - Will not acquire and does not anticipate acquiring any property or pecuniary or other benefit by reason of the death; and
> - Is not in partnership with the practitioner who completed the death certificate.
>
> It is an offence to make a false statement in the Certificate of a Registered Medical Practitioner Authorising Cremation.

If you are not using a funeral company this is can be a little complicated as many doctors will not offer home visits. If a death is imminent speak to your doctor ahead of time, if you would like to arrange this yourself without the use of a funeral company.

Contact the nearest relatives.

Contact the police if the death was violent, accidental, unexpected, if there are unusual circumstances or if the cause of death is not known. If the police are called, do not touch or move anything in the home.

If the deceased wanted to donate their body, or body parts, you will need to contact a doctor quickly.

Contact a celebrant or clergy when and if you want to.

When someone dies in hospital

The charge nurse will usually contact the nearest relative or next of kin and arrange a convenient time for them to attend the hospital.

If you are the nearest relative or next of kin, you may be asked to:

- identify the body, if the person was not a patient of the hospital;

- consider authorising a post-mortem examination, although such authorisation is not needed when a post-mortem is legally required;
- sign the required documents to allow you to take away any personal possessions;
- tell the hospital staff if you know that the person wanted to donate parts of their body for organ donation;
- advise the hospital staff if the entire body is to be donated to 'medical science';
- contact a funeral company, if you want one involved, who will arrange for the removal and transportation of the body. Do not rush this decision on which Funeral Company you choose. (If desired family/funeral advocates can direct you to a funeral company who meets your needs).
- Get a death certificate. The funeral company will handle this if you appoint one.

Keeping the body at home

In Australia there are no regulations to stop a family from having the deceased person stay at home until they are taken to their final resting place. It is becoming increasingly common for families to want to keep the dead person at home, at least for some time, like they used to years ago. Some families will choose to have the deceased stay at home for some or all of the period between death and the ceremony. This can be organised with the assistance of a funeral company or the assistance of a funeral advocate, or a celebrant who is offering this type of home service.

I met with Deb Cairns from State Of Grace, Auckland, New Zealand, a few years ago at a conference at which we were both speaking, and I was encouraged to hear that she had started up a funeral director service that offered a different option for families in New Zealand. <www.stateofgrace.net.nz>

Their website states, "Deb Cairns and Fran Mitchell, two women who are passionate about enabling families to personally care for and make specific home-based funeral arrangements for their loved ones. We also believe in the principles of sustainability and that the processes should be as natural as possible. However, we can also provide you with a more traditional approach should that be your preferred option."

Recently I asked State Of Grace for information on how many families want to care for the deceased at home between death and funeral. They confirmed that 10% of people are now choosing to have a deceased loved one at home, unembalmed, for the entire time. State Of Grace tries to negotiate for the deceased to remain at home for at least the day and night before their funeral, once they have had time to stabilise the body. This accounts for around 20% of their clients. Their embalming rate is at 4%, almost the reverse of the national rate.

Having a home vigil

Having a home vigil can be one of the most beautiful experiences. We hear far too many stories where people have been traumatized as a child when they hear that people they loved had died and they'd just disappear from their life. Taking the body home for just a day or a few days is possible in most instances. This type of ritual can assist people in their grieving and make death a part of every day life. Often people die away from their home – and just never return. Having a home vigil can bring them home and allow them to leave from the family home to their final resting place. By the time family and friends have spent this intimate time with the deceased, I believe they feel more at peace and well-equipped to accept the death.

It was only two generations ago where it was common for people to be invited into a home to show their respects and sit with the dead. Thankfully I am seeing a resurgence of this experience and what I am noticing is that those that attend have a huge sense of gratitude that they were given this opportunity. I try to encourage families to open this option up for discussion.

The home vigil can be as simple or elaborate as you want it to be. There are some key elements that must be considered and planned - the body may need to be attended to, to ensure it is in the best state it can be for those who visit (this may require the constant monitoring of discretely placed ice packs etc). And of course those who attend need to be supported at all times. I find that ensuring there are a number of other activities for people to do assists them in this time. For example you might suggest they visit the deceased in a room that has been presented well – (eg a bright room, soft music, soft lighting, candles, greenery etc.), then move them on to another room where they might write in a journal – which has been specifically placed in a room that is conducive to encouraging people to write about their experience which also becomes a beautiful and important memento for family. I then suggest they move into another area where tea and coffee are set up and people can gather – or something like I did for a 39 year old who died and wanted to be cremated in a shroud only – we asked everyone, including children, to get down on the floor and decorate her shroud. They moved out into her beautiful garden and spent time reading her quotes which had been carefully placed around the garden, and tasting the fruits of her labour.

I appeal to you to think about whether a home vigil might be something you'd like to do.

A Family Undertaking (documentary)

http://www.pbs.org/pov/afamilyundertaking/

I would highly recommend this documentary. It shows a trend for home funerals in the United States and makes it abundantly clear that the heart of today's home funeral movement is the desire to rescue funerals from the impersonality of a mass-market industry, and to reshape them according to personal beliefs and family and community traditions.

Transporting the body

If the death occurs away from the family home, that is at a hospital or a nursing home, then there will be a requirement to transport the body to a place where it can be stored. Hopefully this occurs after a respectful time where family and friends have had a chance to have some time with the deceased. Sadly, too often we hear of families being rushed at this sensitive time, so that the hospital bed can be vacated. This seems a very inconsiderate policy. I have been woken for advice or assistance on numerous occasions when a distressed family has lost a loved one overnight and has been given four hours to vacate the bed. Consequently they have been rushed into making important decisions that they really were in no emotional or physical state to make.

If a family wishes to move a deceased person interstate there will be state laws and regulations that need to be checked. As long as all the legal requirements have been met, a body may be transported interstate. A private individual can do this. No special cars or coffins are required, but a standard of decorum should be maintained.

Organ donation

The Australian Organ and Tissue Donation and Transplantation Authority began operation in January 2009 and established, for the first time in Australia, a nationally coordinated approach to organ and tissue donation.

The heart, lungs, liver, kidneys, intestine and pancreas are organs commonly donated. Bone, tendons, ligaments, skin, parts of the eye such as the cornea and sclera and parts of the heart, including valves, can be transplanted.

Families faced with giving consent to organ and tissue donation are dealing with loss and grief. Under such circumstances prior knowledge that their family member wished to benefit others can help them. When a family is grieving the last thing they want to be worrying about is whether the deceased wanted their organs or other tissues donated.

Where organ donation has been specified, timing is critical. Tissue can be donated up to twenty-four hours after death, regardless of where or how the donor died. The tissue is stored and called upon when needed.

The way in which a person dies will generally determine what they are able to donate. In most cases, organs such as heart, lungs, liver, pancreas and kidneys, can only be donated if a person has died in an intensive care unit under special circumstances. Generally organ donors are on a ventilator that keeps their organs functioning artificially for a limited time. Many organ donors suffer a stroke or bleeding in the brain or have had an accident or head trauma that causes brain death. The very nature of these circumstances means there is usually no chance to discuss donation with the person, leaving the decision to the family.

When someone dies in circumstances where they can become an organ or tissue donor, sometimes the family itself raises the topic of donation. However, it is more likely that the intensive care medical team will raise the possibility of donation, with the family.

Medical staff need to make sure that families are given donation information and sufficient time before a decision needs to be made, if this has not been previously considered and determined. Families will be supported by a trained organ donor coordinator and receive bereavement support by professional counsellors, usually at no cost.

The Australian Organ Donor Register is checked. If the person registered 'no', donation will not proceed. If the person registered 'yes' or had not registered, a donor coordinator from an organisation such as DonateLife will meet the family to talk about the possibility.

In New Zealand the organisation is Organ Donation New Zealand. In New Zealand the process for registering is done at the time of an individual's driver's licence renewal. The driver's licence can then be checked if death occurs and the family does not know the wishes of the deceased.

Thankfully most families abide by the wishes of the deceased if those wishes are known. If the family agree to the donation, there is some paperwork to confirm the donation and which organs and tissue may be retrieved. After the organs and tissues are donated, the donor coordinator keeps in touch with the family to tell them about the success of the transplants and to provide support for them during their time of grief.

Funeral arrangements are not affected by organ donation. Organ and tissue donations will happen quickly after death. You will still be able to have an open coffin funeral, if you wish. The body will appear as if it had undergone normal surgery. Bodies are clothed for a funeral, so stitches or surgery are not visible.

If you are considering becoming an organ or tissue donor please look into it. It is certainly worthwhile and can save another life or give someone a new lease of life. The details can be found on the Australian Organ Donor Register website, or call 1800 777 203 or fill out a form at any Medicare office. http://www.humanservices.gov.au/customer/services/medicare/australian-organ-donor-register

In New Zealand, details are given on the Organ Donation New Zealand website. http://www.donor.co.nz/

Mortuary care

Some people are content not to know too much detail about the preparation of the deceased's body for disposal and may not wish to be well informed in this regard. However it can be beneficial to discuss some of the types of preparation of the body that may be required in the mortuary.

A mortuary or morgue is a place where dead bodies are kept before final disposal; cremation or burial. A mortuary can be found in some major hospitals and private funeral homes and separately for a coroner when the cause of death is being investigated. Bodies are kept refrigerated by staff who manage cold-storage, sometimes combined with deep freeze facilities so that bodies can be stored for considerable time if necessary. A mortuary is also the place where the preparation of a body is facilitated in sterile conditions.

Mortuary care predominantly covers the washing, dressing and preparation of the body prior to final disposal: burial, interment, or cremation.

Embalming is the process used in some cultures to preserve the body, or when the funeral is held up for a few weeks. It is also required when there is a repatriation of the body to another country.

Professional embalming is not meant to be the mysterious process often portrayed by the media. Although one may not approve of unnecessary embalming, the methods used to prepare the dead for disposal these days are scientifically far advanced from those used in ancient times.

◐ DID YOU KNOW?
Embalming was not always safe for those working in mortuary care or for the environment. The chemical previously used for embalming was arsenic!

There are much better options available now and in many countries we are seeing a big reduction in the numbers of bodies being embalmed.

Embalming and preservation

My own thoughts are that in most instances embalming is not necessary at all. However, research shows that embalming is used for three reasons.

- Restoration of the deceased to an acceptable physical appearance.
- To sanitise the deceased (which may not have any scientific backing. Most of us do not need sanitising).
- To preserve the deceased from the time of embalming to the time of final disposal. This is the primary reason it is used in most instances, especially if repatriation interstate or overseas is required. Preservation can be adjusted to deal with longer periods of time, as needed.

Professional embalming ensures the preservation of the deceased if the funeral is not going to not take place immediately. If there is going to be a lengthy delay, or if the deceased lives in the tropics, this allows adequate time for people to arrive from distant locations, for the bereaved to come to terms with the death, for more time for the arrangement and planning of the funeral, and adequate time for the bereaved to say their 'goodbyes'. Preservation also allows the deceased to be transported to a distant point without arriving in a decomposed state.

How is the deceased embalmed?

Embalming involves the replacement of bodily fluids with a sanitising and preserving solution. This solution is distributed through the circulatory system of the body. The diffusion of this solution throughout the body tissues retards deterioration and restores a natural appearance.

Embalming can also involve washing and disinfecting bodies to prevent deterioration and infection, removing fluids and gases from the body and replacing them with injected preservatives, washing and arranging hair and applying cosmetics and using plaster of Paris or wax to restore the appearance of a body after injury.

Generally speaking embalming fluid is a compound of formaldehyde, methanol, ethanol and other solvents. The percentage of formaldehyde found in embalming fluid ranges anywhere from 5% to 29%. The percentage of ethyl alcohol varies from 9% to 56%.

When formaldehyde is used for embalming it breaks down and the chemicals released into the ground after burial and ensuing decomposition are inert. The problems with the use of formaldehyde and its constituent components in natural burial are the exposure of mortuary workers to it and the destruction of the decomposer microbes necessary for breakdown of the body in the soil.

Fortunately, there are now several formaldehyde-free embalming fluids, including one made entirely of non-toxic and biodegradable essential oils. This recently earned the Green Burial Council seal of approval. Some organisations have now taken the initiative to replace their embalming fluid with more environmentally friendly chemicals considered far less toxic than formaldehyde. However, because even these have some environmental risks many consumers who are concerned about environmental issues choose to forgo embalming altogether these days. If the health of our environment is an important factor, and embalming is necessary, you should ask the funeral company what chemical it will use.

Restoration

The goal of restoration is not so much making the deceased look 'lifelike', but rather to try to remove the devastation caused by many long-term diseases and illnesses. Other purposes include restoration from trauma, chemotherapeutic drugs and the removal of visible post-mortem changes that may have begun to appear.

Sanitation

The argument is often made that embalming be used as a sanitary or public health safety measure, to prevent the spread of disease. However, this reasoning has never been substantiated by any scientific study and has been widely discredited.

Decomposition

The decomposition of a dead body depends on many factors, any of which can affect the time necessary to break it down. If a body is buried in a coffin deep in the ground, for example, it could take as long as fifty years for all of the tissue to disappear. But if it is exposed to the elements it will decay very quickly. The most important factor in decomposition time is how much exposure the body has had to bacteria and insects. Exposure to air or water will speed up the process of decomposition dramatically. When a person's heart stops beating at death, the body's cells and tissues are deprived of oxygen and die. Brain cells are the first to die, usually within three to seven minutes. Blood then begins draining from the circulatory system and pools in the low-lying areas of the body. Stiffening of the muscles, rigor mortis, sets in after about three hours, and by the time twenty-four hours have passed the body will have lost all of its internal heat, a process called algor mortis. The muscles will begin to lose their stiffness after about thirty-six hours and the stiffness will be completely gone after seventy-two hours. Meanwhile, as cells die, bacteria living in the body begin to break them down.

Preparing the body

Families may choose to get involved in some elements of the preparation of the body, such as washing, dressing and preparing the person's hair, makeup and so on.

If a recent photo is available the body can be made to look very natural. Conversely, if the mortician or makeup artist has nothing to go by, a person can be made up to look anything but himself or herself and this can and does upset family members. For example, a person's hair may be coiffed so it doesn't look real, or makeup and lipstick may be applied when in fact the person never wore it.

In the mortuary, it typically takes around an hour to dress the body and carry out any cosmetic work. The body is washed with cool water, often containing a soapy, germicidal solution to kill viruses and bacteria. The fingernails are cleaned using solvents to remove any stains, and other chemicals are applied to remove scaling on the hands and face. Any blood in the hair is removed either by washing or with chemicals. If chemicals are used the hair is then washed.

Any hair stubble on the remains is shaved with a razor. Facial hair and any visible nose hair is removed from all bodies, including those of women and children who may have excess facial hair because of medications they received. Ear hairs are sometimes removed and any unsightly facial hairs are removed or trimmed. Care must be taken with beards and moustaches since, once accidentally removed, they can be difficult to properly replace.

The body is dressed, using clothes provided by the family. It is common to use a full set of clothing, including underwear, socks or stockings, and sometime even shoes if desired. Cosmetics may be applied to the face and hands. Usually a special mortuary cosmetic is used, although normal cosmetics may be used also. It is through the proper application of cosmetics that a more life-like appearance will be acquired. This is a true art. Too much or too little make up has a definite effect on the appearance of the remains. Proper colouring must be determined, and the cosmetics adjusted correctly.

The final step is to place the body in a coffin, or a casket, if one is being used. The main difference between a coffin and a casket is the shape and the way the top is attached. A coffin is wider at the shoulders and tapers from head to foot. It has a top that is not hinged. A casket is a rectangular box and may have a split lid for viewing. The lid is hinged at the side. Coffins and caskets can be made by families if they wish but they will need to ensure that they meet health regulations.

Final careful adjustments to clothing, hair and cosmetics, and properly arranging the material that surrounds the body, are so very important. This final step is usually very time consuming and must be done properly. The family and loved ones want to see the person presented in the best possible and most authentic way.

The relationship between nursing homes and funeral companies

I always find it perplexing that on entering a nursing home families are asked to nominate a funeral company. The timing of this decision does not make any sense. If a family member is well and there is no death imminent, why would a nursing home require this information at this time? Families tend to feel locked into this decision, which is often made without much thought. In some cases the nursing home has a direct connection to a funeral company and makes a recommendation at the time that this is their preferred option. Nursing homes generally are reluctant to discuss why this is necessary. This decision can surely be made at a more appropriate time. A family should never feel compelled to use the funeral company nominated on the nursing home form, when it is possible the form may have been completed fifteen years before the death of the family member. Families need to know that this requirement has no legal basis and they are able to change their minds upon the death of the loved one. Don't ever let a nursing home or funeral company pressure you into making a decision that you are not comfortable with and don't feel you have any control over.

Even though a funeral company may be listed on your loved one's form at the nursing home you can easily change that decision at any time once you have researched the information to make an informed decision.

Even if you use a funeral company to pick up the deceased and 'store' the body you are not committed to using their services for a funeral ceremony. They may charge you a small 'pick up and storage' fee, but this is minimal compared to the cost of most funerals. Basically the family and friends can handle everything if this is what you wish, or alternatively you can engage a funeral company for specific elements of their usual services.

Pre-paid funerals

According to the Australian Funeral Directors Association a pre-paid funeral is where the family and funeral director establish the funeral requisites and services they wish to contract and pay for now, at today's prices, for provision at a future date. The cost of the funeral is fixed, regardless of future price increases. All states except Western Australia, the Australian Capital Territory and the Northern Territory have enacted specific pre-paid funeral fund legislation. These state Acts regulate the investment activities of funeral funds ensuring that pre-paid funeral monies are managed at arm's length (independently) from the funeral director.

If the funeral company goes out of business the money you pay for your pre-paid funeral plan is held by an independent entity and therefore is completely protected. It is invested in a separate fund in your name. It is not accessible by your funeral director until your funeral service has been provided. In the unlikely event that your original funeral director is no longer in business, you can organise to have the plan transferred to another funeral director.

If you sign up with a funeral company and then decide for whatever reason that you want to transfer that to another funeral company, you can easily transfer an existing pre-paid funeral plan to another funeral company. This is not widely known nor advertised, but it is the law.

I was on the inaugural board of the Funeral Industry Ministerial Advisory Council (FIMAC), which came about after a review of the funeral industry by the state government. The functions of the council were to review and monitor the industry and to keep the Minister for Consumer Affairs informed. The council was disbanded four years later following a change of government.

Pre-paid funerals were one of the things the FIMAC looked at closely. To this day pre-paid funeral agreements can still provide headaches for families when trying to determine what is included in the agreement. The legislation on this topic is very clear: the contract must be absolutely clear and transparent and must itemise what services and components are included under this investment, as well as those that are not.

NSW Fair Trading states that the following rules are in place to protect consumers:

- A funeral fund must invest all the money paid to it in secure investments.
- All registered funeral funds must lodge annual reports with NSW Fair Trading. However, it is advisable to seek your own

- independent financial advice as to whether the fund is financially sound and viable.
- The funeral fund provider must be separate from the funeral director who is to supply the service. This ensures that your money is secure if the funeral director goes out of business.
- A funeral fund provider must provide a client with a thirty-day cooling-off period when they enter a pre-paid funeral contract. However, the client will be subject to a $50 penalty fee if they cancel the pre-paid contract during the cooling-off period.
- A funeral director must provide a client with information on each component to be supplied under the contract and the costs of those components before they enter into a pre-paid contract. This information should also detail the services not covered by the contract and state clearly the terms and conditions of the contract.
- A funeral director must transfer money received from a client who has entered a pre-paid contract to a registered funeral fund within seven days.
- A funeral fund provider must provide a client with annual reports that include particulars, which will reduce uncertainty about the nature of entitlement to be paid.

The Federal Department of Human Services has information on pre-paid funerals and funeral bonds (also called funeral investments). It is worth checking.

See <http://www.humanservices.gov.au/customer/enablers/funeral-bonds-and-prepaid-funerals>.

Things to do before the funeral

There are a number of things a family needs to do in trying to coordinate between the moment of death and the funeral.

It is one of the most difficult times when a loved one dies. We are frequently dealing with a range of fluctuating emotions alongside the practical necessities of what needs to be attended to. The emotional loss is compounded by the myriad of tasks that need to be fulfilled in order for the deceased to be laid to rest and for the family to continue with their life. The following is a list of tasks that may need to be addressed when arranging a funeral and a resting place.

(a) Consult the Will of the deceased for instructions on any special funeral arrangements to be made.
(b) Inform the following people as quickly as possible:
- the deceased's relatives and friends;
- the deceased's employer;
- insurance company;
- the doctor(s);
- the cemetery or memorial park;
- any organisations, clubs, or unions to which the deceased may have belonged.

(c) Arrange the funeral service:
- choose a funeral company (if desired);
- arrange a meeting with the funeral organiser;
- choose a location for the ceremony;
- decide on a time for the ceremony;
- choose a type of ceremony (for instance, religious, alternative, personalised, military);
- choose a clergy or a celebrant to officiate the ceremony;
- decide on burial or cremation, if not previously specified:
  - choose a casket or urn;
  - choose a vault or crypt;
- flowers;
- music;
- create the funeral car list and if you want to use specific cars;
- choose an outfit for the deceased;
- decide on whether to have a viewing or not;

- choose the following members to participate:
  - pallbearers (if necessary);
  - readers (if not to be performed by celebrant);
  - deliverer of eulogy (if not to be performed by celebrant);
- provide relevant information (such as, surviving family members, location of ceremony for the newspaper and online notices;
- specify a charity for donations in lieu of flowers;
- ensure that multiple copies of the 'Proof of Death' are ordered (for life insurance claims, survivor's benefits and so on);
- make arrangements for a caterer or organise friends and family to help if you are having a gathering after the service;
- arrange for babysitting of very young children if necessary;
- organise room and board for out-of-town relatives and friends.

(d) The following information will be required in order to request and process the Proof of Death certificate:
- name, home address and telephone number of deceased;
- name of business, address and telephone number of deceased;
- occupation and title of deceased;
- veterans serial number or pension number;
- date of birth;
- age at time of death;
- date of death;
- location of death;
- place of birth;
- citizenship;
- father's name;
- father's birthplace;
- mother's maiden name;
- mother's birthplace.

When the body is with the Coroner

In Victoria there are some of types of death that must be reported to the Coroner's Court. These are:

- accidental deaths or deaths resulting from injury;
- 'unnatural' deaths, i.e. deaths not due to natural causes or a medical condition;
- the death of a second or subsequent child of a parent.

Coroners do not hold criminal trials and cannot find a person guilty or innocent of a criminal offence. In circumstances where a coroner's investigation into a death involves a homicide, he or she examines the circumstances surrounding the death in order to establish whether it could have been prevented.

The role of the coroner is to investigate certain deaths to determine how and why they happened in order to help prevent similar deaths from occurring. It is their role to determine as far as possible:

- the identity of the person who has died;
- the cause of the death: how the death occurred and, in some cases, the circumstances surrounding it;
- the particulars needed to register a death with the Registry of Births, Deaths and Marriages.

The Victorian *Coroners Act 2008* requires coroners to investigate all deaths defined as being 'reportable' or 'reviewable' deaths. There does not have to be anything suspicious about the death for a coroner to be involved. Many investigations involve people who may have died due to natural causes.

What is a reportable death? According to the Coroners Court of Victoria a death is considered reportable if:

- the body is in Victoria;
- the death occurred in Victoria;
- the cause of the death occurred in Victoria;
- the person ordinarily resided in Victoria at the time of death; and
- the death appears to have been unexpected, unnatural or violent, or to have resulted, directly or indirectly, from an accident or injury;
- the death occurred during a medical procedure; or following a medical procedure where the death is or may be causally related to the medical procedure and a registered medical practitioner would not, immediately before the procedure was undertaken, have reasonably expected the death to occur;
- the identity of the person was not known;
- a medical practitioner has not signed, and is not likely to sign, a death certificate certifying the cause of death;
- a death has occurred at a place outside the state of Victoria and the cause of death is not certified and is unlikely to be certified;
- the person, immediately before their death was a person placed in 'custody or care' or a person immediately before their death was a patient within the meaning of the Mental Health Act 1986;
- the person was under the control, care or custody of the Secretary to the Department of Justice or a member of the police force;
- the person was subject to a non-custodial supervision order under section 26 of the Crimes (Mental Impairment and Unfitness to be Tried) Act 1997.

◐ DID YOU KNOW?

Families are not obliged to use the funeral company who transferred the person into the care of the coronial jurisdiction. A funeral should not be completely organised until the coroner releases the person from the care of the court. Funeral arrangements can be started but clearly a date and other details cannot be confirmed, as there is no way of knowing how long the Coroner's Court process may take and when the body may be released.

Amanda's story

I met a family in 2012 to organise a funeral for their twenty-eight-year-old son Nick who had died suddenly. His mother, Amanda Pryce, told me some five months later, that the only thing she felt on hearing the news was numbness. She was sitting in the lunchroom of the school where she worked when a message came through to ring Nick's girlfriend urgently, as there was an emergency. On making that call she was surrounded by work colleagues, all of whom were supportive but nonetheless she was shocked to then have to deal with this herself. The usual process at this school was to handle any calls like this through the main administration department and the call would be taken in the office with the appropriate support. The school would then do as much as they could to assist the member of such news.

Amanda says, "I felt sorry for the admin lady who gave me the news. I think she had a fair idea that it was very bad news. Her body language told me that something awful had happened. That in itself filled me with dread".

"I could not think straight, when I first got the news, I sat down in the office, my mind went blank, and I wondered, what happens now? Nobody suggested I go to where Nick was. I had no idea where Nick might be. I didn't know if he'd be at his home or that he might be at the funeral director's or that he might have to be taken to Melbourne, I didn't think far ahead. I thought his body would be somewhere else."

"At that moment my head was all over the place. I had no idea what to do or where to go, so I just said: 'Take me home'. The staff member with me replied: 'Are you sure you don't want to go where Nick is?"

On hearing this question Amanda could not think straight. Her mind went blank. She had no idea what to do and no one up until then suggested what she might do. Amanda had no idea where Nick would be at that stage, and thought maybe that they had taken him to some other place.

Fortunately a fellow staff member offered to drive her wherever she wanted to go. Amanda initially said she wanted to be driven home, so that's where they headed. Then on that drive home Amanda changed her mind and asked to be taken to Nick's place.

On arriving at Nick's flat, Amanda was somewhat shocked to find many people in attendance. Nick's body was still there in his bed. Amanda does not recall who exactly was there but she remembers that Nick's girlfriend and her mother were there.

"There were a lot of people around. There was a very nice policewoman who gave me a lot of support, and a couple of other police officers, the coroner was there, the doctor had already been there and pronounced him dead and given the time of death. That had already been done."

"I don't remember anyone asking me what I wanted to do, so I just went into his room myself."

Amanda went straight to Nick's bedroom and found a couple of people there. They then left the room so she could have time with Nick. Amanda was astounded at just how cold Nick's body was. "I still have that memory with me of how cold his body was. I had no idea a dead body could be that cold."

"I went back into the lounge where there were a lot of people. The funeral director was there and he gave me his card." Amanda had no idea who called the funeral director, and thought it strange, but didn't feel it her place to question his need to be there, or who might have contacted him.

"At the flat I was asked to complete the necessary forms to acknowledge that I had identified Nick, my son. The whole experience felt cold and calculating and with so many strange people milling around I felt so lost, and yet at the time I did not question who they were or why they were there.

Later on, meeting the funeral director at his office to organise the funeral, he mentioned that he had spoken to me at Nick's flat."

Amanda was then told that Nick would be taken to the hospital for a short time before being taken to the morgue at the coroner's office in Melbourne soon after.

"I stood outside the flat and watched his body being taken out in a body bag but I didn't go up on the road to see what type of vehicle he was being put in, but I was told he was being taken to the hospital. All I knew was that he was being taken to the hospital, so I rang my ex-husband, Nick's dad, to suggest he get to the hospital very quickly to see Nick as he was being taken to Melbourne soon. He only just got there in time."

The co-worker, who Amanda had known for a couple of years, stayed with her during this time and drove her home then offered to sit with her. He gave her his phone number and asked her to call should she need anything or anyone. She was very grateful for his support.

Amanda's experience with the coroner's office

Amanda later said that one of her most prominent memories of the time just after Nick's death was of a representative from the Coroner's Court asking for information. Firstly they asked if Nick was in a relationship.

Amanda replied: "Well sort of, but they weren't living together." However she did mention that Nick had a girlfriend but it was a strained relationship that had been off and on for the last few years. After Amanda responded to the question "how long had they been in relationship? Saying possibly 2-3 years" the member of the Coroner's Court suddenly said, "She is the person I need to discuss this with". He gave the impression that because the girlfriend had been going out with him for more than three years, she was regarded as the senior next of kin.

Although she cannot remember the specifics of this telephone conversation, Amanda remembers it was related to a discussion about any medical procedures or questions the coroner may have relating to Nick's body, and to whom the toxicology report might go.

She says, "This was about day two or three and I was really very angry as I felt my wishes were being overridden, and not being considered at all. I felt that as Nick's mother I should have the right to make any decisions and read any reports and papers rather than this young girl, who had only had relatively little involvement in Nick's life." Amanda felt that her role as a mother was being denigrated and she had supported Nick for many years. Amanda got very annoyed and upset over this, and still felt the same way even months later. She felt her wishes were ignored by a law that made no sense to her.

She tried to argue that she was his carer and as his mother, his next of kin. But the Coroner's office staff member kept referring to the law, which broadly speaking states that if couple has been in a relationship for more than three years then that partner is the person who should make the decisions. Thankfully Nick's girlfriend spoke with the Coroner's Court and at her request, all dealings were then conducted with Amanda.

I spoke to an associate of Coroner Judge Gray from the Victorian Coroner's Court about this and although he would not discuss particular cases he did discuss the Court's usual 'process of determination'. The following information is publicly available from the Victorian Coroner's Court website <www.coronerscourt.vic.gov.au>.

This information relates to what the Court refers to as the 'senior next of kin'. The senior next of kin (or their nominee) is the main point of contact throughout the coroner's investigation. They will be notified of any medical procedures and will also be provided with updates on the progress of the investigation and any medical reports provided to the coroner.

The senior next of kin is usually determined by the following order of priority:

- if the person, immediately before death, had a spouse or domestic partner then the spouse or domestic partner is the senior next of kin;
- if the person, immediately before death, did not have a spouse or domestic partner or if the spouse or domestic partner is not available, then a son or daughter of, or over, the age of eighteen years is the senior next of kin;
- if a spouse, domestic partner, son or daughter is not available, then a parent is the senior next of kin;
- if a spouse, domestic partner, son, daughter or parent is not available, then a sibling who is of, or over, the age of eighteen years is the senior next of kin;
- if a spouse, domestic partner, son, daughter, parent, or sibling is not available, then a person named in the will as an executor is the senior next of kin;
- if a spouse, domestic partner, son, daughter, parent, sibling or executor is not available, then a person who, immediately before the death, was a personal representative of the deceased is the senior next of kin;
- if a spouse, domestic partner, son, daughter, parent, sibling, executor or personal representative is not available, then a coroner determines a person to be taken as the senior next of kin

because of the closeness of the person's relationship with the deceased person immediately before his or her death.

The coroner will talk to you if more than one person wants to be the 'senior next of kin'. The coroner will make a decision if there is more than one applicant.

To understand better how a domestic relationship is determined I checked the *Relationships Act 2008* where 'domestic relationship' means:

(a) a registered relationship; or
(b) a relationship between two persons who are not married to each other but who are living together as a couple on a genuine domestic basis (irrespective of gender).

#POINTS TO CONSIDER

- → If a person dies at home from a pre-existing illness or disease you can spend time with them before you have to call authorities.
- → You can keep the deceased at home after their death until the funeral, or for some part of that period, unless the coroner is involved.
- → You are not required to have any mortuary care if that is the decision made by you, the family or an authorised proxy – e.g. a power of attorney.
- → Embalming is not essential in most places in Australia.
- → Organ donation should be considered wherever possible.
- → You do not have to engage a funeral company.
- → If you are considering a pre-paid funeral check the details thoroughly – and ask for them to be written down.
- → You can decide what, if any, role a funeral company plays.
- → If the Coroner's Court is dealing with your loved one's death, find out the process and know that you have a voice.

PART 3
DIFFICULT AND UNEXPECTED DEATHS

*Only people who are capable of loving strongly
can also suffer great sorrow, but this same necessity of loving serves to
counteract their grief and heals them.*

– Leo Tolstoy

What can we experience when an unexpected death occurs?

The following are some of the first effects we often experience when an unexpected death occurs :

- a sense of shock and numbness;
- messy thinking – not being able to think clearly;
- feeling like we are falling apart;
- a sense of isolation;
- a sense of guilt and/or fear;
- not knowing what to do;
- a sense of losing control;
- feeling that our entire life has changed from that moment;
- feeling as though even the smallest task is completely overwhelming.

All of these feelings are very common. The main thing to remember when this happens is to take your time, don't be rushed into making sudden decisions, locate someone supportive to be with you, know (or take time to find out) your rights, and stop and take a few deep breaths.

Shock and numbness

In cases of sudden death our capacity to cope is diminished. The grieving process can be long and complicated as those left behind are overwhelmed by the grief that follows an unexpected loss. We are shocked and stunned and the loss is so disruptive that recovery is almost always complicated. This is because the adaptive capacities are so severely assaulted and the ability to cope is so critically injured that functioning is seriously impaired.

Roslyn A. Karaban a pastoral counsellor and the author of *A Practical Guide for Ministering to Grievers* says, "Grieving is difficult under any circumstances, but some losses are more difficult to cope with than others. Suicide, sudden loss, lingering illnesses, the death of a child, murders, miscarriages and such unexpected tragedies engender grief reactions that are more intense and tend to last longer than ordinary grief. Such complicated losses are more difficult for grief workers to help and may even impact whole communities."

When I refer to 'unexpected deaths' I speak of events and circumstances that can be quite diverse: accidents; suicides; terminal illness with little lead time; killings and large scale tragic events such as the 9/11 attack on the World Trade Center in 2001, the 2009 Black Saturday fires in Victoria, Australia and the Sandy Hook Elementary School shootings. The tragic loss of 298 innocent lives on board the ill-fated Malaysian Airlines MH17 in July of 2014 is another more recent tragedy that not only caused shock and grief to those families and friends directly related to those involved, but a more wide-spread shock and grief on a much larger, more global scale. Sadly these examples are just a fraction of the tragic events that have taken place around the world over recent years.

Dealing with these difficult deaths adds an extra dimension to the initial shock and to our grieving. Recalling the time when my father-in-law died in a tragic sailing accident in 1979, I remember a tangible sense of shock that it had happened and a sense of unreality, as if we all waiting for someone to drop by and tell us it was a dream. Driving down to Blairgowrie after we received the phone call that there had been an accident and then trying to come to terms with what had happened was quite surreal. It just didn't sink in. We could not make sense of what we were being told. And although I can remember some specifics of that terrible tragedy, the only memory I really have is the numbness and deep sadness that encompassed everyone in this large close-knit family.

The sudden death of a person of any age has a distinct sense of numbness and shock that perhaps isn't there to the same level with a death that has been anticipated. It is important not to assume we understand the grief felt by anyone, regardless of the circumstances of death. I've noticed there are occasions when the death of a ninety-year-old can cause just as much distress to families as a family who has just lost their sixteen-year-old in a car accident.

Sudden deaths predominately do have a level of shock that takes days to subside. Consequently when working with families experiencing a sudden death, I consciously like to suggest they take a few days to let the shock subside a little before they start making any major decisions. It is important that they know that they don't have to make any decisions straight away. This includes not having to make any decisions about a funeral.

In 2012 I was asked to conduct funerals for two families within a fortnight of each other. Both funerals were for two-year-olds who had been run over by their mothers in the driveways of their homes. How do families survive such tragedies? These types of deaths seem so much harder to deal with, to come to terms with. There is no consoling these mothers, fathers, aunts and uncles, grandparents and siblings. Nothing anyone could say or do would return these children; nothing anyone could say or do would make it better. The best one could hope for is that they had ongoing support and love to help them continue in life, to learn how to manage their now changed life.

At the end of this chapter I've included the story of Fiona who lost her mother when a simple operation went wrong. It describes some of the experiences that are common to all when a person dies without any warning and those left behind have to adjust to a whole new life.

Overwhelming confusion

When we are faced with a death that happens unexpectedly our thought process often becomes very muddled and messy. This is a common experience that can affect everyone regardless of his or her age or normal cognitive ability. Regardless of how well we manage each and every day leading up to this tragedy, when this type of death occurs it can render us completely mentally incapacitated. If we find ourselves in this situation we need to work out a strategy that will help us determine what is important and what can be left till a later time. Here are some suggestions of ways to cope during this difficult period.

- Know that it is ok to take our time. Don't be rushed by others or feel we have to rush into making decisions. We simply don't.
- Find a family member or friend who we trust to assist.
- Create a list of what we think has to be done and go through the list working out the priorities. Some of these things can be handled by others, some we may wish to handle ourself – in due time.

Falling apart

It is OK to fall to pieces! Your normal sense of life has been utterly shaken. Putting on a brave face is not always the answer or the best thing to do. It is vital to remember is that there is no right or wrong way to grieve. I understand that falling apart may feel very foreign and possibly not the way we would normally handle a crisis, but falling to pieces is all right provided that at some point we can get ourselves back together and manage. We often put pressure on ourselves to manage and not let this 'change us', but inevitably it will and should change us. So don't be afraid to fall apart if that is what you need or want to do. However, here are some all-important tips on how to pick our self back up again.

- Feed your body with healthy, nutritious foods.
- Get out into the sunshine.
- Get some exercise even if it's just wandering around the back yard.
- Surround yourself with positive supportive people.
- Think positive thoughts.
- Feel gratitude and love every single day.
- Join a group, perhaps a support group for others who have suffered a loss.
- Check out the list of things to do in recovery in chapter 10.
- Allow yourself to mourn.

Feeling isolated

Often bereaved individuals *feel isolated* and alone. No one can take away the pain or sadness of a friend who has suffered the death of family member or friend. We don't have to have all the answers. In fact, sometimes just listening or providing a hug is the best support we can offer a grieving friend. If we are feeling isolated, where possible it is good to surround ourselves with caring friends or family members to help us get through this very difficult time. Sometimes the isolation is a result of fearing shame over someone in the family taking their own life, but there is no shame in this. Don't be afraid to ask for help, many people are just waiting to be asked and often feel as though they are intruding unless asked. Take one day at a time and talk about the death.

Guilt and/or fear

Guilt is a very common reaction after a death and especially so where there has been an accident or suicide. There is an innate sense of "I could have…", "I should have…", or "if only I had…" After a traumatic event, people tend to overestimate their ability to have predicted what was going to happen and this overestimation can lead to an excessive sense of culpability and self-blame. When we stop looking for answers, where there often are none, then we can move on in our life to a new phase, learning how to make the best of our 'new' life.

There is often a sense of fear around our ability to cope without that person. How will we cope on our own? How will we cope financially? How will we cope emotionally? Thankfully this fear usually subsides over time and we start to see that we are actually coping. In time we will find our 'new normal' and the course our life and even our sense of identity will be altered. Ultimately it is up to us how we allow any event to define us. Having supportive people around can certainly hasten the recovery process.

Indecision – not knowing what to do

With the unexpected death of a loved one our life is thrown into extreme disorganisation and our normal coping skills are overwhelmed. It is very normal to feel like we have no idea what to do next. After a death our life gets thrown into utter turmoil and every step seems critical or important. This is where we need to rely on others to help us through, people we can trust to assist with the decisions and to work out what is important. We are not expected to know what to do. This is foreign ground and it often feels as though we are walking on quicksand which is about to give way at any time. Knowing these are common responses can assist us in being able to cope.

Losing control

After a death some of us may feel like we have lost control of life as we knew it. However, even though it might seem as though we have no control, it is important to remember that there are many changes in our life which can ultimately empower us.

At the time of a death we might feel like we have no control over the process, so this is where it is particularly important to know our rights, our choices and the law. This book highlights these in the hope that we are able to gain that knowledge quickly. If ever in doubt, take the time to find out. Ask the questions. Having control, taking control, even some control, over a part of the process is often what is required to make us feel much better.

Feeling like our entire life has changed from that moment.

Facing an uncertain future

Complete loss of our moorings

It is true that our life is changed from the moment the death of a loved one occurs. Life will never be the same again, because we no longer have that person in our life. But that is not to say that life can't be as good, if not better in time. As stated earlier, we all have to find our 'new normal' and of course our life will be different and our sense of identity will be altered. However, many people have found a life after a death which is incredibly satisfying, and they have been able, through this process, to find out much more about their resilience and strength than they ever thought possible.

Even the tiniest of tasks can seem completely overwhelming

Struggling with day-to-day needs

The overwhelming task of functioning/continuing

Because of the enormous grief we feel, or perhaps purely because there are so many things to think about during this time, even the tiniest of tasks can seem overwhelming. When we first hear that our loved one has died, we will probably find ourselves awake crying or staring at the ceiling as we lie in bed hoping that this is not real. Sleep patterns tend to be interrupted after the death of a loved one and as sleep often seems impossible we may feel incredibly exhausted. Death ranks at the top of the most stressful life experiences on many surveys.

One thing we *can* do is to limit our *tasks and know our limitations,* so we *can* be more functional during this time. Take tiny steps, one day at a time. Try and get some sleep even if this means having to resort to speaking with your doctor about appropriate medication, at least in the short term. Sleep deprivation can be soul destroying. In Chapter 10 you will find a list of things to do in the recovery period that can assist with getting us back on track.

Suicide

I am convinced that my father died from a broken heart two years after my brother took his own life. My father was a highly intelligent man and struggled terribly with a sense of misplaced blame and guilt around my brother's death. Sadly, nothing was going to change how he felt about Peter's suicide. Although I understood his *profound* pain and overwhelming grief, I did question his belief that somehow he could have prevented it. Although Peter had tried to kill himself numerous times in his youth, he had gone on to live a somewhat 'normal' existence for over twenty years, without any sign of those earlier suicidal tendencies. He had four children and ran a successful construction company and my father could not come to terms with his death. I remember him saying one night, "A father is there to protect his children and I didn't do it, and I should have been able to." Try as we might to convince him that it was totally out of his control, Dad could not change his view that he had failed in his duty as a father.

Naturally one of the most concerning ramifications of Peter's death was that his children suffered greatly, and in many ways they still do to this day. Children of a parent who has taken their own life are often angry and frustrated that 'he did not love them enough' to stay.

The death of a parent becomes the defining event in the child's life. Such a child often begins to define his or her life in two distinct halves: 'before' or 'after' the death. This has been clearly evident in Peter's two daughters. I am grateful and proud to include the thoughts of my two nieces at the end of this chapter. Rhiannon and Paige were twelve and thirteen at the time of their father's death.

When a parent dies, a young person's sense of security and stability in the world is turned upside down, regardless of the nature of the parent–child relationship. In this case, this was not helped by the dysfunctional nature of the family, who failed on many levels to look after Peter's four children when his wife, their mother, was incapable of doing so.

Large scale deaths

Multiple deaths in a high profile disaster give an added dimension to the grief felt by family and friends and the wider community. Families who have lost a loved one in a large scale tragedy often resent the fact that all the deaths get lumped into an 'event', where the individual is lost. A public memorial is a 'one size fits all' situation, which is rarely of consolation to the individual families. It might play a part in the grieving of the wider community but it does little to console or assist in the healing of the individual families when this happens.

I am glad to say there are exceptions to this. Scarlett Lewis who lost her son Jesse in the Sandy Hook Elementary school shootings in December 2012 did not find that her son's death got lost at all. She says:

> "I have always felt 'tragically blessed' that I have the other families to lean on. They are the only ones in the entire world who understand exactly what I am going through and I feel totally accepted and not judged in their presence. The fact that it was a worldwide 'event' was also a blessing in that I (we the

families) received what I call 'love letters' i.e. sympathy cards from all over the world. Imagine being held up in prayer by an entire world. It made a difference."

"I absolutely did feel that people were expecting me to act a certain way. If you remember, Robbie Parker (another parent) was the first parent to speak to the media, and he smiled and was publicly criticised for it and I think that heightened the other families' awareness of the potential judgment that could be out there."

In her book, *Nurturing Healing Love*, Scarlett describes how she slowly realised that her grief would not be a private matter because the world was watching. I do wonder if this community managed to do things differently and better than we had seen in the past. Each family was assigned a state trooper to protect and help to navigate the sea of international media and curious onlookers that had flooded into their town. Scarlett was also assigned a personal grief counsellor who clearly had a big impact on how Scarlett and her other son J.T. moved forward in their lives.

Rhiannon's story

It was the 29th of August 2001 when my sister and I came home on a Wednesday afternoon to find my brother and two ambulance officers at the front door. Although this was out of the ordinary I didn't feel shock or too much concern. Even as my brother told me 'Dad's passed away.' I kind of flatly said, "You're joking". And let him hug me and cry. It wasn't that I didn't care or expected it, I loved my Dad and it was devastating, I just felt annoyed he had used the term 'passed away'. A forty-three-year-old doesn't just pass away. Your big strong loving father does not just pass away. He had killed himself and was gone forever.

I can't remember the details of what anyone really said after that or how it was explained to me. I remember trying to search within myself for feeling. I think I was numb. And I knew I loved and cared about my father but I didn't know how to feel. I went to my room while everyone was busy and played the angriest song I knew of and then went back downstairs to make tea and coffee for my extended family as they arrived. I just couldn't really make sense of it all at that point.

I couldn't fathom eating but someone kept trying to make me and I appreciated it but it just felt wrong. I took two bites of a potato cake before feeling incredibly sick. I think one of the hardest things at the time was that our entire support network was affected by this; our family, extended family and friends, so with our own grief it was really hard to support one another and find support from one another.

As Dad had taken his own life it seemed to add some more confusion for me at the time. Also there was an anger directed not only at him but the world and life itself in a way. I was thirteen and just starting to try and make sense of the world and I felt it had taken him from me. There was no note, no clues, and no answers. Hindsight was a curse of course as I recalled hints he'd given about life insurance he had or just realising how low his mood had been. For months after I couldn't stop replaying the last time I had with him, he uncharacteristically yelled at me for forgetting to bring him a soft drink and stormed off to bed. He said no one cared about him. I still struggle with guilt until this day.

Mum told a few people he'd had a heart attack and this was very confusing to find out. It made me feel as though I should be ashamed or keep things secret. People would tell me it was my mother's fault and she just cried and cried and cried. She drank every day and replayed the funeral tape over and over. My sister and I went to church once to go and support her and try and find some peace. I remember the minister telling my mother it must be hard for us to also deal with the fact he must be in hell now. Again, I wondered if I should feel ashamed.

I watched as our house filled with flowers and then looked on still as they all slowly died. I felt surrounded by grief and mourning. The curtains were constantly closed, my Mum was too devastated to cook and at school my friends didn't know what to say so most stopped trying to speak to me at all.

I can't say whether or not it was more difficult to cope because my father killed himself. I asked someone once if it was harder and they were kind enough to let me make up my own mind about it. I still think to this day it's always different for each situation. It's hard to have the person you look up to most in the world abandon you in it. It's hard to feel like you didn't mean enough for him to hold on. It's hard to listen to everyone blaming each other without feeling like you then must be at fault too. I think one of the hardest things was trying not to consider suicide as an option once Dad had done it. He was a smart man, a brave man and my hero, why wouldn't I think it an option? I did make a few attempts in my teens, but luckily my family supported me through that too, although I know they resented me putting them through it all again.

It's obvious that my parents had poor coping skills. And probably most of our extended family did too. That combined with the grief of his death gave them little chance of educating us on how to deal with the situation ourselves. Looking back, I know now that I was looking to the adults for guidance about how to feel and how to cope. I remember my cousin taking us out to lunch and making us feel like we could talk about it if we needed to, but basically just going to see a movie. It was the first time we smiled in weeks. I remember being so incredibly grateful to the people that brought over cooked meals or who came around to clean for a couple of hours in the week. That meant more to us than all the flowers in the world and to this day it's one of the first things I do for others in similar circumstances.

You know life goes on, even in the most dreadful times of grief, but if you're surrounded by it everywhere you go you start to forget how to move forward in life without that person. It's all I could think about for a very long time. My mind was trying to make sense of it every single second of the day for a very long time. But slowly I started smiling without feeling so guilty again. I would have an hour or two of positivity every so often and then a whole day and so on. It just took time.

It probably took ten years to really understand how I needed to cope. It changes all the time though - a milestone may come up, or even a personal achievement, and out of nowhere I would feel sorrow or anger or just hurt. I think allowing myself to simply feel how I feel and not act on it in any damaging way is important.

On the anniversary of my father's death and his birthday I might make potato mash with butter (his favourite food) and eat a big bowl of that and tell my partner or friends some stories about him. On New Year's Day each year I watch the sunrise and welcome in the New Year. Something my father and I did together the year before he died and I treasure that memory very much. I love my father and miss him very much. I know my feelings about his death will be forever changing but I also know it was his choice and his alone.

I used to have a constant fear that in spite of my best efforts I would sooner or later do a similar thing: I spent every day living as though I'd kill myself eventually too. Because I was making choices with anger and hurt in my heart I would make terrible ones, making my life harder and harder. It wasn't until I met more positive people, had more positive experiences of my own that I developed some hope. I brought meaning to my own life and stopped defining myself by Dad's death. Now, if anything it is the reason I try to smile each day, to help and encourage others and inspire them to love life too. And if I'm honest, who knows if I would ever have ended up like that if I hadn't experienced so much of death.

Paige's story

When I was told my father had died it was a very surreal experience. There were people everywhere and when I remember back I felt as though I was observing myself being told rather than being in my body. I felt numb, as though I was going to collapse. I was the tender age of twelve which may explain why I couldn't comprehend the meaning of what I was being told, so I was just silent for a long time.

My immediate need was just to be left alone. I needed to get my head around it and try to understand what was happening. People were coming in and out of our house and I went up to my room because I couldn't think with everyone fussing over me.

At that time I experienced grief by retreating to be alone, I didn't cry much but I got angry. I was angry because I didn't understand anything, the why or the how, and because I was so young. I could understand that my life was about to change but it was hard because I had little support or knowledge of how to deal with my grief. The weeks up to his funeral were a blur of being in my room alone mostly and looking after my mum.

I don't think anyone's experience can be seen as more difficult than another. We each have our own experiences and those are what are the best or worst for each of us, because we can only identify with our own experiences. I think it was very difficult because he took his own life, but I think that it would also be extremely difficult to watch someone be ill for a long time before death. Having said that, since his death I have had to deal with issues of not saying goodbye, questioning why he did it, and the stigma of suicide.

I would say that my brothers and sister were the most helpful during that time. Some people brought meals and tried to help in those ways but it was a flash in the pan and didn't really make much difference to me as a struggling twelve-year-old. Getting back to life was probably most helpful, pretending that I was still like other kids. I remember I was devastated the week after he died because I wasn't allowed to go to school and they were making something yummy in home economics class. I didn't have many photos to look back on and I used to spend a lot of my home time with him so, in his absence, I retreated to my room a lot or listened to music just to shut out reality.

It's twelve years since he died and I still experience pangs of grief even now. If I'm having a particularly bad day or, say, on my wedding day, I wish for him, but it was half my life ago so my pragmatic nature makes me think I miss the idea rather than him as a person. It is really just a moment of grief here and there, and I try not to let myself get wrapped up in thoughts of loss. I grieve more over what could have been or what his death made me lose: a normal life, him walking me down the aisle.

I like to focus on the positives I've got from the path he chose. It made Rhiannon and I share an unbreakable bond. I am strong and I know how to speak to someone who is hurting rather than look at everything I lost.

I can't begin to tell you how amazing these two young women are. As their aunt and friend I am so proud of how their lives have turned out. I know their Dad would be equally as proud.

Fiona's story

Fiona Gilroy's life changed forever on Tuesday 1 November 2011. Fiona is the forty-five-year-old only child of Myra and Alex Gilroy. And she describes this date as the start of her never-ending grief.

For as long as Fiona can remember she spoke to her mum every day for a catch up. On this particular day her mother said: "I must go as I am just going out to dinner with the neighbours and I'll call you when I get back".

After having dinner with friends they stopped at a supermarket for Myra to get some milk. As she never liked to keep people waiting, Myra hurried back to the waiting car. In her haste she tripped over the yellow tyre stopper in the car park and cracked her hip.

The ambulance was slow to arrive because it was the evening of the Melbourne Cup. I received a call at work informing me of the accident. The policeman said, "Although your mother is okay she is wanting to hear your voice." I tried to comfort her but she was obviously very shaken."

Eventually she was taken to hospital where we were told that she would need a small pin in her hip, to repair a minor crack.

Fiona called her father who was in Malaysia. He had an important function to attend on Saturday and told her he would return to Sydney after that. The hospital and her mother reassured Fiona that this was a minor operation and there was no need to rush to the hospital. Myra was comfortable and the doctors said they would operate when there was a break in between more urgent cases.

On the day of Myra's surgery, Fiona had flown up from Melbourne and her dad Alex had returned from Malaysia. They arrived at the hospital just as Myra was being prepared for the operation. The nurse was asking Myra to remove her wedding ring. Myra said she had not taken her ring off in thirty-five years and she was not about to start now.

They only had a few minutes with Myra before surgery, but it was enough to show their support and, after all, it was only a minor operation. Fiona remembers that her mum appeared to be nervous and shed a tear. While being wheeled through the doors Myra pointed her finger at her husband and said to him: 'All I ask is for you to look after Fiona'. These simple words made an immediate and lasting impression on Fiona, "I wish I could talk to Mum now and ask her about her feelings and why she said those words". The anaesthetist reassured Myra that that all would be well.

The hospital advised them to come back at midday and they would be able to have lunch with Myra and she would be able to go home the next day.

Fiona had not even returned home when the hospital called asking her to come back urgently. There had been a complication. At that moment Fiona knew she was going to lose her Mum. She picked up her father and hurried back to the hospital.

Fiona wanted nothing more than to see her mum but on their arrival they were asked to wait in a separate, private room. The surgeon, anaesthetist, hospital officials and a counsellor entered. The counsellor was a friend of Fiona's from school days. Fiona's first question was: "Is my mum still alive?" The doctor answered "Yes" and Fiona held out some hope but when she looked at the counsellor's face she knew that things were grim.

The surgeon explained that when they had finished the operation Myra's blood pressure had dropped and that somehow the cement used to hold the pin in the hip had broken loose and the granules were travelling up towards her heart. They explained that they were trying to dilute the cement hoping that it would pass out naturally.

Fiona and her father were taken in to see Myra who was still lying on the operating table. They then went with her to the intensive care unit. Apart from her mother the only other person Fiona recognised was the anaesthetist who had assured her that her mum would be okay and he could barely look at either of them.

After many hours of monitoring Fiona was advised the cement granules were still moving towards her mother's heart and there was nothing more that could be done and it was now just a waiting game till her Mum 'flat lined'. Hearing this terminology really upset Fiona at the time. It was like a TV show where they talk about procedures rather than speaking about the person. It didn't seem real that they were talking about her mother. Fiona went into a state of shock. She was dazed but at that stage not angry as she just wanted her mum to be comfortable. She sat by the bedside not saying much, just holding her hand and stroking her forehead. Fiona and Alex didn't talk much.

At this point a group of students came into the intensive care unit and Fiona heard their mentor say: 'This is a rare case.' When she looked up there were fifteen pair of eyes staring at her sitting by her dying mother. Hearing those words from the mentor doctor, Fiona realised she was never going to talk to her mother again.

No permission was asked by the hospital staff to stand close to her mum's bedside and discuss her scenario, in front of them. Fiona felt that her mum was now a case study for a student assignment. Though they spoke quietly Fiona wanted her final time with her mother to be private. She wanted to say: 'Go away'.

The intensive care unit was an open ward and Fiona and her Dad were always mindful of other patients around. They believe that the curtains should have been pulled around them to give them some private time, but this was only done after Myra passed away.

When the nurse said that her mum had about forty minutes to go, Fiona gave her dad some time alone and she made a few phone calls to family overseas.

The hospital chaplain came in to give his blessing and Myra died at 8pm that evening. As soon as the monitor was turned off, adrenaline and shock set in and Fiona went into organisational mode, without many tears. She signed a few documents that were put in front of her, and then waited for the police to attend. Out of nowhere, Fiona remembered that her Mum had always spoken to her about wanting to donate her corneas should anything happen to her, so she signed the relevant forms.

The police attended and asked was there anything they could do. One important thing for Fiona was to be able to walk away with her mother's wedding ring, which the hospital staff would not allow. Fiona told the police officer she was not leaving the hospital without her mother's wedding ring. The policeman returned with her Mum's ring, put it in her hand and winked. She will be forever grateful for this act of kindness.

It had been a long day sitting and waiting. Now, seeing her Mum as a 'dead person' gave her the shivers. She was scared to touch and hold her but did do this briefly. She and her Dad were clearly in shock and just wanted to get out of the sterile environment as quickly as possible. So much was going through their minds about arrangements and calls that needed to be made. It was their choice to leave when they did. They left very quietly as they were aware that other very sick patients were in earshot. At times they wanted to scream and yell but they didn't want to cause a scene.

One thing Fiona would have done differently, had she known about the option, was to ask the staff to move her Mum to a ward with total privacy. There they could have spoken openly without worrying about other patients and staff. Fiona was also shocked that at no time did any hospital staff ask how they were getting home and if they felt able to drive. Although they did drive that day, Fiona was concerned about her Dad's ability to get them home safely. There was no support given at this time at all.

Fiona said it was so strange to walk out of the hospital and pass other members of the general public who looked at them, not aware why they were at the hospital and why they were leaving. She was comforted that she was holding her mother's wedding ring which somehow made her feel like her Mum was still with her.

Fiona remembers her Dad saying to her while they looked at Myra for the final time: 'It's just you and me now'. At that stage this was not a comforting thought to Fiona, as she and her Dad had never been that close. She immediately thought her Dad would sell up and move to Malaysia as this was where he had always wanted to live. Fiona thought that from that moment on she was going to live life alone, as an only child, with no children of her own and most of her extended family living overseas. She couldn't imagine life without her Mum. These thoughts went around and around her head all the way home from the hospital in the car and she repeatedly asked herself how was she going to cope?

The coroner called Alex and Fiona during that week. It seemed to him that there had been no malpractice and he told them that surgery always carried an element of risk. Even so, he asked if they would like an autopsy and investigation to be performed.

Many people have continued to ask Fiona and Alex: "Was it the fault of the surgeon?" Their reply continues to be: "Who are we to judge?" Although they didn't realise the importance of this at the time of the surgery, they understood later that the form you sign before any operation is designed to protect the doctors to allow them to proceed with what they needed to do.

Alex had met many celebrants when he and Myra played bagpipes at both weddings and funerals. They had become very close to one in particular. It was an easy decision that he should conduct the ceremony. Fiona knew the service would be written with substance and delivered from the heart. She took comfort from knowing that when she was reading the eulogy, at the funeral, she would feel safe having him by her side.

It was a tough week saying goodbye to her mother and her best friend, but she could not believe the support and strength her father gave her during this period. Alex has always been the more dominant person in the family, the organiser, the speaker and decision maker but when this terrible tragedy happened he could not do anything and left all the funeral details and eulogy to Fiona. She felt she knew exactly what her Mum would have wanted in her ceremony regarding music and content but was surprised at the lack of input from her father and she had never seen him so reserved.

The ceremony was beautiful and Fiona was surprised how many people travelled far to attend. The support of friends and the community definitely did not go unnoticed but sadly not long after the funeral all the well wishers and the support started to taper off.

Fiona returned to Melbourne two weeks after saying goodbye to her Mum and thought she was ready to return to work. Unfortunately this was not the case. During those first few weeks she was continuously seeing her mother from a distance and whilst looking at people she kept noticing features in other people that were similar or the same as her Mum. This was certainly shocking and surprising at times, and caused her some distress.

The most positive thing to come out of her mother's death is that she now has the most amazing bond with her father. Alex stayed in Australia and now visits her frequently. Fiona realises that if her mother was still alive they may never have experienced this. Now she receives the daily calls from her father and he is not only her Dad, but also her Mum. He talks to her as her mother would, using exact words and phrases her Mum would use.

Overall Fiona was surprised at how little support she really got. Those who promised to call, visit and keep in touch, rarely did and it was up to her and her Dad to get through this together.

When I asked Fiona about her grieving she said that initially she felt she "didn't have the time to grieve", she was too worried about how her Dad was coping. She cried a lot and spoke to her dad several times a day. Ironically, her dad was very worried about Fiona as she was always calling him in tears at all times of the day and night. He suggested she speak to a counsellor friend of his who lived in Melbourne. As she had always been able to pick up the phone at any time and speak to her Mum, part of what was missing was having a female just to talk to.

Fiona feels very lucky to have her Dad to talk to now and she is more open with him about her feelings. She feels that friends assume you are okay and that you are managing. She and her Dad are the only ones who speak constantly about Myra's tragic passing.

#POINTS TO CONSIDER

- → Some deaths are more difficult to deal with and accept than others.
- → Sudden deaths have a level of shock that takes days to subside.
- → When people take their own life, the grief of those left behind is often complex.
- → Losing an adult child can be as difficult as losing a young child.
- → Don't rush decisions when a death occurs suddenly. Take whatever time you need before making decisions.
- → If you are in a hospital situation:
  - Don't be afraid to ask for a private space or room;
  - Don't be afraid to say no to 'intruders at the hospital' e.g. doctors in training;
  - Do speak up if something is really important;
  - Ask for help if you are not coping.
- → Death can bring us closer together.

PART 4
FUNERALS AND FINAL RESTING PLACES

I can't think of a more wonderful thanksgiving for the life I have had than that everyone should be jolly at my funeral
— Admiral Lord Mountbatten

Don't be rushed into having a funeral

When a death occurs there is no hurry to arrange or to conduct a funeral. There is no law that defines when a funeral must take place. Certain cultures, such as the Islamic community, bury their dead quite quickly, but most others have no such defining rituals. Even if the death was expected there is no hurry to make decisions and organise a funeral.

If a family is being encouraged to have a funeral shortly after a tragic accident I will always suggest they take their time and advise them that there is no hurry. In most instances it is in their interests to wait a few days before making any decisions. There is no law that requires a funeral to take place in the next week, or even the week after that. Families should know this, so they do not feel rushed or even bullied into having a funeral sooner than they want.

I am concerned about a recent trend appearing where a funeral company representative often suggests and encourages a family to arrange a funeral quickly. I abhor this practice knowing that, in most instances, it may not be in the interests of the family and friends. A state of extreme shock is usually the case in the event of a sudden death. Families often need time to recover from the initial impact before any decisions are made.

Sadly, funeral companies usually have their own agenda in these situations: they have quotas to meet. The funeral industry is a multi-billion dollar industry and if you don't think their bottom line matters, I am here to tell you that it does! Being in business myself I understand that the balance sheet counts. However, my concern is that the priority of the families concerned, which always used to come first, has shifted. Now we tend to see that in most situations the bottom line is taking precedence. Can the two goals work together simultaneously? Yes they can. When people work together within an atmosphere of trust and compassion, making the family their focus, they can still make a profit. They always did and, thankfully, many still do.

When a death occurs, not everyone can celebrate the life of that person. Some are not ready to celebrate. If the circumstances around that death were tragic, then the chances are they are simply not yet ready. Sadly, sometimes the client is pushed into rushing into a funeral at such a time, when they are not ready. I have witnessed a funeral arranger telling a family that they are booked up later in the week, so they would have to have the funeral in a couple of days, when in fact they were not booked up at all. This to me screams of meeting quotas with no compassion for the family's interests. In this particular instance I stepped in and got the matter resolved quickly and the family received an apology. Sadly this is not an isolated case.

Allowing a few more days for the family to get over the initial shock allows them time to recover enough to think more clearly about the funeral arrangements, about what their needs might be (and those of the deceased) and to attend to all the necessary details. Sometimes even after a few days a family may not be able to celebrate but they can come together to honour the life, having been given time to consider some important decisions.

Author John E. Welshon explains in his book *Awakening from Grief*, that we tend to turn to 'professionals' such as funeral companies when we have to deal with death. He feels that by using these services we can deny the reality and finality of death, change and decay. Using someone else to make arrangements tends to keep the process at arm's length from us personally.

In Australia, the funeral is most commonly conducted three to five days after the death. In England, one to three weeks is not uncommon, and in many other countries the average interval between death and the funeral is five to six weeks, which means that a wait of a month is not uncommon. People from other countries may find our funerals here in Australia unusual, because we focus intimately on the individual person, rather than the ceremony taking on a standard format regardless of who has died.

Once the cause of death has been ascertained, usually by a medical practitioner, the body may be kept at home or be taken to be stored, funeral arrangements made, and then finally burial or cremation takes place. In practice this almost always means that the body is conveyed to the funeral company who takes charge of the proceedings. However you do have choices about this decision.

What does a funeral look like and why is it important?

Funerals usually bring together all aspects of a person's life. The traditional form is to present a brief biography including family, work, friends and hobbies. The family may consider using a celebrant, showing photographs and videos of the person and having several people speaking at the funeral.

In Australia there are relatively few restrictions imposed by our regulations and laws as to what a family can do to honour a life. The system of using professional celebrants enables flexibility and that, coupled with a professional and caring funeral director whose focus is to facilitate the event, most often results in an authentic funeral that pleases the family.

Dr Alan Wolfelt, author, educator and grief counsellor, writes of his concerns that families, and ultimately society as a whole, will suffer if we do not reinvest ourselves in the funeral ritual. Dr Wolfelt states that, "creation of meaningful ceremonies when death affects us can assist us with emotional, physical and spiritual transformations".

I do question whether we as a society have developed the funeral into more of a celebration, which might not allow the grieving to take place, as it should. Perhaps in some ways we are complicit in trying to turn the funeral into something more positive, more celebratory, than it really is for the bereaved. In the new guidelines for mental disorders, the DSM-5 (Diagnostic and Statistical Manual), grief looks set to be confused with depressive illness. I wonder if funeral celebrants and funeral companies are unwittingly complicit in this when they encourage grieving relatives to focus on a funeral as a 'celebration of life', perhaps at the expense of the painful feelings of loss and separation?

◐ **DID YOU KNOW?**
By participating in a meaningful funeral ceremony, we begin to re-centre ourselves, to make that painful transition from life before the death, to life after the death. Funeral ceremonies help us adapt to change and they can start the healing process.

The difference between honouring and celebrating?

The Oxford dictionary defines celebration and honouring as follows: 'To celebrate' means "to publicly acknowledge (a significant or happy day or event) with a social gathering or enjoyable activity".

'To honour' means "to regard with great respect".

Honouring is most likely to mean that the respect for the person would overshadow any celebration, and is more likely to make for a subtler and less 'over the top' way we present the ceremony. A celebration is more likely to focus on the positives and avoid mentioning any negatives.

While I like the idea that we can celebrate a life, I am also conscious that we need to allow time and space to feel and acknowledge the sadness, to grieve, to 'feel the feelings' and not overshadow or deny them with a celebration. Having said that, I do believe it is possible to both honour and celebrate in a ceremony and to work with the family to ensure we get it right. There needs to be a balance where sadness and loss are acknowledged and yet a life celebrated within each ceremony.

There was a clear example of this in 2011, when I organised a funeral for a baby. His parents were both very young (seventeen and eighteen). Both the funeral arranger and myself were concerned that the funeral was turning into a bit of a 'birthday party' and that the death was being denied. However, working closely with the funeral arranger and a grief counsellor, we found a way to ensure that the death was clearly acknowledged during the ceremony.

It is certainly a celebrant's responsibility to ensure that the family's wishes are followed, but equally important is the celebrant's involvement in creating and conducting a ceremony that will assist them in a healthy grieving process. One way is to inform them of the many options available to them. Obviously this can only happen with someone who is experienced and has the research and appropriate knowledge to advise. This only comes with years of training and experience and it is evident to me that many people who become funeral celebrants choose the vocation because of their experience in grief and other challenging situations. No one without that experience should work outside their role or give advice about people's grief, as it has the potential to cause a lot of harm.

Scarlett Lewis, talking about the death of her son, Jesse, in the Sandy Hook shootings, said:

> "I think the wake or funeral is a good way to accept the reality of death. I dreaded seeing Jesse's dead body and don't think I would have wanted that anticipation for too much longer, but then of course I am glad that we chose an open casket (and thankful that we were able to). I did make my instructions clear that I wanted it to be a 'celebration'. I was able to speak at the funeral and receive guests at the wake and afterwards. So in spite of the shock I was surely in, I look back and do not regret a single thing."

If a family, grieving over the loss of their son or daughter in a car accident is not ready or capable of celebrating their child's life, now or anytime in the near future, we must abide by their wishes and not create a ceremony that is centred around a celebration. It is the celebrant's role to assist the parents to honour their child's life as best they can, even by such a simple technique as using appropriate, sensitive terminology and words throughout the ceremony.

Funeral options

A public or a private ceremony, or both?

Location options: chapel, home, park, reception venue, restaurant, golf course, beach or any other location. The options are endless and the choice is yours.

The coffin

Decorated or not? Environmentally low carbon footprint? Building your own? Again, there are many more options than people realise.

In Victoria, in most instances, a coffin or casket is required for both burial and cremation. However, other options are starting to be available, such as people being buried or cremated in a shroud only, without need of a coffin.

The Cemeteries and Crematoria Regulations 2005 (Victoria) specify that a coffin must be a hygienic, closed receptacle, soundly constructed of substantial wood or other approved materials and in such a way as to prevent the escape of offensive liquids or exhalations. There are now many options of different materials that can be used to make a coffin, so if you prefer a more environmentally friendly option there are plenty to choose from. For example it can be made from recycled cardboard, untreated pine-ply, wickerwork, or even wool. 'Eco coffin' suppliers can be readily found on the internet.

The New South Wales Office of Fair Trading states that it is not illegal for an individual to organise a funeral, burial or cremation as long as they comply with the relevant local government and health regulations. They state, however, that the process is complex, demanding and involves specialised resources that may be difficult to obtain. I disagree with this attitude. I think it best to advise families of the legal requirements and let them determine if it is feasible for them to comply.

Coffin makers often refuse to sell direct to the public and some funeral companies are unwilling to accept coffins from families. There needs to be more transparency about this because most people are unaware that many of the larger funeral companies either own or have shares in the coffin manufacturers. By law, as long as the coffin fulfils certain requirements, it can be constructed by a private individual. Fortunately, there are increasingly more organisations and people, such as celebrants, who can obtain coffins for families at a much reduced cost.

Technology

A great deal of technology is available for those wishing to include overseas relatives or friends in the ceremony: video, Skype, etc.

Music

Live music, singing, recorded music.

Funeral memorabilia

Stationery, bookmarks and keepsakes. These can be provided by yourself, or you can use a company who specialises in this sort of memorabilia.

Flowers

Flowers can be ordered either directly from a florist or you can bring them from your home.

Celebrant, Clergy, Master Of Ceremonies

The person of your choice can be contracted privately without having to go through the funeral company.

Mourner involvement

Escorts for the coffin into and out of the ceremony.
 Family or close friends to place flowers or other items such as photos on or around the coffin.
 Communal singing.
 Speakers.
 Performers.
 Mourners to share in the preparation of food or wine

◐ DID YOU KNOW?

It is not a legal imperative to have a celebrant leading the ceremony. But you do need to find someone with the appropriate skills who can control and lead it. It might look and sound easy but I can assure you it isn't, and asking someone who is more emotionally attached to the deceased adds another dimension of risk. I have seen a ceremony done well without using an independent celebrant, but it is a big responsibility. The person leading the ceremony is important on so many levels and they can make a huge difference to the outcome. This is something to consider when you are making your decision about who you will ask to lead the ceremony.

Engaging a professional independent celebrant

It is important to make the distinction between a celebrant appointed by the funeral company and an independent celebrant. Some funeral companies use a staff member to be the celebrant. While some funeral company staff may be well intentioned, this does not automatically mean they will make a good celebrant. Many funeral company staff are paid a very low salary and are then expected to act as celebrant, often working outside their normal daytime hours, for no extra remuneration. This scenario is fraught with danger and often leads to burnt out and frustrated staff who consequently end up leaving. Another little known fact is that in some situations the funeral company then keeps the money you have paid for a celebrant.

Simply accepting the celebrant appointed by the funeral company may also not be ideal. One would like to think that they would consider matching you with a suitable celebrant from their list, but I can honestly say that this is rarely done. The funeral companies have a list of celebrants to choose from and they will just work down that list until it is exhausted. In busy times this could mean you are allocated a novice celebrant who may never have conducted a funeral, or, worse still, has no training or skills. There is no requirement for any celebrant to be trained to conduct a funeral.

The best option is to choose an independent celebrant not connected to the funeral company. They work independently and are therefore not so likely to be concerned about working within the funeral company model. They are autonomous and will not be under the direction of the funeral company. Celebrants who gain their work through a funeral company naturally are concerned about upsetting the funeral company, for fear of losing work. To my mind this is a conflict of interest for you as a client. You need a celebrant who can work with you on all the elements that are important. The funeral celebrant then works with you to ensure your needs are met. In addition, you pay that celebrant direct, just as you would if you had chosen to purchase your own flowers, or make your own coffin. Most independent celebrants work for an hourly rate and they are very transparent about the rate at the outset.

Why it is in your interests to consider appointing an independent celebrant - not appointed by the funeral company?:

- you are able to choose the person yourself;
- they are easily found via word of mouth, by recommendation or online;
- you get to appoint someone who fits with you and your family;
- they are often more flexible and do not work within confined and defined rules;
- you pay them directly, so you know what you are paying for;
- they can assist you without any conflict of interest.

A word of warning! Be wary of engaging someone who is only dabbling in the work. Sadly, the repercussions of using someone who is not skilled can be devastating for everyone, and can have long-term effects. Recently

I was asked by a palliative care worker to meet with an elderly gentleman whose wife was not expected to live more than a few days. He wanted assistance and advice on how to handle the ceremony himself. I asked why he was considering conducting the ceremony himself, and he said that he had attended two funerals of late, both facilitated by celebrants, and that both were very poorly conducted. This is a sad indictment of our industry, but not uncommon. To place this stress on an unwell, grieving person is dreadful, but clearly the impact of a 'badly planned and presented funeral' can be profound and should not be underestimated.

Choose wisely and do not just allow the funeral arranger to choose for you. Meet with the possible celebrant and decide for yourself if this person is the right person to create and present the funeral you would like. You always have the choice of bringing in your own independent funeral celebrant. Thankfully people are starting to understand they have a choice. I have received calls from people who have decided to 'sack' the celebrant who had been engaged. While it is sad that this was necessary, it is positive that they chose not to settle for less than what they wanted.

A celebrant should be well trained in:

- working with grieving families;
- listening and checking in on the needs of the family;
- gathering information;
- constructing a professional ceremony;
- presenting it well.

Funeral company or not?

If members of the deceased's family or friends decide on a DIY funeral, they can reduce costs substantially. This option, however, is rarely known. If you do decide to arrange a funeral yourself, I suggest you get hold of a funeral advocate who can guide and assist you on the best way to handle it.

Although a significant number of people are becoming more aware of the options and possibilities available when making funeral arrangements, more education is still needed. Some families do now understand that they can use a funeral company for some or all of the funeral arrangements, or they can handle everything themselves if they choose. Regrettably, however, the majority is still unaware of all the options available. I believe it is the responsibility of people like myself to make others aware of the many options available, so that families can make an informed decision about what is the best way to handle the final farewell.

Naturally, it is easier to leave the arrangements to someone else, however for those who want to participate in this last significant rite of passage and the final resting place, it can be an enriching and life-affirming experience.

The list of things to do can be quite daunting, so when you are deciding whether to use a funeral company or not it is probably wise to clarify what you as a family are capable of handling under the circumstances and what sort of outcome you hope for.

Here are my 'pros and cons' of using a funeral company or doing it yourself (with or without assistance). Remember you can always engage a funeral company to do only part of the service they would usually offer. Alternatively, you may choose them to take charge of all the proceedings

Advantages of using a funeral company

- Everything can be handled by the funeral company on your behalf.
- It relieves the burden of planning and decision making.
- You are handing over to people experienced in the field.
- It can reduce stress.

- You are able to concentrate on yourself and your family without the worry of organising everything.
- Some small independent companies have the flexibility to tailor their services to suit families' needs.
- Many funeral companies offer a 'one stop shop' for all things funereal.
- Some funeral companies offer good value for money.
- Some funeral companies are very empathic and will be with you every step of the way (what you should be looking for is a company whose professionalism is built on trust and compassion because they truly care about the individuals and the families that they have the opportunity to serve).
- Some funeral companies give very good advice and do have your interests at heart.
- Funeral companies can easily arrange for repatriation of a person to another country or state if required.
- Some funeral companies truly understand both the cultural and religious needs of various communities.

Disadvantages of using a funeral company

- The cost can be very high and can place great financial burden on the family. A tip: funeral costs can vary significantly, so while it may be difficult at this time, it is important to shop around and compare quotes.
- Many funeral companies have a service fee that is quite high regardless of what services you actually want or use. It is not always easy to work out what is included in the service fee and what is not.
- Some funeral companies are very inflexible, and it is becoming more apparent that larger organisations adhere to a strict process and model and are not interested in working outside this model. With these companies you just get to tick their boxes.

- Many funeral companies only offer limited or no options.
- Most companies do not allow you to bring in your own funeral-related goods and services such as coffin or caterers.
- Some insist you use a particular funeral celebrant who they have on their books.
- Many funeral companies will pressure you into making decisions.
- Many pressure you into having a funeral quickly, which may not suit your needs.
- On the day of the ceremony a funeral company will often send a representative with whom you have had no previous contact prior to the funeral. This happens when their roster does not allow the person you have been dealing with to attend your particular funeral ceremony.
- Some funeral companies will restrict the time allocated to you and your family for the ceremony. For instance they will only allow a 30 to 45 minute ceremony option (in some places it is even less).
- Some funeral companies will not have resources, such as a hearse, available for use on the day.
- Most funeral companies add a commission to anything they organise for you: for example, the newspaper announcements may incur more than a 100% mark up for simply emailing your advertisement through to one email address at that newspaper, so if the newspaper fee is $400, the funeral company may charge you $800.
- Some funeral companies pay commission to the funeral arranger on the price of the coffin sold to you.
- Most funeral companies will not assist or encourage you in having your loved one at home anytime between death and the ceremony.

Doing it yourself

There are many ways to 'do it yourself'. You can handle it all yourself, you can arrange for a funeral advocate to do part of it or you can do some of the work yourself and employ a funeral company for the rest.

Advantages of doing it yourself

- It dramatically reduces the cost in most situations. You pay for what you need and nothing more.
- It gives you enormous flexibility.
- You can source your own funeral related goods and services, such as coffin, caterers and other elements.
- You can choose your own independent funeral celebrant or clergy.
- There is no pressure to make decisions.
- You decide when and where it is convenient to have the ceremony.
- You choose a venue of your liking that has no time limits, such as a reception centre, the park, your home, a restaurant with a private room, the local golf club.
- There is no commission on anything you yourself obtain, such as caterers, coffins, room hire, newspaper advertisements, etc.
- You can decide if you want your loved one at home anytime between death and the ceremony and you can engage people to assist with this.

Disadvantages of doing it yourself

- There may not be anyone in the family willing to 'take this project on board'.
- You do not have the experience to know your options.
- You do not have the time.
- It is easier to just hand over to the funeral company.
- It is easier to keep doing what you have done in the past.

Using a funeral advocate

There aren't very many funeral advocates in Australia. My own funeral advocacy service for families has been available for many years and there are others who also offer this service. Families can engage an advocate to work for them as their independent support and not necessarily as their celebrant. While this role can vary it is likely to include:

- selecting a funeral company if one is required. This is discussed later in this chapter;
- selecting a final resting place and finding natural grounds;
- working out what funeral arrangements are required: flowers, location for the ceremony, advertisements and so on;
- assisting the family to keep the body at home for some or all of the time until the funeral;
- dressing and preparing the body;
- sourcing funeral products such as coffins and ashes urns;
- referral to other people in the death care field.

Funeral advocates are independent and wll give you the information you need to make choices. They work from a blank canvas and together with the bereaved create something that is authentic. They don't have set models so there are no constraints on the way you wish the funeral to be conducted. They are very versatile and will personalise the ceremony, resulting in an authentic outcome that will meet your needs.

Disposal of the body

There are a number of options with regard to the final resting place chosen.

- Traditional style of burial.
- Alternative types of burial, for instance burial at sea or natural

burial ground (discussed later in this chapter)
- (<www.environment.gov.au/topics/marine/marine-pollution/sea-dumping/burial-sea>).
- Cremation.
- Spreading of ashes.
- Promession (freeze drying and vibration).
- Resomation (rendering to liquid).
- Cryomation (freeze drying).
- Donating the body to science.
- Grave decorations.
- Greener, more environmentally friendly options.

You can choose the venue for the funeral from any of the available options. We have been conditioned to believe that the only choice is to sit in a dreary dark chapel. This is certainly no longer the case. There are many beautiful venues that offer a different and wonderful alternative. Why not consider a special venue, even one outside?

On Page 312 we look at a sample structure of a funeral ceremony and later in the book I have included a number of different types of funeral ceremony, by various celebrants.

Burial or cremation

Cremation is the preferred option over burial in many countries, and I believe the most popular reason is cost. Also, today it is the preferred choice for ecological reasons, as it saves land space. However, it is now questionable whether Cremation is in fact better for the environment than burial.

There are, of course, some cultures where burial is preferred. Religious and cultural beliefs play an important part in this decision. Except for Orthodox Judaism, Eastern Orthodox Church, and Islam, most religions accept the process of cremation.

In most instances - for a body to be cremated it needs to be in a coffin type vessel and the container then slips quickly from a rack of rolling metal pins into the primary cremating chamber, also referred to as a retort. We are starting to see the viability of shroud cremations only.

There are options with regard to the choice of a final resting place. Some people are choosing more creative options such as scattering the ashes or burying them at sea. Some people are choosing to have part of their remains sent into space: Celestis Incorporated will place ashes in a sealed capsule which is then placed on a spacecraft and launched into space. Prices range from about $1,000 to $12,000. Some people choose to have ashes made into a work of art or jewellery. In fact they can be made into just about anything nowadays. Alternatively, you may choose a traditional in-ground burial, an all-natural green burial, be placed in an entombment or you can be cremated.

Families often do not realise that in many cases you can have the body at home until the funeral, and some even apply to have the body buried on their private property. It is possible to bury someone on your own private property, not in a cemetery, however, it is unlikely that you will receive permission. This is discussed in more detail below.

There are other non-mainstream options for disposal of the body:

'Resomation' is slowly being looked at. In the United States people can opt to have their tissue dissolved as an alternative to traditional cremation. The process, also known as 'bio-cremation,' uses heated water and potassium hydroxide to liquefy the body, leaving only bones behind. The bones are then pulverised, much as in normal cremation, and the bone fragments are returned to the family.

Cryomation is the process of freezing a person's body in the hopes that later medical science will make it possible to revive them, personality and memory in tact. However, be warned, this is an extremely expensive process! Another consideration is that the continued storage requirements certainly don't make it environmentally friendly.

When people are consciously deciding on greener options when arranging a funeral there are many aspects to consider, from the car that takes you to the ceremony to coffins made from woven wicker, plantation pine or recycled cardboard, or maybe just a shroud or a more environmentally friendly garment.

To bury a person on private land there are a few things that need to be taken into account:

Are burials on private property allowed? The simple answer is yes in most parts of Australia but you do need to do some homework and unfortunately this varies from state to state as each state in Australia has its own laws <www.health.vic.gov.au/cemeteries/public/private.htm>. More detailed information on this topic and on cemeteries, cemetery trusts and crematoria in general is given in the next few pages.

◐ DID YOU KNOW?

For the late Barbara Cartland, recognised as the world's most prolific novelist, it wasn't a plot in Westminster Abbey's Poets' Corner beside Chaucer, Dickens and Hardy that she most wanted as her final resting place. When she passed away in 2000, a few weeks shy of her 99th birthday, she was buried in her back garden, beneath her favourite tree. Perry Como's 'I Believe' played as her cardboard coffin was covered.

When you purchase a burial site within a public cemetery do you own the plot of land?

The answer to this question will differ depending on the location. However as a general rule the answer is that you don't own that land. There is a common misconception that a person actually buys the land associated with a cemetery plot or grave when in actual fact a 'right of interment' for a burial is purchased.

Can a cemetery cancel your interment right?

Yes, they can in Victoria, under the *Cemeteries and Crematoria Act 2003*.

Cemeteries, Cemetery Trusts and Crematoria

In Victoria and Western Australia, cemeteries and crematoria are usually owned by government appointed and regulated trusts (state or local). In most cases they are on land owned by the local council rather than the state, though a few were set up on private land which is now usually administered by a trust. The system grew in a very arbitrary way for over 150 years and there are endless exceptions.

In Victoria, the Greater Melbourne Cemetery Trust controls most of the northern metropolitan cemeteries and crematoria between Altona and Fawkner and Lilydale (about eighteen in total).

The Southern Metropolitan Cemetery Trust controls another dozen from Springvale to Brighton to Bunurong (near Frankston), and, for historical reasons, the central Melbourne General Cemetery.

The other trust in Victoria is the Greater Geelong Cemetery Trust, which also administers a dozen or more cemeteries.

A few Melbourne cemeteries such as Eltham have somehow managed to avoid amalgamation and are still run by their own trusts. The City of

Hume also is still responsible for Sunbury and Bulla, and the City of Banyule for Warringal in Heidelberg.

Some monasteries and nunneries still have private cemeteries, however you have to apply for permission from the Health Department to use them. The cemetery at Elaine, south of Ballarat, is an example of a cemetery set up on land belonging to the Serbian monastery for the Serbian community, and since put under a trust in conjunction with the local council and opened to the general public.

There are Class A and B cemetery trusts. The larger trusts that run a number of cemeteries are required to make enough money to maintain some of the smaller, older cemeteries that they have been amalgamated with. These trusts are huge corporations that turn over many millions of dollars per year. They are required to make a profit to invest for long-term management of cemeteries that have been closed. (This was part of the deal when the big trusts were formed from lots of little ones.)

Small cemeteries in country towns that only serve their local communities might only have a few funerals per year. They tend to be run as Class B cemeteries run by volunteers and are only expected to keep themselves financial and operational. Yan Yean is an example of a well run cemetery. Donnybrook is an example of one that was run so badly for years that records of which graves have been sold and to whom, or even who is buried in some graves, are considered a bit hit and miss (although that is being fixed now).

In other states of Australia some cemeteries are owned by the state or local council, or privately, but a number of the large ones now are owned and operated by companies like InvoCare that also own funeral chains. By contrast, some cemeteries have simply set up their own funeral company that operates solely from and for their cemetery.

Can a cremation or burial be organised by the family?

There is a fallacious belief that a cremation or burial cannot be organised directly by a family. In fact most places, such as Victoria for example, have legislation that states that cemeteries and crematoria must accept bookings from families where funeral directors are not involved.

However, the practical restraints still exist. With small country cemeteries there usually isn't a problem with the family organising the funeral, but with the big Class A trusts ... that is another thing altogether.

In a recent case where the family wanted to do everything themselves for a cremation, they found that doing the paperwork, getting the certificates, and arranging for a medical officer to come to the house and inspect the deceased to co-sign the documentation, etc., was beyond them, despite many hours of effort. In the end they managed to locate a wonderfully helpful Funeral Company, who completed the paperwork, arranged the certificates, provided the coffin and did the final transportation to the crematorium for them. They left the family to do everything else themselves that they wanted regarding preparation and service. The crematorium in this instance was relieved that a funeral company was involved because in the past when families had tried to deliver privately they had to send them away at the last minute because the documentation was incomplete or incorrect.

In this instance, the funeral company saved the family several hundred dollars when they checked alternatives. This is purely because the funeral company had the process and contacts to handle documentation on a large scale, whereas the family would have had to source and pay a locum to process and sign the necessary paperwork. In this instance the family was quoted $300 or $400 by a doctor for doing this privately, whereas the funeral company had an arrangement in place for $56.65 for the same service. A company that processes hundreds of medical certificates a year is a good option if you find that the doctor needed to sign the requisite certificates gets greedy!

This is the sort of compromise that is often needed with the big trusts, where, for example, funeral directors have to pass WH&S (Workplace Health & Safety) registration requirements before being allowed on site to do burials, something that families usually can't manage on their own (despite what the legislation says). The 'law' at issue here relates to the big trusts meeting their statutory WH&S requirements, which prevents a family doing the burial themselves, even though the legislation theoretically allows them to do so.

In another example, a family purchased a coffin which they brought to the cemetery in their own car. However, the cemetery trust requested they engage a funeral company to lead it in with their (empty) hearse, demanding that their men be the ones to 'supervise' as the family carried and lowered. That is, as long as the funeral directors, who had cleared their WH&S registration, stood nearby giving instructions, they could satisfy both legal requirements even though the directors never touched the body or the coffin!

So laws – no. Practices - yes.

It is interesting to note that anyone can set up as a funeral director. Although there are requirements for funeral directors in some places such as Victoria, to register with the justice or health departments so there are records of legal ownership and responsibility, there is no funding or regulation to pursue people who don't register (or don't even know registration is required). Registration requirement is not well advertised, however the Justice Department is currently trying to get the funeral directors' associations and the cemetery trusts to tell people who ring up as funeral directors to book in, that they need to be registered. This is another example of holes in the system, and one that unfortunately allows dodgy operators to slip through and then escape charges.

Finally, although there are codes of conduct and rules of behaviour for those funeral directors who are members of professional associations (about 80%), some major players seem to ignore the code of conduct plaques on their wall and, if they are big players, their association conveniently turns a blind eye.

Are burials on private property allowed?

The simple answer is yes they are in some places in Australia, but you do need to do some homework. Unfortunately each state in Australia has its own laws <www.health.vic.gov.au/cemeteries/public/private.htm>.

Under section 121 of the *Cemeteries and Crematoria Act 2003* (Victoria) the approval of the Secretary to the Department of Health is required for burials on private property. Generally such applications are not approved. There are a number of reasons why the department has adopted this position.

A Parliamentary Joint Select Committee recommended in 1987 that burials not be permitted on private property due to:

- no one having responsibility for the creation and preservation of an adequate burial record;
- no one being responsible for ongoing maintenance of the grave;
- there being no guarantee that ownership of land will not change hands in the future, and that the land will not be used in a way which compromises the integrity of any grave;
- difficulties in ensuring compliance with appropriate legislation regarding burials.

This is why the law requires the approval for burials in places other than public cemeteries, and why approval will ordinarily be provided only in the special circumstances outlined below.

Public cemeteries are administered by cemetery trusts appointed by the Governor in Council to administer and maintain cemeteries on behalf of the Victorian government and the community. This framework ensures that the historical significance of cemeteries and burial records is preserved, and that burials comply with the appropriate legislation.

When would an approval be granted for burial outside a public cemetery?

Normally permission for burial of a body outside a public cemetery will only be considered if there are pre-existing burials on that land. This means that if there is a record of another person or persons having already been buried on the land, and the relevant grave or graves are clearly marked and identifiable, the secretary would consider granting an interment approval.

On the rare occasion when permission for burial of a person on private land has been granted in the past, the burial has been made in an established, defined and properly maintained burial site that contains:

- physical evidence of pre-existing burials such as headstones, fencing;
- documented records of other burials that have taken place there;
- an ongoing tradition of such burials.

Additionally, section 124 of the Act specifies that the Secretary may grant approval subject to conditions. These conditions might include consideration of:

- the size and zoning of the land;
- the depth of the interment;
- the standards of construction for any memorial or monument to be erected on the burial site;
- what arrangements exist for the care of the proposed burial site;
- the connection of the deceased to the land;

- the proposed location of the new grave in relation to the existing grave(s);
- the condition of the ground.

Can a cemetery cancel your interment right?

Yes, they can in Victoria. The *Cemeteries and Crematoria Act 2003* Section 91 states:

> When can a cemetery trust cancel a right of interment?
>
> 1. A cemetery trust may cancel a right of interment in a public cemetery for which it is responsible if:
>   a. the right of interment has never been exercised; and
>   b. the holder of the right of interment cannot be found after diligent inquiries.
> 2. A cemetery trust must not cancel a right of interment referred to in subsection (1) until the end of at least 25 years after the original grant of the right of interment.
> 3. At least 14 days before cancelling a right of interment, a cemetery trust must publish notice of its intention to do so in a daily or weekly newspaper circulating generally in the area in which the public cemetery to which the right of interment applies is located.

In New South Wales for example, renewable interment involves the purchase of a right to inter human remains, and for those remains to be left undisturbed for an initial period of time with the option of renewing the right for additional subsequent periods. If an interment right is not renewed, the interment site may be reused after certain requirements have been met. <www.dpi.nsw.gov.au/lands/cemetery-reform/renewable-rights>

In Western Australia the first review of the Cemeteries Act since 1897 produced some significant changes. The biggest change was the legislation regarding the length of the 'Grant of Right of Burial'. Under the revised 1986 Cemeteries Act, the new stipulated tenure of Grants was twenty-five years with an automatic option for grant holders to purchase an additional twenty-five years either initially or at any time during the first twenty-five years. The discretion of all cemetery authorities in Western Australia to issue fifty or ninety-nine year grants was revoked.

<www.mcb.wa.gov.au/OurCemeteries/1986CemeteriesActReview.aspx>

Natural burial

There are two components that make a natural burial: the burial environment and the burial process itself. Natural burial means no headstone, no embalming, no fancy furnished coffin, and no 'six feet under' either. The Australasian Cemeteries and Crematoria Association (ACCA) defines a green burial as "the interment of a body that conforms to the usual or ordinary course of nature and adds to the biodiversity of the area" (ACCA 2008, 5).

I am a committee member of the Natural Death Advocacy Network (NDAN) in Australia <www.ndan.com.au> and as a diverse group of people in the industry we are working together to offer a resource of greener and more natural death options, all located on the one website. At the moment our focus is concentrating on developing natural burial sites and setting Australian standards.

The Natural Death Advocacy Network is an advocacy partnership of community facilitators, non-government organisations and professionals working to deepen the experience of dying and death. We are committed to empowering people to bring dying and death into the light. The Network advocates end-of-life journeys that honour the dying and heal the living. It is creating a facilitative, innovative and transparent organisation advocating holistic approaches to dying and death, through independent research and action. We are committed to enabling individuals, families and communities, with the assistance of professionals, to choose humane and ecological pathways at the end of the human life cycle.

NDAN's philosophy is to empower those for whom death matters through the consolidation of the independent investigations and research conducted by all of its members. They are working to create a seamless network of people who are able to facilitate, inspire and work with families and communities to transform care of at the end-of-life.

The best place to start if you live in the USA is the Green Burial Council. I have met with one of the leaders of this organisation, Joe Sehee who is the founder of the council and was the executive director from 2005 to 2012. He oversees outreach and advocacy for the council and heads the newly formed GBC International. A senior fellow with the Environmental Leadership Program, Joe consults on green burial projects that further ecological restoration and landscape-level conservation. The Council is doing admirable work. <www.greenburialcouncil.org>.

There are several hundred natural burial grounds in the United Kingdom and half a dozen sites across the USA, with other 'eco cemeteries' planned in Canada, New Zealand, South Africa and China.

In Australia there are no standard guidelines for those dealing with the burial location environment and the burial process itself. There is also relatively little research being conducted in this area.

Natural burial is an approach to burial methods that considers environmental sustainability and recycling in natural ways. It proposes new methods to decrease the amount of wood, steel or other metals used in making coffins and to prevent pollution of the environment with chemical treatments of the corpse during burial. It also encourages protection of the natural landscape as well as the fauna and the flora at the time of planning the cemetery and choosing its location.

Natural burial or green burial sites often uses grave makers that do not intrude on the landscape. Graves are marked with markers native to the landscape like trees, shrubs, or flat stones. In some cases, graves are unmarked and surveying techniques such as GPS are used to identify the plots.

Natural burial can involve use of a biodegradable coffin or the wrapping of remains in a shroud. Bodies are not usually treated with any chemicals. Plantings are often made at a burial site in place of the traditional headstone.

In June 2013 legislation was passed by the South Australian parliament to recognise natural burials. Attorney-General John Rau said it would mean consistent regulations for dealing with human remains. He said: "These laws reflect modern technologies, industry practices and community expectations, including the recognition of natural burial grounds". The use of natural burial as an alternative to more traditional forms of burial is now, for the first time, recognised under law in South Australia. There are two natural burial grounds in SA – Enfield Memorial Park and Smithfield Memorial Park.

Bushland Cemetery in Lismore Memorial Gardens, New South Wales which is located approximately 700 km north of Sydney, offers several greener options. You may choose to be buried without a coffin, instead wrapped simply in a shroud of biodegradable cotton. You can ring them direct to organise a burial. http://www.lismore.nsw.gov.au

Wirra Wonga, South Australia's first natural burial area is a tranquil bushland environment offering a unique final resting place.

Kingston Cemetery in Tasmania was the first in Australia to offer 'green bushland burials' in which bodies are buried in open bush using recyclable burial materials.

In Victoria the Kurweeton Road Cemetery is located in the Corangamite Shire southwest of Mt Elephant. It offers the opportunity for an upright burial (buried in a vertical plot that is 10 feet deep and just over 2 feet wide) in a rural setting using a simple approach that considers the environment and minimises the financial burden for the deceased and their family. They state that this cemetery aims to leave the lightest possible carbon footprint on the earth. Their burial process allows the body to be placed in a biodegradable body bag then lowered in the plot.

In mid 2014, Carlsruhe, a small rural town in the Shire of Macedon Ranges, just outside Melbourne, made a decision to put aside 600 of a total of 2000 plots in its bushland cemetery specifically for the development of a natural burial ground. A local holistic funeral director, Libby Moloney, has approached the Class B cemetery trust with a plan to convert this section of land. The Trust is very supportive of NDAN and adhering to the principles. I look forward to watching this develop into what might be termed a hybrid cemetery. It appears that some families have already made plans for moving current plots from the older section of this cemetery into the new natural burial ground when it becomes available.

The Lilydale Cemeteries Trust also has two sites with natural burial options alongside traditional burial sections; Lilydale and Healesville. I have assisted families in burying their loved ones in the Lilydale cemetery wrapped only in a shroud, no coffin. It is worth noting that method was not chosen for any particular religious reason.

A few other cemeteries offer burial grounds, which depart from the granite headstones and manicured grounds of the conventional cemetery. The Metropolitan Cemeteries Board (Western Australia) has established a natural burial area at Fremantle Cemetery. Natural burials at Fremantle Cemetery are located within an elevated grove that overlooks the cemetery's splendid bushland gully. Their website states "Pinnaroo cemetery is widely considered to be the most environmentally responsible cemetery in Australia. The park, which received its first burial in 1978, has been developed and maintained as a natural bushland cemetery planted only with native species. No monuments are permitted but each grave is marked by a flat bronze plaque". http://www.mcb.wa.gov.au/OurCemeteries/Pinnaroo.aspx

In the USA there is a 'Natural End Pledge'. The Natural End Funeral Service Provider Network <www.naturalendmap.com> is a free online service created by Cynthia Beal of the Natural Burial Company and sponsored by supporters of natural end-of-life products and services. Providers or suppliers to the funeral industry can sign an agreement and get a listing and customers (i.e. the family of the deceased) are able to leave feedback on the website, creating a self-regulating system for monitoring the quality of the products and services being offered. The 'pledge' covers things such as:

- being able to provide your own coffin;
- offering 'natural funeral' services, which means no embalming;
- promoting biodegradable coffins and urns;
- offering vault or outer burial container-free burials and shroud burials with no coffin;
- supporting the family in using natural options.

For more information on natural burials I suggest the following reading:

- Green Burials in Australia and their planning challenges, a paper by Nancy Marshall and Rennie Rounds, UNSW, Sydney New South Wales, Australia; and
- The ACCA Mentor Report – Natural Burials (2008) by Glenys Parton (Australasian Cemeteries and Crematoria Association).

The challenge when making a decision is having the right information about how green or environmentally friendly the final disposal options are. How do you compare:

- being cremated in a traditional coffin; to
- being cremated in an environmentally friendly, smaller carbon footprint coffin; to
- being buried in a traditional plot, in a coffin, after being embalmed; to
- being buried in a traditional plot, in a shroud, no embalming; to
- being buried in a natural burial ground, in a coffin, after being embalmed; to
- being buried in a natural burial ground, in a shroud only, no embalming.

I have spent many years trying to get clear objective statistics about comparisons of body disposal. However, so far I have been unable to obtain clear figures. If you are after minimum impact on the environment, then the last option is the one I would recommend. It can allow for the body to be a natural fertiliser for the soil, without the decomposition of materials such as timber coffins and without any toxic liquids being leaked into the soil below.

The story of Moora Moora's community's sanctuary

Moora Moora is a cooperative community located some ninety minutes north-east of Melbourne, just outside Healesville. The intention at Moora Moora is to provide the opportunity for all stages of life, from birth to death and burial, to take place there in ways that are consistent with the community's philosophy.

Some people have had the privilege of being born at Moora Moora. At the other end of life they would like to have the choice of being buried there, so where they have lived becomes their last resting place. Burial of one's body as part of local reforestation is a choice that makes a positive environmental contribution to the planet. That this can occur at Moora Moora adds to community empowerment and celebration.

Moora Moora's story with local community green burials began in its early days, with the spreading of the ashes of Wilby Rackham in the late 1970s. The location is around a large gum tree overlooking the Yarra Valley. A stone plaque was placed on a nearby rock.

Revegetation of this site began with the planting of hundreds of gum trees, many of which have survived. A working party was created and its research showed that it would be difficult to make this site legal and would be disruptive to the community as it was a long way from the entrance to allow for visitor access.

After many discussions over the years and with the ageing of the community, in 2013 members decided to find a better site. They stepped up their efforts to provide for the bodies and ashes of past, present and future members. A site called the 'Copse', closer to their community centre and one in need of regeneration, was identified.

A group drew up a proposal to put to the community and the following resolution was passed unanimously: "That Moora Moora agrees to the establishment of a green burial site for past, present and future members of Moora Moora at the place in front of the lodge near the entrance called The Copse, where ashes and, if approved, bodies can be placed with recognition by a tree, plaque and/or an engraved local stone. (A GPS map would also be used to record these burial sites)."

Ecologically, the cooperative favours burial of bodies left to naturally decompose in degradable coffins. And to locate them so it is possible to plant a tree on top of the body rather than near it, so the organic matter feeds the tree.

Why was this site chosen?

- The area is in need of care and regeneration. It is currently covered with holly, dead trees and blackberries.
- It will enhance the beauty, meaning and extension of the community entrance and centre.
- It is easily accessible to visitors, with little intrusion on the cooperative as it is near the entrance with easy car parking adjacent.
- It is of sufficient size - about one hectare - to meet potential needs.
- It is at least 400 metres away from spring catchments.

Work has begun clearing the weeds and revealing the magic of naturally exposed stone boulders. There is some blackwood, hazel pomaderris, silver wattle and the remains of a mixed eucalyptus forest on a gentle slope facing west from the Mt Toobewong plateau.

To the surprise of members, a current neighbour and ex-member recently said there is a plaque in The Copse designating the place where a previous resident was buried, which as yet has not been found. Another member has spread her mother's ashes in a particular spot at The Copse. The location has no permanent marking.

Members, past and present, are beginning to discuss their intentions with regard to committing to the site and the nature of their interest, as well as beginning to plan pathways, burial sites and revegetation species within a local species framework. Sites will be marked with a plaque on stone or next to specially planted trees.

There is a long history of private burial sites on rural properties in Victoria although this has ceased. However, in South Australia and New South Wales it is legal to have greener burials on private land. One recently occurred at Bundagen Eco village.

The cooperative is preparing a submission to state government agencies seeking permission to follow suit at Moora Moora in partnership with the newly formed Natural Death Advocacy Network of Australia (NDAN). Their intention is clear but it will take considerable time.

Their case is based on:

- being a registered legal entity which owns the land as distinct from it being privately owned land;
- the long history of settlement on Mt Toobewong. The place was previously only visited for summer hunting by the Wurrundjeri, and tourists, up until the mid twentieth-century and then as a hobby farm. Moora Moora cooperative community was the first to take up permanent residency.

What the community is undertaking is part of a larger movement to empower citizens to be more in charge of their own passing, in ways that make a contribution to the wellbeing of families, communities and nature.

Dr Peter Cock, for the Moora Moora Sanctuary working party says, "Maybe our site can be a place for the community on top of Mt Toobewong. For what we are working towards is the creation of recognised community neighbourhood burial sites as middle grounds between purely private and public burial places that honour the community members and the ecology of their places."

#POINTS TO CONSIDER

- → Families want choices and today many options are available to them.
- → Families can always choose who leads the ceremony, regardless of what the funeral arranger tells them.

- → A funeral does not have to take place quickly.
- → When you are ready, you determine if and when you want to hold a ceremony.
- → There is a difference between honouring and celebrating.
- → Not all families are ready and willing to celebrate.
- → Families are demanding the truth about what they can and can't do when arranging a funeral.
- → Families are considering their 'natural death' options.
- → A person can be buried in a shroud, without a coffin, for non-religious reasons.
- → There is no independent data on what is greener: cremation or burial.
- → A funeral advocate can help ensure that you get all the information you need to make a fully informed choice.
- → Don't put up with a funeral company that is not offering options. You can take the funeral away from them at any time.

MY NOTES

MY NOTES

CHAPTER 6

THE CHANGING LANDSCAPE OF FUNERALS

Things change. And friends leave. Life doesn't stop for anybody.
— Stephen Chbosky, *The Perks of Being a Wallflower*

The face of funerals is always changing. However when it comes to arranging a funeral, we tend to be creatures of habit. Our choices are mostly influenced by what we have experienced before, and often follow on from previous decisions made in our own families. I do think this will change in the near future with the baby boomers demanding a much more life-centred celebration with more inclusiveness and flexibility, interwoven with more informed decisions made around what is best for our environment. Perhaps more than most previous generations, it seems the baby boomers are challenging the traditional ways of doing things and creating new traditions.

Over the last five years the content of funerals has become far more authentic. We are far more accepting of mental health issues and depression and this is being openly acknowledged at funerals. More often now the 'elephant in the room' is mentioned. As recently as five years ago a family would be firm in their decision to not mention things like suicide or mental health issues, but today people are aware that talking about these types of matters openly is healthy for all concerned.

Families are now much more likely to:

- ask questions and not be rushed by funeral companies who simply want to take their money and rush them into having a funeral;
- take time and effort to celebrate the death of a family member with as much authenticity as possible;
- take time to find out their choices and rights;
- ask about green and natural death options, and care about the long-term effect on the environment.

Defining what elements of a funeral and which type of final disposal is better for the environment is actually quite difficult. There is little data available – and very few standards, but we do know that the number of trees being cut down around the world for funeral pyres and coffins is astronomical and is not sustainable. For example in India alone, out of the 10 million people or so who die each year, close to 85% of the population practice cremation, according to the latest UN statistics. This results in the cutting down of an estimated 50 million trees and the production of approximately 8 million tons of carbon dioxide each year.

Whenever possible we should minimise the overall impact of the funeral.

Some of the things you can consider are:

- **Coffins:** There are many options that have a lower impact on the environment. Or better still don't use a coffin – use a shroud;
- **Embalming:** Say no to embalming;
- **Clothing:** Use sustainable biodegradable clothing – or use just a shroud;
- **Venue: Gather outside in a natural setting;**
- **Vehicles:** Make arrangements for carpooling from location to location during the funeral;
- **Programs:** Use only recycled paper products for order of service;
- **Flowers:** Source any flowers from organic, local growers, or from the garden of your guests;

- **Refreshments:** If the deceased was an environmentalist, the chances are they enjoyed local, organic food. Look at organic options or simply ask everyone to bring a plate of food;
- **Final Disposal:** Look at natural burial ground options.

To find out more about greener options please visit the Natural Death Advocacy Network http://www.ndan.com.au/ or the Green Burial Council website http://greenburialcouncil.org/

Auckland researcher Sally Raudon in her paper *Contemporary Funerals and Mourning Practices* says:

> "Currently people's willingness to consider alternative death practices is limited by real uncertainty about what they can and can't do. It is not widely understood, for instance, that in New Zealand anyone can organise the disposal of a body by burial or cremation, and that embalming is rarely required. That coffins, like funeral directors, are optional. Or that any person can conduct a funeral, and there is no legal requirement for any particular form of ceremony.
>
> "In short, New Zealanders have broad choices available for paying homage to the deceased and for offering comfort to the bereaved. However, though reformers suggest we may find novel practices more relevant or more comforting, most of us adhere to typical practices amongst this wider range of possibilities. It may be because there is currently no comprehensive resource for New Zealanders regarding what to do when someone dies. What information does exist is fragmented and difficult to access, and is usually published by funeral directors themselves."

The majority of funerals follow a fairly familiar pattern, and decisions are based on perceived assumptions rather than law or on traditions. They tend to have little reference to religion, as Australia is now predominantly a secular society. Funerals can be the ultimate celebration. With far less formality than a religious ceremony, they are now more of a social and learning experience for the audience.

And I believe as a result of our society becoming more secular we now see funerals appearing to bring the wake into the funeral ceremony. By that I mean our ceremonies are full of stories and tributes which years ago would only be heard at a wake, after a funeral that often didn't talk about the person in any detail.

It was Dr Alan Wolfelt who said, "Throughout our grief journeys, the more we are able to 'tell our story' of the death itself, of our memories of the person who died, the more likely we will be to reconcile our grief. Moreover, the sharing of memories at the funeral are memories that we have not heard before. This teaches us about the dead person's life apart from ours and allows us glimpses into that life that we may cherish forever."

Sally Raudon, in an investigation of five secular countries, concludes that about 29,000 people die in New Zealand every year (Statistics New Zealand, 2011). The ageing population of Australia and New Zealand, and other countries, means this will increase as the famously individualistic group of baby boomer plans and participates in funerals much more keenly, as their parents, partners, sometimes children and, finally, they themselves die.

There is an interesting debate as to whether returning a body to the land after typical cancer treatment, when it has been treated with toxic medications, has less impact than say EcoPrep which is a technique that combines environmentally friendly preparation to restore the dead body to a more natural chemical free state for burial or cremation. It is a discussion that I think will become more prevalent as people start to think more about the environmental impact of death and disposal of the body.

Today the majority of Australians and New Zealanders no longer attend church regularly, if at all. Our de-ritualised society offers bereaved families few guidelines, so increasing people's awareness of different funeral practices is one way of helping them navigate the decisions they will inevitably have to make.

To see what a typical funeral looks like in certain countries I suggest you download Sally Raudon's paper, which is readily available on the web.

A funeral director's perspective on current practices

It is refreshing to work alongside caring professionals in the death care industry. Two such individuals are Anne Gleeson and Steve Lamb from MacQueen's Funerals, Terang in Victoria. I have worked with Anne and Steve for some time now and find their approach of an inclusive, transparent, warm and friendly style is loved and appreciated by families. I asked them their thoughts on current practice in the funeral industry.

Q. What do you think has changed most over the time you have been in this industry?

> The divide between small independent funeral homes and the big businesses. Corporatisation in many regions particularly in the metropolitan areas has led to more centralised and business-focussed practices. That often means less flexibility and a lack of continuity of care, which at the time of profound grief and distress matters so much.

What do families care most about?

> Naturally every family or partner is different, but from comments received afterwards, it would seem that the way a family

has felt supported throughout the time of dealing with us is one of the most important aspects for everyone. In various emails, notes and visits we receive, families express their appreciation of the helpfulness, of not being pushed into decisions, of having the differing views of families listened to and brought together, the sense of professionalism and taking the worry of organising the funeral away, being comfortable, being looked after. These are some of the services people look for.

What seems to matter a great deal are that the bereaved families deal with one or other of us and that they feel the funeral home is a welcoming place. People need to feel free to vent or grieve or query. After the initial visit, the family feels comfortable to drop in and sometimes, even months or years later, one of them will come to tell us about something significant happening in their lives.

Q. Is there a shift towards having the body at home for some of the time between death and funeral?

This is something that was commonplace two generations ago, so it's within the memory of many older residents. To some extent, it is through listening to them that we have moved in the direction of offering different options for greater family based care. But usually when we do offer to bring people back home, most are surprised. It is not something most people are choosing, but for those who do, it seems remarkably special and poignant.

More people are choosing multiple or extended time with the deceased person at our funeral home. It is a warm, cosy, two-roomed space arranged in a way so that people can spend as much or as little time with the deceased person as they want but still be part of a family gathering. Sometimes someone will come in and have a beer with their Dad; another might massage or anoint their Mum. People can have a drink and something to eat, if they choose, and stay as long as they like, so it's very relaxed. Many times families come in from different parts of Victoria and have a sad farewell but a great catch-up with each other. These family gatherings have become a hallmark of what we do.

Q. If there is a shift to having body at home - why do you think this is?

As death has become more medicalised, people have lost the natural instincts of how to deal with death so there is a certain lack of confidence. It is interesting though that when people rightfully assume or are given back control, they seem to know how to care for a person transitioning from life to death, just as most do with a new soul entering into life.

Q. Do you think funerals have changed much? If so why and how?

Funerals have changed, but not everywhere. Because as a society we have changed so much, particularly in the shift from traditional religions and consequently religious practices. Once people feel safe to look at different options, they tend to be very ready to look at different structures, venues and formats. Then other less common decisions often follow from that. One family might have a farm funeral, another a quiet organic goodbye with no formal service, another a community gathering or a ceremony in a person's home or garden. A number of people choose a combination ritual where community singing, an Aboriginal ceremony, a street parade, and a traditional religious or a contemporary service are combined. Many families make a distinction between the public and private goodbyes.

Q. Do families ask more questions now?

Yes, it is a notable feature when working with baby boomer decision-makers (those born post WWII, between 1946 and 1964). Once people feel safe, secure and supported in their thoughts and ideas, they tend to be willing to think outside the square a bit more, to come up with something appropriate for the deceased and for those likely to be part of the farewell.

Q. What do you think are the immediate needs of the bereaved?

People in profound grief need to be looked after, especially if the death is a shock. Sometimes information can help too, such as explaining some of the physical reactions of grief and shock so they do not become impatient with themselves. Apart from practical arrangements of funeral care, ensuring these people have the professional support they need is also important.

Many people come in overwhelmed by the thought of organising a funeral so working quite 'matter of factly' can help, especially if there is division within the family. People will often express relief as various decisions are made.

For some the physical care of the body is important so it can be reassuring for people to know that massage, or oils rather than chemicals, have been used or their mother's hair can be washed and coloured or their grandfather's moustache trimmed. Often people will ask how the person looked when we collected them, so it is a relief when the staff has cared for them beautifully. There are places where the person who has died is prepared very respectfully and lovingly. I wish it could be the same for everyone.

Some people want to help with this physical care but most do not. It is quite common though for family members to want to wait until we arrive if their family member has died in care. When someone dies at home, families tend to be more physically involved.

Keeping in touch with people after the first meeting and throughout the process also seems to help as each aspect is organised and confirmed. This can bring relief or diminish the burden of worry. It may seem like an obvious point, but it is not being taken for granted. Giving reassurance is doubly important at a time of such vulnerability. I like to think people feel they can rely on us to 'make it happen.'

Q. Do any families call you before a death to ask questions about what they can and can't do when a person dies at home?

Yes, this is common. Often a family or the person concerned will contact us and their questions are not limited to death at home. Some want to know the practical aspects of after death care; others are more concerned with setting up their own farewell ritual or telling their story the way they want it told.

We love this work. To establish a relationship with the person you are going to care for and ensure their wishes are carried out is an utter privilege, but it does bring with it such a sense of responsibility. We are really trying hard to counter the dreadful relentless pre-paid and insurance funeral marketing by providing a very different form of end-of-life care.

Q. What do you consider the most important thing to think about when spending time with someone who is close to death?

- The agenda is theirs, so listening.
- Being comfortable with silence.
- Creating a relationship of trust.

Q. How do you ensure you meet the needs of the grieving families?

- By listening carefully.
- Sometimes by supporting quieter members to have their say (strategy and diplomacy).
- Working hard to get the things they want. This can take time and relentless negotiating.
- Education in a whole range of ways.
- Learning from the experience of others; the bereaved, the dying, professional colleagues in allied industries and the funeral industry.
- Professional reading from others involved in end-of-life care.
- Professional developments to do with end-of-life care.

I have been witness to how Anne and Steve work with families and can honestly say, with some sadness, that it is rare to find such caring and loving individuals who really do put their clients' needs before their own. They will attempt on every occasion to provide the very highest level of care for everyone concerned, and are highly respected in their community. We should all be grateful for such loving and compassionate people who will work alongside families at this difficult time.

In my first book, *The Heart and Soul of Celebrancy,* I discussed the changing aspects of the industry. But in this rapidly changing world, that book, published in 2009, is out of date with the reality of what is happening now. As people, especially the baby boomers, continue to learn more of what is possible they will continue to challenge and question the dying and after death processes. So I expect to see even more changes over the next five to ten years, in the way we manage and handle death in our culture.

There is enough evidence available now to suggest families will consider:

- being more involved in the end-of-life decisions;

- being present at a death;
- caring for a person at home at end of life;
- allowing a death to occur at home if possible;
- keeping the person at home for some of the time between death and funeral;
- looking at options available to them for a funeral and shopping around for the option that suits them best;
- look at greener, environmentally friendly options;
- not engaging a funeral company unless they want to;
- if they do engage a funeral company, choosing one with the knowledge that their wishes will be followed;
- ensuring that the wishes of the deceased and the family are catered for.

In 2012 I received a phone call from a frustrated young couple wanting to arrange the funeral of their grandfather. I could tell immediately that they had come across some difficulties in planning the funeral. Nothing was coming together for them and they were not being given much assistance from a funeral company who wanted nothing more than for them to 'tick boxes'. (Names have been changed to protect their privacy.)

This is the letter I received from that client in 2013.

Dear Sally,

You might remember you worked with us last April to create a wonderful celebration of a life in the gardens at Heidi for Dale's grandfather, Donald.

We are finally writing to say a long overdue, and very heartfelt, thank you. We've been meaning to write to you for some time but it is only recently that we have really been able to put our finger on the difference you made and to articulate it. Quite simply, you made the process of saying goodbye, human.

Until we spoke with you, organising a tribute for someone we loved felt like a business transaction. There was a mechanical process to go through, a set script with a limited range of 'choices' to be slotted into the blanks. None of which seemed to have anything to do with Donald. Nor did they feel 'right'. Dale said at the time that none of the 'choices' we'd been able to come up with so far would leave him feeling glad that we had done them. All it felt like we were doing was ticking someone else's boxes, none of which meant anything to us.

When we called you, the first thing you asked was whether we had any ideas about what we might like to do. At our tentative suggestion that we wanted to create something that might be a bit different to what seemed to the be norm, something outside in the sun where Donald had spent his whole life, possibly in the gardens at Heidi near where he had lived, you said simply 'that sounds wonderful, I'll do everything I can to help'. Doing something meaningful for Donald suddenly felt not only possible, but also perfectly natural and expected.

Thank you for meeting with us at Heidi that same afternoon, for your encouragement; for your support of each of us; for working with us over the weekend at such short notice; for helping us expand the funeral director's view of what's possible; for your sensitivity and humour; and for writing and then delivering a beautiful service for Donald that acknowledged both the joys and the heartbreaks of his life.

At the end of the day, after everyone had left and we were walking through the gardens back to the car on that beautiful, sunny, autumn afternoon, we both couldn't stop smiling. We felt sad but also incredibly proud of the tribute you helped us create for Donald, for us and for everyone else that Donald was special to.

There's just one more thing. We've been finalising all the paperwork recently and we noticed on your invoice that you only charged us for the amount you initially quoted, not for the full number of hours you spent working with us. We appreciate your professionalism in sticking to the quote but also feel you couldn't have done a more wonderful job and we appreciated every hour. We weren't sure you would accept payment for the extra hours but we hope you will accept a thank you gift. We hope you will enjoy a meal with your family at Chateau Yering, one of Donald's favourite places.

Our heartfelt thanks again and our very best wishes.

Jane and Dale

I cried when I received this letter because it is such a validation of what I believe is important. A client is endorsing everything I believe in, everything I have worked towards for twenty years. What is important is that every family's voice is heard, every wish is addressed and that every client receives the assistance they deserve in creating a farewell that is authentic. As I explained to Dale and Jane at our first meeting, as long as their wishes are respectful and safe I would assist them in anything they wanted.

The voucher was an unexpected bonus and meant that I could share this time with my family.

Funeral professionals are faced with even more challenges as they are forced to venture out of their protective, traditional bubbles: they need either to find a way to adapt to today's needs or face extinction. A sad indictment is that only a handful of these companies are adjusting well; most are not. And families are seeing beneath their veiled compassion and untruths about the services they offer. For instance, families who will do the research and demand clear answers will catch out companies that advertise themselves as environmentally friendly and claiming to offer greener options when in fact they offer nothing like a green option.

What is emerging as the 'must haves' for today's funeral?

- clearer and more easily obtainable education on what is possible;
- information on where to obtain certain services and products if people wish to obtain that themselves;
- people demanding a more inclusive, flexible ceremony that is authentic;
- the ability to include technology as part of the planning stage and the ceremony itself;
- clear, transparent costings.

What has changed that is not necessarily for the best, that affect the families? The emerging changes that have been detrimental are:

- the lack of information for families;
- the lack of choices (because the funeral companies generally want to offer only what suits their business model);
- the increase in cost but reduction in services being offered;
- lack of transparency about the individual items being offered within the overall cost of a funeral;
- lack of awareness about what is included in a pre-paid funeral;
- funeral companies not bothering to inform families of the resources they are entitled to access, such as hearses and funeral cars, that will be available on the day of the funeral;
- funeral companies not informing families that the very person who has been arranging the funeral will in fact not attend on the day of the funeral. Families are rarely informed of this prior to the day.

◐ **DID YOU KNOW?**

Funeral company staff are often paid a very low wage, and some funeral companies pay their staff commission on products, e.g. the cost of the coffin sold. Worse still, at the family meeting, when the families are arranging the funeral of a loved one, pre-paid funeral plans for their own 'future death' are being discussed by the Funeral Arranger!

Have you ever considered having a living wake?

An idea which I find very helpful and which has become more common of late, is to have a celebration of life before an imminent death. When a person of whatever age becomes aware that they will die in the foreseeable future, they can chose to share in a celebration of their own life with those closest to them. This may be something that is formal or informal but it focuses on being able to thank people and share memories.

We can explore rituals that involve family and community to celebrate the end of a life in many ways. They may be termed

- a living wake;
- a living funeral;
- or a living farewell.

Probably the most famous examples of this type of celebration are in the story *Tuesdays with Morrie,* Mitch Albom's story about the life of Morrie Schwartz, and the film, *'Get Low '* where Robert De Niro throws his own funeral party while still alive. Bill Murray plays a baffled funeral director who has never heard of a living wake.

Why wait until the person is dead before we gather to celebrate their life? Some may think this type of celebration is morbid. But many are starting to consider that this might be a far better option than a ceremony or wake conducted after death.

What form the ceremony takes depends on the person whose life you are celebrating. They may want a large gathering in a more formal space or it could be a few people gathered at a park or favourite place. The format will be unique to each person. Here are some possible scenarios you might choose:

- 'A day in the life of';
- You might like to all bring something that is indicative of your connection with this person and share with everyone;
- You might have someone write and deliver a story about the life of that person, similar to a eulogy;
- You might have an 'open floor' where everyone gets a chance to talk about the deceased and the effect they have had on your life.
- You might have a shared meal.

With so many options to choose from these days, it seems rather sad to wait until after a death to acknowledge what a difference someone has made to our life. It is something I see often at the funerals I conduct - families who are saddened that they did not get the chance or to make the opportunity to tell their loved one how much they were loved, or to thank them for what they have done in their life. It is rare that there are no regrets.

Although it was not intended as a living wake, a memorable sixty-fifth wedding anniversary celebration comes to my mind. It was for a couple in their late eighties. I was asked by their three children, all in their fifties and sixties, to come along to the anniversary celebrations and surprise the couple with a 'renewal of vows' ceremony. I trusted the children to know their parents well enough that this was not going to cause either of them any health problems and that it would be a positive experience for everyone. And yes, it had the happy ending it merited.

It was a ceremony that I will remember until I die. We were all gathered at the retirement village waiting for the right moment to announce what was about to happen (which as it turned out was between 'the mains and dessert'!) Family and friends had gathered together to celebrate the anniversary and were about to witness something special. I had worked with the children and grandchildren to create a truly wonderful event - we tried to re-enact as much as possible of the couple's original wedding ceremony. We had their original vows, a bouquet made to match the original, the original bridesmaid and groomsmen, both of whom had flown in from the UK and we were surrounded by their closest family and friends.

I spoke about their life together and what an amazing story it was. One could say an ordinary life lived by ordinary people, full of good and bad experiences and humour where appropriate. I had suggested during the planning that family could be involved in many ways. People participated in readings, a unity candle ceremony, and a community ribbon ceremony.

The couple sat beside me for the entire time holding hands right throughout the ceremony; and cried during their exchange of vows. They were a very happy couple having weathered sixty-five years of marriage. We celebrated their life story with them. We talked of work and play and relived precious memories.

It was a celebration for all of us. How sad it would have been for the lives of these two people, their family and friends, had they let this opportunity slip by until one of them had passed away.

After the couple had died, their family said that the 65th anniversary was like having a living wake for the couple.

Celebrants are asked every now and then to conduct a significant birthday, but it would be wonderful if we were also asked to conduct something more formal and celebrate a person's life before they pass away.

Although it may be difficult to be involved in a gathering where you know the death of a loved one is imminent, the end result can be an enormous relief and a wonderful celebration if handled well. So if an opportunity arises please don't let it slip by without having considered whether this might be appropriate.

#POINTS TO CONSIDER

- → Funerals are ever changing.
- → Baby boomers are questioning tradition.
- → Funerals are becoming far more authentic and honest.
- → Families are less likely to be rushed into decisions.
- → Statistics tells us we will have a major boom in the death industry over the next twenty years.
- → Funerals in Australia are predominantly secular.
- → We see far less flexibility being offer by the larger funeral companies than ever before.
- → Funerals continue to increase in cost and there is a vast difference between costs from one company to another.
- → Please know you don't have to adhere to a model that a funeral company may offer because you can do far more than just tick their boxes.
- → Funerals differ greatly as to where they are held and how the ceremony, if there is one, is conducted.
- → You do have choices.
- → You have a right to know what the funeral costs include and these should be clearly itemised and transparent.
- → You have a right to know if a funeral arranger is being paid commission.

- → For some people having a celebration of their life while still alive is a wonderful idea.
- → The ritual may take many forms: formal or informal.
- → The main aim is to share in the memories of a life with the person still here with you.

MY NOTES

MY NOTES

MY NOTES

CHAPTER 7

CONSIDERING THE IMMEDIATE NEEDS OF THE BEREAVED

Have you ever lost someone you love and wanted one more conversation, one more chance to make up for the time when you thought they would be here forever?
If so, then you know you can go your whole life collecting days, and none will outweigh the one you wish you had back.
– Mitch Albom, *For One More Day*

The immediate needs of a person who has just lost a loved one can vary greatly. Undoubtedly there is a feeling of shock and numbness; often there is anger and guilt. But whatever the feelings, there are things that need to be attended to. Many people struggle with questions like: what are the immediate needs of a bereaved person, how would you talk to someone who has just lost someone close to them, what's appropriate and what is not, what words are the right ones to say to a grieving person, and what about extended communities of friends: who attends to their needs?

In such situation people often use clichés because they either don't know what to say. They may be concerned that they might upset the bereaved or that they themselves might become upset. In fact, the person who has lost a loved one often wants to talk, but those around them don't feel comfortable doing so.

Doris Zagdanski (<www.allaboutgrief.com> and <www.mygriefassist.com>) is an educator in the field of grief. After one of Doris' workshops on 'How to Talk to Grieving People', I took away a very important lesson. After Doris' workshop I realised that although listening is extremely important, the most critical factor is understanding the crucial significance of the response we give to a grieving person.

Doris spoke about the different levels of building a relationship. When we talk to someone we don't know well or who isn't particularly close, we tend to use clichés, and go into automatic pilot: 'Hi, how are you?', 'Well, thanks and you?' 'Isn't it cold today'. Easy conversations that do not require much thought and have standard acceptable responses.

The highest level of communication is when we are able to share our feelings. This requires a high level of trust and it is this level of communication where we are able to share our innermost feelings with someone else and where there is comfortable listening and a real understanding of the other's pain. When we reflect, there are probably only a few people in our life with whom we can have this level of communication.

When we think about our lives, it is interesting to think about who you have that is close to you, who would be able to sit with you in your grief and let you talk about your pain at the level you wanted to share, comfortable in knowing that they would really listen and acknowledge that pain for you, and be able to respond in a way that was not a cliché, and able to respond to your pain in a way that you really knew they understood how you were feeling.

It is very sad, but quite true, that although you might have one hundred people at a funeral, out of those one hundred there are probably fewer than a handful who might be able to have this level of communication with you.

A person does not want to hear:

- Everything happens for a reason;
- Time heals;
- You're young. You'll find someone else;
- Are you over it yet? It's been over a year;
- Be strong;
- Don't cry, you'll only upset yourself more;
- It was for the best, they've gone to God;
- They've gone to a better place;
- It was not meant to be;
- You can always try for another baby;
- God doesn't give you more than you can handle;
- I know how you feel!
- Try to look for the positive in the situation;
- If you think this is bad, I know a family …

These clichés are not helpful at all. How could any such comment comfort a bereaved person?

The most important suggestion I can make is to listen, hear what matters most to them, and respond with empathy. Understand what it is that the person wants to hear you say.

For example:

- I can hear that for you that feels like …;
- It sounds as though you are feeling like …;
- I can hear how much you are hurting;
- Your life has been turned upside down;
- It sounds as though you would like to turn the clock back and say …

These empathetic responses show the grieving person that you are listening and in some way understanding how they are feeling.

So what are the immediate needs of a bereaved person?

- Sometimes it is to see the body of the deceased person.
- Sometimes it is just to talk. They may want to talk about the person and this may seem never ending to you, but they clearly have a desire to talk and keep talking about the person who has died. Grieving people want and need to be heard, not 'fixed'.
- Sometimes all they need is silence. Allow for moments of silence and reflection. Don't try to fill in conversations with a lot of general chitchat. The home after a death can be chaotic and crazy. So silence can be very helpful.
- Sometimes they just want to be left alone, given some space and not be fussed over.
- Sometimes all they require is a listening ear from someone who is non judgemental and accepting. Don't imply that the pain is not real.
- They do not want you to suggest you know how they are feeling because no matter what you think, you don't know. Loss and the feeling it creates are very personal and unique. Even people who have lost the same person feel things differently because they are each different and their relationship to the deceased was different. They feel whatever they feel, and that is okay.

Other practical needs may include:

- A place for relatives to stay;
- Transportation to or from the airport for relatives;
- Your physical presence. Just being there can be very helpful;
- Transportation to doctor's appointments, shops and so on. It can be very difficult to drive in the first couple of days and weeks because you feel numb and in shock and not able to concentrate;
- Assistance with housecleaning;
- Assistance in planning and organising the funeral or memorial service;
- Practical and emotional support. Help minding children, cooking a meal, writing thank you notes, even walking a pet;

- Mention the deceased person's name and encourage the bereaved person to talk about them;
- Offering (or managing their) invitations to coffee, dinner, a walk, or a visit;
- Childcare so they can rest without having to worry about the needs and safety of their child or children;
- Information about and attending a grief support group (including times, place);
- Non-perishable food items;
- List making and record-keeping so that thank you notes can be sent;
- Addressing and stamping envelopes for thank you notes;
- Answering the phone or the door. There are usually endless phone calls and visitors so being there to assist can be very helpful.

Viewing the body

Is it appropriate to suggest the closest family members view the body regardless of the age of the deceased? If I believe it is in their long-term interests to do so I will try where possible to encourage the family to view the body. There are a number of reasons why I suggest this but predominantly it is about coming to terms with the reality of the situation.

◐ DID YOU KNOW?
In general, my experience has been that family members who do view a body seem to come to terms with the death better and they tell me afterwards that they are glad they chose to view the body. Even those who initially said they didn't want to expressed how grateful they were that they had changed their minds, as they found the experience very beneficial.

Remember if you are going to encourage a person to view a body, it is important to have a discussion about that experience beforehand to ensure they are as prepared as possible. Talk to those involved about what state the body might be in and always in terms they can understand. Explain that the person will be in a coffin (if indeed they are) and answer any questions they may have in layman's not medical terms. It is important to let people know that the body may be a lot colder than they may imagine or expect. This is one thing that often upsets people and stays with them for a long time if they are not prepared for it.

Naturally, it is not advisable to leave a frail or young person alone at this time. Ensure they are supported by another family member, or at the very least offer to be there with them during this time. Give them time and space once they are comfortable. This is often the time that they will say their goodbyes and tears are very likely. At all times we want to avoid shock if possible, so take your time and try and prepare them as best you can. Let them express their grief during this time, as it will inevitably assist them. And give them time to talk about the experience afterwards if it is appropriate.

Doris Zagdanski relays a story about a request that came to her many years ago, when she had just starting working for a funeral company as a funeral arranger. A man approached her to ask to be allowed to sleep alongside his dead father the night before the funeral. He wanted to lie near to his father who was in the coffin. At the time Doris was very new to the industry and was unsure of the protocol or whether her managers would allow it. However, she facilitated the request, placed the coffin in an interview room and made the son comfortable on a couch to sleep the night next to his father. The feedback from the son was that spending the night with his father was so important as it gave him a chance to talk to his Dad for the last time. I think this type of empathy goes a long way in assisting a person in their grieving.

In stark contrast is the experience of Scarlett Lewis after her son

Jesse was killed in the Sandy Hook Elementary shootings in 2012. In an interview with Scarlett after the release of her book *Nurturing Healing Love*, she told me:

> "Yes, to this day I wish that I had been able to spend the night with Jesse. One last night lying next to him. I was told that it was not 'standard procedure' but it felt more like the funeral director just wanted to go home. I didn't need him there and opposed every argument but in the end allowed my family to lead me out because I knew I probably wouldn't get much sleep and I wanted to be as present and in the moment as I could the following day for the public wake where thousands of people would attend the funeral, burial and celebration afterwards, at my mother's house. I was surprised at how comfortable I was with Jesse's body. I moved my hands all over him, trying to memorise every little curve of his precious little body. There was a scene that the editor took out of the book where I sat beside the casket and held his little right hand until it began to grow warm and I thought it almost felt as if he were alive. I then tried to warm it up so I could feel it one last time as if he was alive. I studied every little detail of his fingers even noticing the dirt underneath his fingernails, which always told me that he had been having a good time."

When I was interviewing Amanda Pryce about the death of her son Nick, I asked her what was important to her at that time. "I really wanted to know was it a deliberate overdose or accidental. I wanted to know the cause of death. That was important to me at that time." There was no note left and Amanda had many questions, none of which could be answered at that time, and possibly never will be.

It is a sad indictment of the business that some people working in the funeral industry seem to lack compassion or an understanding of a family's need for access to the body or other similarly natural requests. After the drowning of a five-year-old child I was called to see if I could assist with some difficulties the family were having with the funeral company who had their son's body. The family was furious that it was being 'prevented' from seeing their son's body. Staff at the funeral company had said it was not in their interests to see the body. I was asked to intervene so the family could indeed have their request granted. This intervention should not be necessary, after all the funeral company are only minding the body; they do not own or have any rights over the body. When I checked with the funeral company, they confirmed that they had not given permission for the family to view the body as "they did not believe it was in the family's interests, because the child's body was swollen".

I explained that the family was fully aware that their son's appearance may cause them some distress but they were adamant they wanted to sit with him. The mother had previously spoken to the funeral company and explained that they had already seen the son since he died, at the scene of the accident and at the coroner's office, and they knew his body was swollen. It was only after my intervention that the funeral company agreed to the family's request. The staff's lack of understanding of the consequences of this type of decision is lamentable. The staff needed to have had an honest discussion with the family and let them make the decision. It is not the company's role to take such decisions. It doesn't matter what state the body is in, it is the family's prerogative to view the body if they wish to do so. Of course I will always advocate for a discussion about what they will be confronted by, but it is their right to have access to the body. No family should have to suffer this unnecessary stress. The family's requests were very normal and in no way would inconvenience the funeral company.

◐ DID YOU KNOW?

You have every right to have whatever access to your loved one's body that you want. The funeral company is just there to store the body, it does not own it.

If someone we know dies and we don't have an opportunity to express our own feelings of loss and grief then we can still be suffering a long way down the track. Apart from the needs of the family, often the needs of close friends are not met either.

It is interesting that when reading up on 'funeral etiquette' we learn about what happens up to and including the funeral but very little about the follow up. What about the weeks, months and years after a death?

I am continually astounded by the number of people who after having experienced a loss find they suddenly lose friends. They stay away because of the palpable awkwardness and discomfort they felt in seeing the bereaved person after a death. It seems many people don't know how to converse with someone experiencing grief so they just disappear from a person's life. They fear saying the wrong thing, and so the easiest thing to do is to stay away.

The closest loved ones are often left floundering within weeks of a death because we as a society don't know how to interact with the grieving.

It is the friend who is always there, regardless of whether they say the 'right' thing or not, who matters most.

What can be helpful:

- Don't stop visiting;
- Don't stop calling;
- Don't stop talking.

Ask the bereaved what would be helpful. And don't stop asking. Sometimes it does take time for a person to feel comfortable in accepting your help. Some of the simplest things in life can make a big difference to a grieving person: a simple phone call, a bunch of flowers, a meal dropped off at the front door. Offering to sit and have a 'cuppa' with them and just allowing them talk. Such simple acts can be extremely helpful.

#POINTS TO CONSIDER

- → Viewing the body is your right, regardless of the circumstances surrounding the death.
- → Check with the bereaved as to what will assist them most at this time.
- → Listening to a grieving person is important, but your responses are just as important.
- → Clichés are not helpful.
- → Practical assistance is usually extremely helpful.

MY NOTES

MY NOTES

CHAPTER 8

GRIEF – A LITTLE WORD WITH A BIG PUNCH!

No one ever told me that grief felt so like fear. I am not afraid, but the sensation is like being afraid. The same fluttering in the stomach, the same restlessness, the yawning. I keep on swallowing.
At other times it feels like being mildly drunk, or concussed.
There is a sort of invisible blanket between the world and me.
I find it hard to take in what anyone says.
Or perhaps, hard to want to take it in. It is so uninteresting.
Yet I want the others to be about me. I dread the moments when the house is empty.
If only they would talk to one another and not to me.
– C.S. Lewis, A Grief Observed

The death of a loved one casts one into foreign territory. There is no map, no direction, it can feel like quicksand at every turn and it can be very dangerous for some. How grief is felt is different for every person, and for every loss in our life. Thankfully we aren't always consciously aware that grief and loss are part of everyday life for many people. Over a lifetime we experience many losses. Loss is the disappearance of something cherished, such as a person, possession, position or property. There are many different types of loss which are part of the process of living. Although many of these may be related to minor aspects of our life they may still affect us in varying degrees. We know that many losses that occur during childhood and adolescent years can remain unresolved as we move into adult years. Even though some of these losses may occur when we are under the age of ten we might still be grieving about them, consciously or subliminally, well into our senior years.

I remember many years ago attending a workshop on loss and grief. I was asked as part of that course to complete a 'grief indicator chart'. I was shocked at how many ticks I had marked on the completed chart. I was asked to identify the losses experienced by my family, my extended family, my friends and myself.

The losses were listed as: forced to stop work, multiple relationships, divorce, family break up, loss of home, loss of job, loss of a promotion, forced to retire, adopted out, fostered out, loss of body shape (obesity), being burgled, bankruptcy, empty nest, domestic abuse, suicide, multiple schools, loss of dreams and hopes, loss of neighbours, loss of a business, serious car accident, loss of limbs, loss of culture, loss of school friends, loss of personal identity (motherhood, sisterhood, fatherhood and so on), loss of children, experience of crime, loss of freedom, rape, premature birth, miscarriage, stillbirth, infertility, terminal illness, HIV/Aids, sudden death, substance abuse, intellectual disability, loss of finances, murder, physical abuse, loss of vehicle, homelessness. The list went on and on.

Completing this list had a profound effect on me and brought home the realisation that every day we may experience some type of loss in our life and that the accumulated grief of our lifetime may rise to the surface when we least expect it. I am always aware when I ask others to complete this form as part of the funeral celebrancy course that I facilitate, that the students may be as shocked as I was. However, along with the shock comes the self-evident and candid awareness and understanding as to how this may continue to affect our lives.

There is a myth that grief somehow has an 'end date', as though there is an indeterminate date when for some reason people expect us to be 'over it', be it six months or one year. The reality is one will never be over it, nor should one be. If someone spent years loving another person, the pain of that person's death simply will not be removed due to a date on the calendar.

Dennis Klass wrote in *Death and Religion in a Changing World* that if we are not attached to someone, we do not grieve when he or she dies. 'Attachment' is medical jargon for what we call love in common language. Grief then, is the price we pay for love.

I think healthy grief enables one to maintain a continuing bond with the deceased. The process of grieving proceeds with a person retelling the stories of their loved one. A loss never stops being a loss. Even when we recover from it to the point where we can function, the most we can hope for is that it can eventually be integrated into our ongoing life. However, our life won't ever be the same again, so we need to learn to adapt to our life without that person, understanding that there will be a new 'normal'.

Grief is an extremely complex emotion that has a more profound impact than we often realise. As infants we are able to cry or have a tantrum when we feel like it. But as we grow we learn to repress our feelings. I can still remember my parents saying to my brothers: "You're boys, you don't cry" and worse still: "Stop that crying or I will give you something to cry about." My sisters and I were told to 'get over it, you'll be fine'. As young children we are all taught certain ways to react; we raised boys to be tough. So males 'wear' toughness (and believe it to be true), and the society perpetuates the myth that men can only be hurt physically, not emotionally. Publicly they present a facade of equanimity and restraint. I remember being told as a teenager that 'big' boys and girls don't cry. So we learnt quickly that as we grew up, crying was unacceptable, and displaying those difficult emotions, and burdening others with our feelings was not acceptable. In my generation, and that of my parents, we've been taught from an early age not to acknowledge or show our feelings. This then begs the question: if we can't acknowledge our own pain, how can we begin to deal with someone else's?

It is interesting to note that many books and references refer to the different 'styles' of grieving between genders. Researchers suggest that there is what might be called a 'male model' of grief and a 'female model' of grief. However, all women do not necessarily display the 'female model'; nor do all men display the 'male model'. Phyllis Silverman, who did important work on grieving at Harvard, explained that people, women or men, who follow the 'male model' prefer to 'get on with life' and quickly involve themselves in work or other activities. Careful studies done on the grieving process indicate that men are more likely to grieve privately. Followers of the 'female model' are more inclined to display grief to others, reach out to one or more people around them and talk more openly about the loss.

Often we hear that men just want to do something, get on with life and put the event behind them, and so they often return to work quite quickly after a death. Whereas women tend to want to talk it over and take much longer to grieve. So we see two people grieving over the one death in very different ways. In many cases this causes their relationship to suffer because they mourn the loss so differently and because they are unable to understand the other's manner of grieving. This can then lead to a distancing between them where they are unable to comfort and support each other.

In many cases the woman might have been the main carer of the dying person and a great deal of their time would have been spent in this role. When the person dies that time is then often spent in mourning and grieving. Moreover, I do think women have a natural propensity for mourning. What is considered self-indulgent for men may be necessarily cathartic for women.

However, it is more likely that conditioning, rather than a lack of feelings, sees men favour what is commonly referred to as 'instrumental grieving' and women tending to 'intuitive grieving'. Instrumental grief includes more thinking than feeling, expressing grief through doing something, through being physical. Intuitive grief includes strong, affective reactions and expressions that mirror feelings.

It is a sad fact that in our society we often deny our true feelings. We tend to avoid saying how we are really feeling, automatically responding with such clichés as, 'I'm fine'. In general we are a society that is uncomfortable with displays of painful emotion. This in turn perpetuates a fear of showing the natural feelings that accompany emotional loss. We learn to conceal the tears, the pain and the anger. And we often do it well. But those feelings are always there, often lurking just beneath the surface and whenever we are faced with a major loss in our life the suppressed grief accumulated over a lifetime can rise to the surface. And boy, can that be an incredible experience if we let ourselves feel the hurt.

Katherine Ashenburg in her book *The Mourner's Dance* asks, "Would it remove a cruel burden if an intuitive griever didn't have to hide his tears, and an instrumental one wasn't constantly being nudged by her friends to talk about her feelings?" Absolutely.

It is wonderful to see that in more recent times the gender specific model of grieving has moved on and men and women are more likely to grieve in a way that suits them and not in the prescribed or expected way. These days it is not uncommon to see men crying in public over a death and wanting to talk about it. This was something one rarely witnessed in the past.

I like Alan D. Wolfelt's model of grieving, discussed in his *Healing Your Grieving Heart* series.

Need 1 – Accept the death.
Need 2 – Let yourself feel sad.
Need 3 – Remember the person who died.
Need 4 – Accept that your life is different now.
Need 5 – Think about why this happened.
Need 6 – Let others help you, now and always.

Julie Beasley said in *It's Grief to Me*:

"Life brings death and, along with that death will bring grief, an active, violent emotion that lives and breathes in one's life for days, weeks, months, and sometimes years. Grief waits its turn patiently, through births, accidents, illnesses, but sooner or later it will visit you. It will come like a thief in the night, a knock on the door, the ringing of a phone, perhaps even a letter. At first you will not acknowledge me. You will deny me, avoid me, run from me, but rest assured, I will become your unwanted guest.

"At first I will feel a wave of emotion like none ever experienced before. You will weep, you will find intense anger, and you will be physically sick, become unbalanced and sometimes literally lose your sense of being. Friends at first will spend much time with you. They are relieved it is you feeling this pain and not them. It is their duty to offer you a shoulder to cry on, a pan of lasagne, and sympathy cards. But their lives have not been disturbed and they will leave your house without me. As the days pass, everyone around you has gone back to being normal. They haven't forgotten you, but they have either not experienced me or have forgotten me. You, on the other hand, are walking in a fine fog of my making. If you think, I will be there. If you run from me, I will be waiting. Your days are spent trying to act normal and your nights are spent alone with me.

"As I begin to weaken and start the process of leaving, you may at first become frightened. You will fear that you are not being true to your loved one or will forget. Sometimes this fear will strengthen me and I will linger longer. At other times, I know it is time for me to spend time with someone else. It is time for you, my friend, now, to move on."

We accept a loss in stages, quietly closing one door and moving on to the next. Healing is a process, gradual and slow. Grief is not linear, nor is it predictable. It's anything but smooth and self-contained. Grief goes in cycles, like the seasons. Everyone experiences grief at some point. It's an inescapable reality of human existence. And I believe everyone should follow his or her own grief journey, not in any prescribed way or following how others might suggest it will be for you. It is your own journey.

The five-year period of grieving often referred to, does not mean that it will necessarily take a full five years to recover one's 'old self'. With each day that passes we move further and further away from that initial shock and grief, so we don't feel the same several months or two years later as we do in the beginning. It is a gradual fading.

The grief I felt with the death of my father remained painfully close to the surface far longer than I imagined it would. Finally, I no longer had the strength to suppress my feelings and the persistent grief caused my defences to crumble. I had thought that because my brother's death was two years earlier we would be able to bring Dad around, that we would be able to fix his broken heart. In the event, I had almost no control over the way I felt and no control at all over my father's death.

I'd just been through an emotional earthquake, and the aftershocks were going to continue for a long time. Eventually, I gave myself permission to feel whatever I needed to feel. It was okay if I couldn't cry and it was also okay if I cried all the time or at inappropriate moments. I just allowed it to happen.

An article in the Australia Centre for Grief and Bereavement's journal, *Grief Matters*, says that:

> No one seriously debates the notion that loss changes life. The often-repeated phrase that 'life will never be the same' is certainly true, but some of those 'not the same' characteristics

of loss can be revolutionary. People gain new passion. Their purpose for life and in life is reignited. Great movements are begun. In short, the identity of the grieving person can be utterly transformed.

Grieving involves many different emotions, actions and expressions, all of which help the person come to terms with the loss of a loved one. It is important to keep in mind however that grief doesn't look the same for everyone. Every loss is different, and everyone will grieve over each loss differently.

The way we think and feel, the way our body functions, and the way we interact with others may all be affected. Grieving is important because it allows us to 'free-up' energy that is bound to the lost person, object, or experience, so that we might re-invest that energy elsewhere. Until we grieve effectively we are likely to find reinvesting difficult; a part of us remains tied to the past. Grieving is not forgetting. Nor is it drowning in tears. Healthy grieving results in an ability to remember the importance of our loss, but with a newfound sense of peace, rather than searing pain.

The bereaved often struggle with many intense and frightening emotions, including depression, anger, and guilt. Often, they feel isolated and alone in their grief. Having someone to lean on can help him or her through the grieving process. It is common for a grieving person to feel depressed, confused, disconnected from others, or as if they are going crazy.

When you grieve you can feel both physical and emotional pain. People who are grieving often cry easily and can have:

- trouble sleeping;
- little interest in food;
- problems with concentration;
- a hard time making decisions;

- extreme fatigue;
- physical ailments – vomiting, diarrhoea;
- hyperactivity.

The most important point here is to look after yourself and those close to you. Surround yourself with loving supportive people who can assist you in those early days to just get through the days. Remember you can call your GP to assist if you feel things are getting the better of you.

Research shows that most people can recover from loss on their own. However, sometimes a professional in this field can help you cope with your feelings and find ways to get back on track. Grief counsellors and other associated professionals can help people build their resilience and develop strategies to get through their sadness.

If the bereaved person's symptoms don't gradually start to fade, or if they get worse with time, this may be a sign that normal grief has evolved into a more serious problem. If you are supporting a person through their grieving encourage them to seek professional help if you observe any of the following warning signs after the initial grieving period, especially if it has been a few months since the death:

- difficulty in functioning in daily life;
- inability to enjoy life again;
- withdrawn from others;
- a constant feeling of helplessness;
- alcohol or drug abuse;
- neglecting personal hygiene;
- excessive anger, guilt or bitterness;
- extreme preoccupation with death;
- talk of suicide.

A client recently told me, when I checked in with him a week after the funeral, "I had a good session with a grief counsellor yesterday where I 'unloaded' the background of my past few months". This is such a healthy sign. Asking for help is not a failure and joining a support group may be very beneficial.

A resource that I often recommend for families and my students is *Coping with Grief* by Mal and Dianne McKissock, a small but powerful and practical book on grieving.

Preparatory grief

Grief can be experienced differently due to the nature of the loss. If we know that someone we love has a terminal illness we can, and often do, start our grieving process while they are still alive. This can be difficult because of an indeterminate or inaccurate medical estimate of the time to death, so the grieving can go on for quite some time. Generally this time can be very useful in allowing you to grieve with loved ones, and in many ways it prepares you for what is to come. That is not to say that the feelings felt about that imminent death are diminished. But it can affect the way in which we then go on to grieve over that loss.

James Hellenbeck, author of *Palliative Care Perspectives*, says that the term 'anticipatory (or preparatory) grief' is somewhat confusing. It is not as simple as preparing for a future event, such as a wedding. People are not preparing to grieve at some time in the future, they are grieving in the present, relative to a process of loss currently being experienced and projected into the future. In facing the death of a loved one, the grieving pay a great deal of attention to both the past and the future. In looking back, people often carefully examine not only themselves and their relationship with the dying person, but the dying person's accomplishments and missed opportunities. It is as if they are reviewing a long story they have created, one full of heroes and villains, tragedy, comedy and romance. How well was this story written? In this person's death, how will it end? If impending death is viewed as coming prematurely, part of the grief process can be thought of as a rewriting of this story.

It can be vastly different from the grief people experience when a loved one dies suddenly, in that preparatory grief requires constant adjustments to ongoing changes and losses.

Elisabeth Kübler-Ross's model of grief, within her 'depression stage', based on the 'grief cycle' model first published in *On Death and Dying* describes this process as preparatory grieving. In a way it's the dress rehearsal or the practice run for the 'aftermath' although, naturally, this stage means different things to every individual involved. It's a sort of acceptance with emotional attachment. It's natural to feel sadness and regret, fear and uncertainty. It shows that the person has at least begun to accept the reality of death.

There is a moving passage in *Hannah's Gift*, a book written by Hannah's Mother, Maria Housden, where she speaks of an incident at the hospital one Christmas, where Hannah had just undergone chemotherapy. She and Hannah were trying out Hannah's new Christmas present in the hospital hallway. This to me is an excellent description of how she experienced grief.

> 'Look out below!' she shouted as we rounded the corner by the elevators. She coasted to a stop and hopped off her bike to turn it around. As I untangled and readjusted the IV tubes for the return lap, I noticed a small crowd of people weeping and whispering outside a rarely used room at the end of the hall.
>
> 'What's happening down there?' I asked a nurse who had broken away from the group and walked towards me. 'The little boy in that room was hit by a car this morning and just died' she said softly.

I felt as if I had been punched in the stomach and, at the same time, lucky in a way that I would have hated to admit out loud. I couldn't imagine losing Hannah to death so suddenly and unexpectedly, without time to prepare her or myself for what was coming, without a chance to savour every last drop of her before she was gone. Had this boy's parents even had a chance to say good-bye?

No matter how intense and frightening the months since Hannah's diagnosis has been, I felt grateful for every moment I had shared with her. Even the darkest ones had contained slivers of savage joy. I now knew that there was something simple yet exquisite about the gift of time; time to savour, time to remember, time to say goodbye.

The death of an adult child

For some reason, society seems to think losing an independent, adult child is less difficult than losing a dependent, younger child. But grief and loss cannot be measured.

Losing a child no matter what their age is devastating.

Losing a child at any age goes against the 'normal' life cycle that we expect. The reason I say this is that when I'm working with families I see that sometimes the grief of parents who've lost an adult child seems less important than the grieving of those younger than themselves.

I remember working with a family in 2011 to prepare a funeral for a man in his early fifties who had died after battling with cancer for a year. I was surprised to see that most of this man's family did not recognise the loss felt by his parents. There seemed to me to be no acknowledgement of the magnitude of their loss. The father had lost the only other man in his family, and his best mate and he was suffering terribly. I decided to include in the ceremony a few words of comfort for them in the hope that they could see that others did acknowledge their grief. This is what I said:

> "For Julie and David, our sympathies go to you both. This is one of the most unnatural things that can happen to a parent. As a parent you invested many years of your life loving and supporting him. You endured the young and teenage years and in return saw him grow into a charming young man. Peter then became one of your best friends."

> "There is a special bond between a parent and their adult child that is priceless and special. And when you lose that child to death, it goes against nature and no parent is prepared for a child's death, regardless of their age. You are not supposed to outlive your child. To Julie and David our thoughts are with you. When I sat with David recently and talked about Peter, he said to me that: 'Peter was an all time good person and even though I have lived much longer than he, Peter has achieved far more than I ever will."

> "David, just rememeber that our children start with the lessons we teach them and the values we pass on to them as they grow to maturity, so you both had a very big impact on the man he went on to become. And remember relationships are eternal; there is no end, they are of the mind, not the body."

Grief when a person is suffering dementia or Alzheimer's disease

The grief and sadness surrounding loss through Alzheimer's disease and dementia is perhaps more subtle but no less undermining, because the person you know and love is gradually taken away. As this happens, you will mourn him or her and may experience the loss over a very long time. Grieving is an up and down process. In the earlier stages, you may swing between despair and wild optimism that a cure will soon be found. You may even deny that anything is wrong with the person and try to suppress your feelings. A person with dementia suffers a series of losses – loss of a life, relationship, a sense of self and memories. As memory fades, other losses follow – work, driving, hobbies, skills, abilities and finally independence. I describe these losses as 'mini deaths' because at each stage the person's loved ones go through the realisation that 'part of the person' will never return and naturally they will grieve these mini deaths along the way, while the person is still living.

When I'm working with families who have lost a loved one to Alzheimer's disease or dementia, it is clear that they have already suffered a series of losses regarding their loved one. Often at the funeral they are dealing with the death of a stranger, because that person at the time of death was nothing like the person they knew during their life. Some find that they have grieved so much during the course of the illness that they have no strong feelings left when the person dies. However, strong feelings may surface at a later time, sometimes quite unexpectedly.

The Alzheimer Society of Canada says in its publication *Ambiguous Loss and Grief in Dementia*:

> "As a caregiver you may grieve the loss of your dreams and plans for the future, the loss of a confidante and partner, the loss of shared roles and responsibilities, and the progressive losses in the life of the person with dementia. The ambiguous loss that you may feel caring for a person with dementia can make the caregiving experience even harder.
>
> "Ambiguous loss is different from the loss and grief of death because closure is not possible and your grief cannot be fully

resolved while the person with dementia is alive. But this ambiguity and the mixed feelings that it can stir up are a common and expected experience for caregivers of people with dementia."

Ambiguous loss is the loss you feel when a person with Alzheimer's disease or dementia is physically here but may not be mentally or emotionally present in the same way as before.

Grief when someone dies suddenly

A look at some examples of sudden and unexpected death might help us to understand the grief which often results from these types of sudden loss.

Suicide

Firstly I am concerned about the use of language when we refer to someone committing suicide. I do bristle each time I hear the expression: 'committed suicide'. Historically, laws against suicide and mercy killing have developed from religious doctrine, claiming that only God has the right to determine when a person dies. Thankfully, individual suicide has now been decriminalised in most western societies, although the act is still stigmatised and discouraged in most places.

The grief process is always difficult, but a loss when someone takes his or her own life is like no other and the grieving can be especially complex and traumatic. Suicide is a difficult subject to discuss due to the added element of people looking for answers that simply aren't obtainable. Family may be reluctant to confide that the death was self-inflicted. And when others know the circumstances of the death, they may feel uncertain about how to offer help. Suicide is sudden, sometimes violent, and usually unexpected, even if the person has tried unsuccessfully in the past. It can shatter the things you take for granted about yourself, your relationships, and your world. There is still a huge stigma attached to suicide and mental health problems and this type of death may deeply affect not only the closest family but a number of others directly or indirectly related, bringing pain to more distant relatives and acquaintances such as extended family, cousins, friends and co-workers.

Bereavement after someone has taken their own life is distinct in a number of significant ways:

- those left behind struggle with more questions about the death;
- they experience higher levels of guilt and blame;
- they experience higher levels of rejection and abandonment;
- the grief can be more complex;
- the way society treats the people left behind. There can be a feeling of isolation from community;
- the impact suicide has on family systems.

When someone takes their own life they leave those behind with an enormous array of feelings: disbelief, shock and horror, blame and anger, wondering how they could have prevented it and why they didn't see it coming. It brings pain to anyone who knew the person; which is quite often far reaching down to counsellors and teachers, not just family and friends. There are lots of questions about 'why?' and a deep sadness about missed opportunities. There are many theories on why people take their own life and it is impossible to speculate because quite frankly the only person who might have an idea is the one who has taken it.

A person grieving over someone 'taking their own life' may struggle with guilt and this sometimes takes over from their ability to grieve. Feelings of guilt can even lead a person to avoid telling others the true cause of death. The shame factor for many people is huge and debilitating. The funeral can be heart wrenching because people have to face so many of their family and friends when they cannot cope with their own feelings. Surviving one day at a time in such a situation is all that is possible.

Many people in this situation get stuck in their grief and don't cope well. Guilt, unless dealt with carefully, can be one of the most destructive emotions a person can have to bear. And, as referenced earlier regarding my father's inability to cope, bereaved people can find it almost impossible to realise that much of the guilt is imagined and unfounded.

Grief from a tragic death

Nick Pryce died in 2012 as a result of an unintentional overdose. His mother, Amanda Pryce said:

> "I was numb for a while, and then resigned. I was surprised that after all the things that he'd been through over that ten year period, that he hung in that long really. He would say to me: 'The only reason I'm alive is you'. It was not a serious conversation we were having. I think he struggled so much with his depression that he was being brave. He was really struggling with it for ten years because he didn't want to upset me. Recently, I realised, when I was depressed, how horrible it is, and how hard that would have been to put up with it for ten years, despite his outward show of strength."

I asked her how she experienced grief at the time of his death. She replied:

> "I did not feel the five stages of grief mentioned by Kübler-Ross.
>
> I remember thinking about those five stages that everyone talks about; denial, anger, bargaining, whatever that's meant to be, depression and finally acceptance, and I remember thinking about those stages when a co-worker asked me: 'Do you feel angry'. My response was: 'No, why should I feel angry?'

She had jumped to the conclusion that because he was twenty-eight he had committed suicide, but it annoyed me that she had assumed Nick had committed suicide.

Generally speaking I know I do not have to grieve in any particular way. I am happy about this and reading more about it, which is helpful."

The loss of a baby

I contacted Kate Kripke, a Licensed Clinical Social Worker, from The Postpartum Wellness Center of Boulder, USA. <katekripke.wordpress.com>. She has kindly allowed me to reproduce this article she wrote for Postpartum Progress, an organisation dedicated to helping women with perinatal (the later stage of pregnancy and early post-natal stage) mood and anxiety disorders such as depression.

> I have worked with countless women in my office as they try to manage the unfamiliar emotions that surround loss, and I have learned a great deal from these phenomenal moms. I also have a dear friend and colleague who lost her daughter hours after birth and she, too, has honoured me with her insight, pain, and eventual healing. With the information gathered from both my clients and my dear friend (who is now a clinician in San Francisco specializing in perinatal loss), this post today is written for all of the mothers out there who are trying to navigate the unfamiliar postpartum experience while also grieving the loss of a child that never made it home or past that first year mark. For these mothers, the process of grief complicates postpartum distress, and sometimes it is hard to make sense of what goes where in this unimaginable puzzle.
>
> So, if you are one of these women, here is what I want you to know:

Some women who lose babies through miscarriage are able to move through this loss freely, while others feel deep despair at this loss. There are no 'shoulds' in this. No right way to feel. If you feel strong and grounded and ready to move forward after a miscarriage that is totally valid. If you feel deep loss and grief then that, too, is appropriate. No one gets to tell you how you feel except you.

Any time a body goes from being pregnant to not being pregnant, there is a significant shift in hormones that can affect brain chemistry. Postpartum depression, anxiety, and other mood disorders can affect a 'mum' regardless of the point at which a baby is delivered. You are likely in a position where you need to process through grief while also having vulnerable brain chemistry. This can make the experience of healing feel impossible for many.

Grief is a normal process and includes a shifting of emotions such as denial, anger, bargaining, depression, and acceptance. Grief felt after the loss of a baby is not necessarily depression and while there may be some overlap, it should not be treated as such. If you feel angry one day and dissociated from your loss the next, this is normal.

If you are not aware of a shifting through the stages of grief and continue to feel debilitated by your suffering, there may be an element of clinical depression or anxiety that needs to be addressed. 'Healthy' grief moves, but sometimes it can develop into relentless depression that requires more specific treatment. Many mothers will experience depression that includes feelings of guilt, shame, self-doubt and sometimes suicidal ideation. Regaining a sense of self, hope, and trust is important to one's healing after a loss such as this.

Identity shifting is a huge piece of the postpartum experience for every new parent, and yet mums who lose their babies are not able to show the world their mother-ness. If you feel like a mum, and yet are not able to participate in the experiences that the mothers around you are included in, know that this is a shared experience and that, whether or not the world can see this, we value you as a mother too.

Loss can often beget feelings of loss. Many women who lose their babies become suddenly afraid of losing everything else, be it their sanity, other relationships important to them, their faith in the world, or any hope for the future. Many, many women who go through this loss feel a deep need to grab onto other things in their life for fear of losing those, too. If this is happening to you, let those close to you know.

Relationships with spouse/partner, family, and friends will be impacted by your loss. It is important to be aware of the tendency to isolate during this time. Receiving appropriate support will be imperative in your healing and there may be work to do in relearning your relationships given this new reality. If you are unable to get the support that you need from loved ones, reach out to a therapist who can help.

While you desperately want your spouse/partner to understand what you are going through, he/she may not. People grieve differently. Often, losing a baby is a very different experience for a birth mother than it is for her partner, as she was the one who felt the development of this baby and feels, still, the physical loss as her body adjusts to no longer being pregnant. Give space for your own process as well as your partner's.

You are likely to learn who your truest friends are during this time. Some people's insecurities and fears around loss and tragedy may interfere with their ability to be there for you. It is entirely appropriate for you to spend time with those who are able to give you what you need, and to take distance from those who do not.

It is normal to feel triggered into sadness and despair when you least expect it. You may find reminders in the places where you least intend them to be. Seeing other pregnant women, babies, holidays and anniversaries, playgrounds, doctor's offices, advertisements for baby-related items, may bring you to tears even when you feel strong. This is normal.

People don't always know what to say. Many of you will want desperately to talk about your babies, to bring them to life through your words and memories, to make room for them in conversation and in your experiences. Some people will worry that bringing your baby and your loss in conversation will be upsetting to you. It is helpful to let the people in your life know what you need.

Just because you are ready to feel whole again, are healing, and may decide to have more children, this does not mean that the baby who you lost is forgotten. Regaining strength does not mean that you have 'moved on' and will no longer think of what might have been. Your pregnancy and your baby will always be a part of you. However, you deserve to be well and the feeling that you must keep grieving in order to stay faithful to your baby will not serve you. Finding a way to honour your pregnancy or your baby through ritual or event is often a lovely way of incorporating that being into your life as you move forward.

And finally, find others who have experienced something similar. As mentioned so many times on this blog, community is imperative and I am certain that there are others out there who can offer you the kind of solace, strength, and integrity that you will need as you continue to heal.

Babies can die both before and after their birth. There are several organisations devoted to helping those who lose a child. A list is provided at the end of this book, under 'Organisations and their roles – Support organisations – Loss of a child.'

At the end of this chapter I have included stories of couples who have lost their baby. The story of Oscar, whose mother Tennille had to go through the process of a stillbirth at thirty-three weeks gestation; and the story of Susan who lost her baby at thirty-two weeks

Children and grief

In the past children experienced life and death much more first hand, when a number of generations lived in the same house. It was not uncommon to be surrounded by illness and age as well as birth and new life. They watched as people grew older and they often assisted their parents tend to the elderly and then watched as their grandparent or some other elderly family member died. During these times children understood that they had witnessed a significant loss. Unfortunately children in more recent times don't tend to experience that privilege. Today in this grief avoiding culture, children are sometimes still prevented from being involved in these types of events, and often children are lied to about the state of health of a parent for example. It is no wonder then that children find death difficult. Children need to know that death is the natural end of life; it is inevitable and final. Parents should try to include their children in all stages of life – from birth through to death - because it is a natural and much healthier state for the children to experience. Trying to protect a child from these experiences is not beneficial to them! Children are often the forgotten mourners.

Death of an important person, especially a parent creates a continuing sense of emptiness in a child's life. It leaves an indelible mark and can become a life-defining event. In many instances, other significant occasions are remembered as before or after the death of a loved one.

Research shows that when children in crisis are not heard or protected, they are more vulnerable to harmful behaviour and substance abuse in their teenage years. There is also evidence of a direct link to later failed marriage and to a deterioration of wellbeing in children, including sexual abuse, family violence and a dramatic rise in self-harm for twelve to fourteen year-olds, as documented by Professor Patrick Parkinson in *For Kids' Sake.*

Rainbows Australia is a national organisation with about 750 volunteers providing support to grieving children and teenagers in Western Australia, the Northern Territory, Queensland, New South Wales, Victoria and Tasmania. It endorses the views expressed here, based on their experience of providing programmes to assist grieving children and adolescents in Australia for more than thirty years. Suzy Yehl Marta, founder of Rainbows, states in her book *Healing the Hurt, Restoring the Hope* that "bereavement rocks the foundations of children's lives; their confidence in the world they know is destroyed and they experience confusion and anguish. It can be an acutely sad and difficult time, to the point of being overwhelming. Emotional responses can be particularly confusing when young people are also experiencing rapid physical growth and bodily change. Grief interferes with the normal process of growing up".

Novita Children's Services was established in 1939 as the Crippled Children's Association of South Australia, to care for children diagnosed with polio. It is also has done a great deal of research and work with children in grief

From these beginnings, Novita has grown to become a major South Australian children's charity, and a recognised and celebrated world leader in the research, development and provision of quality services to children and families living with physical disabilities and acquired brain injuries.

Novita currently provides essential therapy, equipment and family support to more than 1300 children, and through broader work with families and communities, has a direct impact on more than 10,000 South Australians.

It is with their kind permission that I offer these tips on 'How to deal with children around times of grief'.

When dealing with children, keep in mind that:

- children may often go through similar experiences of grief as that of adults;
- however, even though this may be the case, they may not express this experience in the same way;
- in many cases, children haven't developed the same ability as adults to understand what is happening and may not easily be able to talk about their feelings;
- how children understand and react to loss will depend partly on their age and developmental level;
- how children understand and react to loss will depend partly on how others around them behave and cope.

General tips

Keep it simple: Children need to be told about death in language that is clear, simple and at a level that they understand.

Be honest: Children should be offered opportunities to ask questions and should have their questions answered as honestly as possible. Honest answers may sometimes include admitting that there is no answer or we don't know the answer to that question yet. If honest answers are not given, children may try and make sense of things by making up an explanation for themselves. This can lead to some children blaming themselves in some way. When choosing language to explain death, try to avoid connecting death with lifelike activities, for example, saying "So and so has gone to sleep for a very long time". This may only confuse the child and may cause a child to fear going to sleep.

Ensure those closest to the child provide information and support. If children don't find out the details of a death from a caring relative or friend there is always the risk they will be given misleading information from others. However, sometimes the most caring people are dealing with their own grief and may not readily see the child's needs. In such cases, someone close to the family but not so directly affected can take on part of the role of informing the child. **This should not be done without consulting with the family first.**

Protect the child from public curiosity. Where a death has a 'public interest' element the media may become involved. Care needs to be taken to protect children from exploitation by media operators.

Avoid giving confusing and contradictory messages. Sometimes children get mixed messages about what is acceptable in expressing their grief. They may hear 'Now, now there, don't cry' from one person while another person may encourage them to express their grief quite openly. Also, there can be unreasonable expectations placed upon them to be strong for their parents or others in such a situation.

Provide reassurance. Reassure the child that the world has not completely changed. Return to as near as possible to normal routines as soon as possible. Children may need reassurance that death is not contagious or catching.

Be aware of the other losses associated with the major loss or death. Other losses may include:

- loss of income;
- loss of family network;
- loss of household if a move becomes necessary;
- loss of security.

Most importantly, let the child talk. We often think that our role as adults is to tell children what to think or believe. In fact we need to listen to what they want to share with us.

Early intervention to help children and adolescents who have suffered trauma from violence or a disaster is critical. As parents, teachers and mental health professionals, we can all do a great deal to help these youngsters recover.

Oscar's story

Tennille and Mark Welsh were expecting a baby just before Christmas 2011.

Early in November, Tennille became worried that she had not felt the baby move and went to the doctor, hoping to be reassured. Unfortuantely, her worst fears were realised when they could not find a heartbeat. Oscar was stillborn at thirty-three weeks. This was something that no parent ever expects. In fact it was the farthest thing from their minds. However, much to their surprise, the research says that in Australia 1 in 140 babies are stillborn every year. They were surprised by this dreadful statistic and by the general silence around the subject. Since losing their baby they have heard numerous stories from others about their own loss, and they wanted to share their memory of Oscar. He is, and will always be, a part of their family.

When the midwife couldn't find a heartbeat, Tennille remembers being very calm and talking positively to herself in the few minutes between the midwife examining her and the obstetrician arriving.

She didn't want to get 'worked up' unnecessarily. Yet when she found out her baby had died she remembers screaming and then her doctor helping her to call her husband, Mark. She remembers saying 'The baby has died' and for some reason she wanted to know if the baby was a boy or a girl. Tennille remembers being thankful that the obstetrician just said to her: "We will find out at the birth".

Tennille also asked him to check again, just to make sure this wasn't a mistake. She couldn't believe this was happening. Her cousin (who was also pregnant) was in the waiting room and sat with Tennille until her family arrived. Mark called her parents, who in turn called her sister.

Tennille had had no idea that anything could be wrong. She was told that reduced movement was normal later in pregnancy and she had never even thought that a stillbirth could be a possibility. She had had an uneventful pregnancy and had assumed that at this stage if there were any difficulties with her baby then it would just be delivered early.

It was three days from finding out that Oscar had died till he was born. These three days seemed like an eternity but in retrospect, it was just the right amount of time. They went home, made arrangements to go into hospital to be induced. This allowed them to begin processing what had happened and to make some decisions about how they wanted to remember Oscar. The care from her obstetrician was outstanding. Mark and Tennille want to make special mention here of his generous support.

Without his availability and advice, including referral to support services, this time would have been very different.

During the several days in hospital before Oscar was born they received a great deal of printed information from various support services, memory services (such as hand and foot print services) and information about funeral homes. The day of Oscar's birth they did nothing but spend time with him. However, the following day they needed to start attending to all these things.

Oscar was born on Saturday 12 November at 6.55 am, just as the sun was coming. He was perfect in every way. They were very fortunate to have time to bathe, dress and cuddle him. Their families all came and met Oscar and this was a happy time for them. A friend of theirs, who is a professional photographer, came in and photographed Mark and Tennille with him and these photos are very comforting and special. The three of them stayed together in hospital until Sunday night.

When Oscar was born, Mark's and Tennille's mothers were there. The photos really do show their happiness and pride in their new son. In the days leading up to his birth Tennille had cried so much, so uncontrollably but on this Saturday she just looked at him, cuddled him and smiled. Oscar was placed on her tummy and they were able to hold him and bathe him.

Tennille's sister took responsibility for telling their friends and family about Oscar. The baby shower was planned for the day that Oscar was actually born so she needed to make many phone calls. Mark and Tennille were very appreciative that they did not have to do this but they know it was a difficult experience for her and can remember sitting at home the night they found out, hearing her make phone calls and then vomit.

Tennille is a teacher and her school, students, colleagues and parents were also remarkable. At school she dealt with many students across all year levels so the school prepared a statement to tell the students (high school age) and also prepared a balloon release for the staff and students she taught, to occur concurrently with the balloon release the family had planned for Oscar's 'party'.

They decided even while in hospital to refer to Oscar's funeral as a 'party': kids don't have funerals, they have parties. It was important for them to remember this day with happiness and love for Oscar, even though it was heartbreaking. They had a small service, conducted by the chaplain who married them at the same church in Ceres. Their families attended and they were able to sit on the floor in the church. They read Oscar a bedtime story, released blue balloons and enjoyed cupcakes with blue icing. The weather was warm and there wasn't a cloud in the sky. This was a very peaceful day. They have been overwhelmed with the photos of family and friends setting off balloons, literally all over the world.

Any child born after twenty weeks gestation is required to be buried or cremated. They were supported by the funeral home and the chaplain to have the service they wanted. Tennille knows at the time the chaplain was unsure about reading a light-hearted story book (Hairy Maclary) but he has told the family since that it was absolutely perfect. He has also recommended this to other families who have lost a child. Only family members attended this ceremony and everyone read a page from the book. As it was passed around they were able to share a small laugh and smile.

Sometime later Tennille and Mark spoke at length with their obstetrician who didn't believe a cause would be found, even if they conducted an autopsy. A baby who dies in utero is not required to have an autopsy, which is different to any child who dies unexpectedly as their death is automatically referred to the coroner. Tennille was very worried about 'leaving' Oscar. She felt very protective of him and couldn't bear the thought of him being left alone. Oscar did not leave their room for the entire two-day stay in hospital. In fact, when the funeral home came she wrapped him up and walked him to their car, placed him in the bassinet on the back seat and watched them drive away.

Tennille and Mark are very clear that they wouldn't have done anything differently. They are grateful for the advice to take their time when Oscar was born. They took lots of time to look at his hands, feet and hold him. They encourage parents to speak up about what they want to do with their baby in regards to photos, funeral arrangements and so on, and to make the most of their time together.

Although generally they are at peace with how things unfolded, several aspects still haunt them today. Tennille often wonders if she had gone to her doctor the day before she did, when things didn't quite feel right, if this may have made a difference and in the months following Oscars birth she did a great deal of research, reading and talking with other bereaved parents. One thing that became clear from this research was that having an autopsy improves the chances of finding the reason(s) for unexplained stillbirth. In hindsight they now feel they would have preferred to have had an autopsy, so that Oscar's brief presence could have contributed to the ongoing research into this tragic phenomenon.

Tennille says there are times when she experiences grief more intensely, especially missing Oscar, and other times when she is more removed. While she doesn't cry for Oscar every day now, she still thinks about him every day and always looks for ways to incorporate him into her life. When she comes across friends or family who are experiencing grief she thinks she now looks for ways to help them live through the grief, rather than just sending commiserations and waiting for them to 'feel better.' When she talks about living through the grief she means talking about their loved one, doing something to remember them, finding out what they loved most about them.

Tennille and Mark now have an eighteen month-old son, Angus, and are expecting another child in a few months. Angus knows who the baby in the pictures is and can say 'Oscar'. In the years to come they imagine there will be some difficult questions, both for them to explain and for Angus to understand, but they will continue to give Angus information about his brother, as he is able to understand it.

Susan's story

I read with interest an article written by Susan Simpson who lost her baby at thirty-two weeks. The article includes letters she wrote to her child. In the letters she talks about finding out there was a problem with the growth of the baby as early as the twelve-week scan. By thirty-two weeks it was known that there was a build up of fluid in the baby's body and it was determined that the baby had died in utero. The medical staff decided to deliver the baby by caesarean section after Susan came down with a sore throat, which ruled out an epidural anaesthetic.

Her letters to her child were both comforting and heart wrenching at the same time. She told of the disappointment in not getting the hospital photographer to take more photos, and not letting her other children see the baby, and she regrets not asking the staff to unwrap her child so she could see all of her instead of only her perfect face and hands. She goes on to say that just a few days later she was celebrating her other daughter's birthday, showing the brave face that she felt she had to. She wanted to give in to her grief, to crumble.

Susan said: 'Sometimes I wish I could collapse into a sobbing heap and let go of the agony bottled inside. I know I can't and I won't. People ask: "How are you?" and I wonder how they'd react if I told them I feel utterly spent and incomplete without you. I am thankful to those to whom I can simple answer "Ugh" and they immediately understand.'

#POINTS TO CONSIDER

- → Grief is different for everyone.
- → Grief is a normal, natural and healthy part of life.
- → The effects and symptoms of grief can be extremely difficult and debilitating.
- → Grief is more complex than we think.
- → We are conditioned on how to react.
- → Although we can prepare for a death it does not mean that we won't grieve when the death occurs.
- → Look for support and assistance when you don't cope with a death.
- → Ask for help if you think you need it.
- → Look for professionals who can assist with your grieving.

MY NOTES

MY NOTES

CHAPTER 9

HAVING THE CONVERSATION

Our lives begin to end the day we become silent about things that matter.
– Martin Luther King, Jr.

Now we are informed let's have the conversation

While working with families I have noticed a change over the last few years in the increasing number of families who have had a conversation with their loved one about some of the basic aspects to consider regarding death, such as a preference between burial or cremation. People are beginning to leave clearer instructions about their end of life in general and to discuss their thoughts on what might or might not occur in relation to a funeral. Having said that, unfortunately these are still the minority. Nowhere near enough people are having this conversation even though many of them, when questioned on their end, agree it is important to talk about it.

How this conversation unfolds depends fundamentally on the person initiating the conversation about death and the situation itself. Each conversation naturally depends on the respective situation and each will look slightly different.

We've talked in chapter three about when this conversation might occur, but let's recap:

- When no one is unwell and no imminent death;
- When someone is unwell or elderly;
- When someone is diagnosed with a life-limiting illness;
- When a death has occurred.

The conversation has to cater for whatever stage of life the family is in.

- A family with teenage children would have a different conversation than say;
- An elderly couple;
- A young couple with a terminally ill child;
- A middle aged couple that find out the mother or father has a terminal illness.

It might also be helpful to explore what our role might be when having these types of conversations, how we will manage that experience. Our role might be something quite simple or quite challenging or onerous, and at times throughout the conversation/s our position might change.

It might be a role where we:

- simply sit and listen;
- are asked to do something;
- might support a person when they attend medical appointments;
- might be a sounding board;
- might be a mediator;
- might lead the conversation;
- might be a resource person.

Important things to note about having this conversation:

- it's never too soon to have this conversation and it is a lot better to start this conversation long before health deteriorates;
- perhaps we could find a friend or family member to have a practice conversation with us before the real conversation takes place;

- this is a difficult conversation, so don't rush it and take care by easing into the discussion;
- this should be the first of many conversations;
- don't be judgemental about anything that comes out of the conversation as it may differ completely to what we believe: we may find it frustrating when we don't agree with the terminally ill person's view;
- everything is changeable so make sure the person we are talking with understands that they can change their mind at any time.
- above all, be respectful.

If the conversation is with someone who is dying or elderly the most important things to remember are:

- don't assume we are supposed to know what to do;
- make it a priority to demonstrate our love for the person who is dying;
- respect the authority of the dying person to make his or her own decisions;
- accept that he or she is dying and don't fight against it;
- contribute to maintaining a peaceful environment;
- we all respond to information about death and dying differently;
- we are often initially in shock and so our response can be quite emotional;

In the previous chapter we looked at the many reasons 'why' and the excuses 'why not'. Now let us think about how we actually go about 'having the conversation'. Naturally there are many ways to approach this sensitive topic and have the discussion but fundamentally it should come from a place of honest concern and empathy. It is important that everyone feels comfortable about sharing his or her feelings. There is no right or wrong way, everybody is different and if it comes from the heart it will be all right. I would ask you to consider the following questions before you have this conversation.

The best format

A comfortable discussion about dying and death can be had in any of the following ways:

- a private conversation;
- a family meeting;
- meeting of friends;
- writing a letter;
- a DVD or audio recording.

Who to include?

Our deepest thoughts and feelings are not meant for everyone. Hearing them is a huge privilege and we should consider who is the best person to share this information with. We need someone who can hold that safe space for us and love and support us no matter how the questions are answered.

What are some of the topics you might introduce?

- Working out what is important will avoid confusion at a later date (understanding the person's wishes is high on this list).
- Determining basic practical outcomes, for example burial or cremation? Funeral and spreading of the ashes, or leaving one's body to science?
- Determining what the he/she perceives as 'quality-of-life'.
- Determining what medical care is appropriate and what is not. For example, does he/she want to be resuscitated and, if so, under what circumstances?
- Is organ donation desirable?
- Fears and anxieties around end of life, death and dying.
- Understanding choices around end of life, death and dying.
- What matters most?

- What decisions he/she wants to be involved in?
- What decisions he/she wants family and doctor/s to know about?
- Clarifying who exactly he/she would like to be informed.

When is a good time to have this conversation?

As mentioned earlier, the sooner the conversation is held the better. If there is health crisis or knowledge of a terminal illness, then the conversation should go ahead at the earliest possible opportunity

What is the ideal location?

Do you want a place that is private where you won't get interrupted?

Finding a place where everyone is comfortable and getting their needs met will help make interaction between those present an experience that you can treasure.

Getting Started

This conversation is confronting for everyone because it brings to the fore the reality of life and death, and possibly the hardest part is getting started.

Conversation starters

It can be awkward starting a conversation about dying and death. Here are some suggestions as to how one might approach the subject.

If it's the elderly or dying person who wants to initiate the conversation

- I know this might not be easy but I'd like to have a chat with you

about some of my thoughts and feelings, if not now, when would be a good time?
- There's something I wanted to talk to you about ... When I think about ... I feel ...
- How would you feel about having this conversation?
- How would you like us to have this conversation?
- Would you be happy to listen to what I am feeling?
- I'd like to have a conversation with you where I could express my feelings about ...
- Remember when (name) died, do you think he died a good death?
- I need to think about my future, and I would love your help.
- I've been thinking about my own end of life and wondering what your answers might be to those same questions?
- What do you think a dignified death is?
- When I think about my end of life care and treatment, there are things that I'd prefer didn't happen, or, there are things I prefer did happen.
- When you think about the end of your life what do you think would be the most important things for you?
- Is there a way that we can talk about this that would be comfortable for you?
- I'd like to talk to you about what is important to me at the end of my life.
- I'm frightened of crying or upsetting you but there are things that I need to talk about ...

If it's the family member who wants to initiate the conversation

- This might be really uncomfortable, but I am feeling ... and wondering how you are feeling about this?
- I know this might not be easy but I'd like to have a chat with you about some of my thoughts and feelings ... if not now, when would be a good time?
- There's something I've wanted to talk to you about ... when I

think about ... I feel ... How would you feel about having a conversation about it?
- How would you like us to have this conversation?
- Would you be happy to listen to what I am feeling?
- It's really important to me that I know (or I am aware of) your preferences when things get worse.
- I'd like to be able to support you during this difficult time, I'm wondering if we can take some time together to discuss some important details.
- I'd like to have a conversation with you where I could express my feelings about ...
- Remember when (name) died, do you think he died a good death?
- Remember when (name) died, do you think he had a good funeral?
- I need to think about your future and I would love to talk to you about some things that have been on my mind ...
- I've been thinking about my own end of life, and wondering what your answers might be to those same questions?
- What do you think a dignified death is?
- Have you ever given any thought to what would happen if ...?
- When you think about the end of your life, what do you think would be the most important things for you?
- When you think about end-of-life care and treatment – are there things that you'd prefer didn't happen? Or did?
- When you think about the end of your life it's important that I know your thoughts and wishes.
- I was reading the other day of the importance of letting family members know your wishes should anything unforeseen occur.
- I'm frightened of crying or upsetting you but there are things that I need to talk about.

Irrespective of what we see as our role during this process, the important thing is to listen and be actively involved in the discussion, and to learn the right responses rather than trying to avoid the person's pain and suffering. I have come to learn that it's not just listening that's important. Equally as important is having the right responses so that the dying person really sees that although we may not be able to understand their sadness and grief and/or any other feelings they may wish to share with us, we are empathetic and acknowledge that their feelings are very tangible for them.

I believe that 'mindfulness' is the core of everything, and it is especially appropriate when being with the dying. It is the deep attention to what is happening in the present moment, in the mind and the body, as well as the surroundings. It is being mindful of our responses and the associated feelings that arise in reaction to the discomfort and pain felt by the person we are sitting with. Those who have the privilege of spending time with people who are dying and/or grieving can learn such profound lessons from the experience.

If you are talking with a person who has been given a terminal diagnosis, or a person approaching death, the single most important thing to remember is to ask them, having the illness, what is important to them and what you can do that would assist them the most. Don't be surprised if the answer is a 'nothing at this time' because that may simply be the truth. The other response that you might surprise you is that they just want some practical help - assistance with housework, minding children, cooking meals, or helping them to give 'stuff' away.

This type of response might feel very strange to you, but a friend of mine, Ginny Bydder, who died whilst I was writing this book, was a very practical person and every time I visited she would 'gift' me things. One time it was nail polish, another time it was a beautiful range of skin care that she loved. She knew I would love it, as I did, but she also wanted to give her things away so that her husband did not have to be bothered with this after her death. Initially I had a problem with this, but I came to realise that it was so important to her and the only reason I was having difficulty with it was that I then had to face the fact that she was not going to survive the cancer. So for me it was a reality check; for her it was housekeeping!

I asked Ginny what was important to her during this time and these are some of her responses.

- People who respected her wishes and loved her regardless of the choices she was making.
- Getting everything done in a practical sense, such as changing bank accounts and the names that appeared on household bills.
- Leaving instructions for her husband.
- Giving away things so that we could have a 'piece of Ginny to remind us of her.
- Recycling anything that she could was important.
- Giving away clothes to friends who could not afford the beautiful clothes she had sitting in her wardrobe.

Just sitting with a dying person in a comfortable manner allowing them to talk freely can be very liberating and healing. Speaking with an oncologist recently I heard him say that just giving the person your time is precious. Allowing them to chat to you without you having a time frame – because some of these conversations take time. Some patients feel that their family can't have the discussion so some of the medical and nursing staff will go out of their way to sit and listen.

It seems perhaps the current younger generation is able to approach these conversations more easily than previous generations. A few years ago my daughter, Jess, spoke to me about her choice to be an organ donor. She wanted my assurance that I would comply with a decision that she had made. I assured her that I would always follow through on any decision she had made like this when her time came to leave this world. I was pleasantly surprised that at her young age of twenty-seven she had thought about this decision and wanted to share that with me. I felt honoured that she wanted a commitment from me that I would follow her wishes. Thanks to a concerted public education programme, particularly about organ donation, my daughter's generation seem far more accepting of thinking about big decisions like this. It was a matter of fact conversation we had – nothing morbid or sad – simply checking in with me about her wishes.

A friend told me that she is fortunate to stand in a good place on this topic, because her mother is so positive about the future 'experience of death'. They have talked about it often, with regard to both the practical and the philosophical aspects.

However, when she thinks of her niece and nephew who lost their five-year-old daughter from a brain tumour and the heartbreak that was involved for everyone who knew that Tessa's death was inevitable, then initiating a conversation about death and dying takes on a whole new meaning and depth. The ripple effect on the family and friends was naturally indescribably painful.

An example of how this conversation can have a positive outcome

Jill Thackray shared: "When my mother was diagnosed with ovarian cancer and was told she had only weeks to live, I asked how she felt about it and did she want to talk with me about it. At first she didn't so I asked if it was okay for me to talk about what I was feeling. She seemed happy about this; almost relieved, as she didn't want to upset me if I wasn't ready. By sharing my feelings, she told me, I helped her to acknowledge her thoughts and feelings. It opened up a 'magical' time between us. Pure honesty at its finest. She was able to tell me that she wasn't scared and knew it was time. She expressed her love of family and the life she had lived. I honestly believe that opening up the discussion gave us both much comfort. This may not work for every situation but I believe that she was hoping I would initiate the conversation".

Catherine Bearsley, a palliative care community nurse for ten years, agrees with Jill. "A diagnosis of a terminal condition can be a lonely experience for both men and women. The feeling that no one around truly understands your fears adds to the pressure to 'be positive', which can be isolating. Hair loss and body changes may add to the feeling of being different. A wish to protect others, especially close family, from distressing grief may contribute to feeling isolated. No matter how supportive close family and friends are, loneliness remains a challenge. Some might even find that not being able to discuss the many aspects of dying causes fear and anxiety to increase. Finally, being able to courageously share concerns and feelings can be an important step in experiencing trust - and giving and receiving love. Speaking from the heart may bring shared tears – and longed for understanding."

I believe that our readiness to die can inform and invigorate how we live and how we relate to one another. If we can face death with grace and the comfort of family and friends, then death will hold less fear.

Remembering the words of a dear friend Susan Stretch who once said to me, "Why is death any different from having the conversation around any travel we do – we always research, discuss and plan, and I see death as the next adventure in my life, an opportunity for discovery and learning. So I will put the same effort into that adventure, that I would any other". Well said my friend!

#POINTS TO CONSIDER

- → We live in a death-denying culture.
- → At a very basic level it is important to try to have conversations about death when a death is imminent.
- → Most people still fear death.
- → People who are dying need to have the right team around them, a team that is helpful and facilitates the process and the end-of-life passage.
- → Have a discussion about what is important to the dying person.

MY NOTES

MY NOTES

MY NOTES

CHAPTER 10

THE ROAD TO RECOVERY: MANAGING AND ADAPTING AFTER A DEATH

The emotion that can break your heart is sometimes the very one that heals it.
— Nicholas Sparks, *At First Sight*

People who are grieving often feel as if they are dissociated from the world around them. C. S. Lewis described the sensation as "...having an 'invisible blanket' around him". He could see the world going on as usual, but he wasn't a part of it.

After a death you walk a road to recovery. Regardless of the previous losses in your life, it's not a road you have walked before. It can be a very slow process, one which is extremely painful. Every death in our life is a wake up call to get us to live more fully and more in the present. I don't like the terminology 'moving on' but I do think you need to believe you are getting back to some type of 'new normal', whatever 'normal' might mean for you.

I become concerned when people think 'you just have to move on with life'. Move on? Move on to what, or where, exactly? Some people think that after a certain time, say a year, that everything should be better. Most grieving people would probably resent the expectation that they and their families should just move on. However, I do believe that it is never too soon to address your grief and make a start on your path to recovery. Loss is an inevitable part of being a human being, and ultimately our choice is either to remain in pain and suffering or to learn how to use the experience to develop a richer and more fulfilling life. Grief and loss can be our biggest teachers in life. They certainly have taught me much about who I truly am.

We all suffer loss as we journey through our life but ultimately we can make the choice, a commitment, to live abundantly, happily, joyfully, gratefully while we are still alive. We all suffer. Everyone experiences their share of traumas, hardships, difficulties and suffering in life. It's how we choose to handle these that determines who and where we will be in five, ten or twenty years from now.

Scarlett Lewis said:

> "One of the lessons my grief taught me was that healing takes time, and its path is unpredictable."

Scarlett explained that getting back to any form of 'normal' can be difficult for a number of reasons.

> "I did feel self-conscious if I was out to dinner and laughed for example, whether people were thinking it was inappropriate or not. Since the tragedy was high profile most people would recognise me; some would approach me at the grocery store and ask to hug me. This was nice except I then burst into tears and had to run from the store distraught. (This happened once). My community kept me going, however, by bringing me dinners and a fund was established, My Sandy Hook Family Fund, with the sole purpose of helping families. They sent out people who helped fix my stove and oven, and even helped take care of my animals and clean my house."

So even though you may want to get back to some type of normal, family, friends and even the public may be evaluating your every move.

Sometimes it's easier to get back to doing the things in life that you were doing before the death, such as getting back to work. At times it's the distractions that you need in order to help relieve the pain of grieving and sadness. But then you don't always grieve as you might if you just gave yourself the time and permission to let it happen. Other times, it takes a very long time to get back into anything remotely 'normal'.

From my own experience and working with grieving families for over twenty years, I think it's about learning how to manage and adapt after your life has been turned upside down. Most of us like to feel in control of our life and when you lose that control it can be difficult to live fully, with any sense of purpose. Sometimes it is unbelievably difficult to adapt to the painful reality of the death of someone important to you. Of course things will never be the same without that person but you can learn how to manage your life and how to adapt without having that person by your side in an everyday sense. And sometimes time does not heal at all. You just want it all back the way it was.

The length of time it takes for someone to adjust varies greatly with each mourner. And how we mourn will depend on a number of things:

- age;
- personal circumstances;
- religious or spiritual beliefs;
- personality;
- cultural background;
- previous experiences of bereavement.

Life will never be the same again after a bereavement, but there should come a time when you are able to adapt and adjust and cope with life without the person who has died. I do believe that getting back into the 'new normal' is a good thing and helps you to "turn the corner to recovery" as Mal and Dianne McKissock put it in their book *Coping with Grief*.

Some tips

It is important to surround yourself with people who will assist and support you in the recovery process. This may be formally, informally, socially or professionally. Your wider community of family and friends will hopefully be there for you when you need them.

Finding a good grief counsellor may also be advisable if you find you are not coping. Specialist bereavement services for individuals, children and families who need assistance following the death of someone close to them are a good source of support and advice. A list of various support groups is located at the end of the book.

Joan Halifax, an anthropologist and Zen priest says in her book, *Being with Dying*, that, "Even grief is transient, and eventually it can pass through us and leave us wiser and humbler for it. Before this transformation though, we must do the slow work of swimming through it."

Some people will never be the same again, especially people who may have been robbed of a goodbye or were not able to go to a funeral, or whose self-imposed guilt, for whatever reason, is overwhelming.

Finding the right support is paramount.

- Look to friends and family members because now is the time to lean on the people who care about you, even if you take pride in being strong and self-sufficient.
- Talk to a grief counsellor or therapist, call on a professional if it gets too much for you.
- Join a support group because having others around you who have experienced something similar can be a great source of comfort.
- Look after your physical health, everything is connected, your mental, physical, and spiritual wellbeing needs to be looked after.
- Express your feelings in a tangible or creative way. Talk to people

who will listen, or write a journal, but find a way to express those feelings. Journal writing can be very helpful during a time like this.
- Plan for grief 'triggers' such as anniversaries, holidays, and other significant times. These can awaken memories and feelings. These times are tough so prepare for them as much as you can. Don't be alone during these times and do try to surround yourself with people who love and support you.
- Don't let anyone tell you how to feel, and don't tell yourself how to feel either. Take your own path and don't expect too much from yourself, especially initially.
- Love who you are.

Looking after yourself

I said at the start that this book was about not just about dying but also about living, so let's look at how you can start looking after yourself.

Recovery has a lot to do with looking after yourself. Remember that you have a duty to care for yourself first. Life as we know is very busy and we often forget about ourselves. How do you ensure you look after you? One way is to ensure you have a list of things that you can do for 'you' – and put time aside to include even one of them in your daily or weekly life. Some of the simple things in life can make a big difference to how you cope. After speaking with many people about this topic I know that the simple task of getting out of bed can be the most difficult things to do when you are grieving, so some of the following might be beyond you to start with. But it is about baby steps to begin with, so don't be hard on yourself if you are just not up to anything in the early stages.

Work out a list of things that would make you more relaxed, feel better about yourself or just generally make you feel a bit better. This list is just a starter.

- Get enough sleep. Sleep is one of the most important elements in life. It is when our body gets the chance to heal. Don't underestimate how important sleep is. It is essential for a person's health and wellbeing. Getting enough good quality sleep at the right times can help protect your mental and, physical health, and your quality of life. Lack of sleep reduces your immune system's ability to deal with infections. It also decreases your ability to function on a daily basis.
- Eat healthy, organic food. Eat fresh fruit and vegetables and plenty of fish, and try to stick with a good nutritional eating plan.
- Get out of the house, even if it is just for twenty minutes. The fresh air will be invigorating. Go somewhere with a friend, a family member, or even by yourself.
- Ask for help. Always know where your support is – this might be formal and informal. For example, a community support group, a specific support group or family and friends.
- Try and stay away from coffee. If coffee is your preferred hot drink then try rotating with different teas as an alternative way of providing your body with a rich source of nutrients. At least once a day, take your tea to a place that is special to you and just sit and drink. Take a book if that helps to unwind for a few minutes.
- Take five minutes in the morning to stretch and breathe. When you first get out of bed try and meditate if you can, even using an 'App' like *Calm* can be helpful. It is simple to download onto your phone, which then makes it a mobile resource that you have with you wherever you are.
- Write things down. Write a worry list. Often things that are bothering us are best written down. It has the effect of transferring your anxieties off your consciousness onto something else, or capturing those things that are important for you to remember but that you now don't have to hold onto, along with everything else.
- Listen to your favourite music. Create a favourite play list of songs that make you feel good. Take time out to listen to them.
- Keep in touch with your friends. Friends are there to support and

assist you, and you will cope better if you stay in touch and allow them to walk alongside you as you journey through the difficult times.
- Write a daily gratitude list. I learnt this from a very good friend, Wendy Haynes, when I attended her yoga retreat in Coffs Harbour a few years ago. She taught us the value of writing a 'grateful list' each day, which I've done since that day. It is incredible the list of things I create every day from the small things to the big things to be grateful for. And surprisingly the content of this list changes daily.
- Make room for rest and always listen to your body. If you need rest, take it. It doesn't matter if it is day or night, your body is the best indicator of your physical, mental and spiritual needs. Learn to trust it.
- Breathe. When times get really tough or you find yourself getting anxious just breathe. If you can purposefully slow your inhaling and exhaling you can avert the stress response commonly known as 'fight or flight'. It is amazing how quickly your body goes into this 'fight or flight' mode and without realising it you have forgotten to take a few deep breaths.
- Exercise. Three minutes at a time, three times a day. It doesn't have to be a long walk, or run or session at the gym. I am a firm believer that if you exercise and get your cardio level up for three minutes, three times a day then that is a really good start and is adequate for many people.
- Keep track of your achievements. Keep a daily journal and write down everything that you achieve, even the tiniest things make a difference. However, don't expect big improvements every day. Take baby steps and reward yourself on achieving even the most simple of tasks. And don't worry if the next day you don't achieve anything; sometimes it is a case of three steps forward and two back.
- Try a Yoga or Pilates class. Find a local Yoga or Pilates class, go along and check it out. Speak to the people running the place and explain what you want from such a class and see what they

have to offer. When you find something that works for you enrol in regular classes.
- Get more sunlight. It is estimated that over one billion people worldwide are deficient in Vitamin D. Not only are physical bodies weakened by a lack of Vitamin D, but also our minds. Depressive symptoms correlate strongly with lower levels of Vitamin D. My son, Ben, who is highly qualified in this area, talks about the importance of exposure to morning sunlight for the regulation of your daily circadian rhythms. This will actually make it easier for you to fall asleep at night. There are photo-receptors in your eyes that are specifically tuned to the blue light found in natural sunlight. Blue light from unnatural sources (TVs, computers, iPads, phones) during the wrong times of day will also activate these receptors, further disrupting melatonin production and your sleep patterns. If you must look at these after dark use amber-lensed goggles once the sun has gone down. These blue-blocking lenses are highly effective in reducing the effects of blue light exposure. Our family has been trialling these for some time now and we have noticed a significant improvement in sleep patterns. Missing the sun in the morning, and watching hours of TV late at night is guaranteed to make restful sleep a difficult proposition.
- Get a massage. Find a person and place that will do the massage that suits you and book in for one regularly. It can be inexpensive and if you find the right masseuse you will find it will make a big difference. You might be amazed at the results.
- Take a hot bath. Did you know that there are wonderful benefits from having a hot bath? It can relax the muscles, calm your mind, detoxify, moisturise, stimulate circulation and clear your lymph system, all with a simple bath.
- Light candles. Candles work for most people. Light a candle with a nice scent and you will find it will uplift your mood.
- Have a good laugh. Even though this is one of the most difficult things to do after a loss and you might think you will

never laugh again, having a good laugh is essential. Research has found that having a laugh can also improve heart health, increase life expectancy and make pain more tolerable. Don't worry about what other people think. It is not disrespectful for you to have a laugh.

- Create some routines. After a loss routines get lost as things can be quite hectic for the first few weeks and it throws everything out. But finding routine in your daily life will assist you in recovery.
- Give yourself permission to feel the feelings. It is very healthy for you to allow the feelings, even though at times you can feel as if your heart is breaking. You can't suppress the bad feelings and feel the good ones. It doesn't work like that. If you try to suppress 'bad feelings', what happens is that effectively you depress 'all feelings'. In fact, it is possible that this is setting up a vicious cycle: you have a painful emotion, you try to push it away. This leads to more painful emotions, which you try to push away, and so on. Intense emotion can be overwhelming for all of us. Learn how to identify and acknowledge your feelings, stay with them briefly, and don't do anything with them, just accept that this is how you are feeling. Also, it is important not to get caught up in analysing your feelings too much, just be aware of them.
- Delegate. Immediately after a loss the smallest of tasks can seem insurmountable. Delegate tasks to your family and friends or a support group. Learn how to ask for help and learn how to accept help. Accept all offers of help and care from others. People around you will want to help, and getting things done will assist you in your recovery.
- Take your vitamins. My son, who is a qualified scientist, and a nutrition coach, has taught me the value of taking vitamins when experiencing stress or poor sleep. Speak to someone who can assist you in working out what is suitable for your needs, and find a good product that will assist you in keeping your levels up. Loss of appetite is very common when grieving and your nutrient

- intake may not be optimal through your diet, so supplements may be a good idea.
- Resist the urge to be busy all the time. Keeping busy is often counterproductive, even though it might divert you away from your feelings temporarily; however it is not wise to be busy all the time.
- Limit your media consumption, especially if your loss is part of a bigger event, such as shootings or bushfires. The continual obsession with media related to tragic deaths or events is not healthy or helpful. Many articles are pure fiction and therefore won't assist you. And there is a limit to how many times we can watch the constant barrage of footage about tragic events without it having a harmful effect on us. There is now evidence to suggest that our anxiety levels and prevalence of trauma-related and depressive symptoms is increased primarily due to the continual consumption of tragic events through the innumerable media networks (Ahern et al, 2002).
- Postpone all major decisions. When you are grieving, making the smallest decision is usually very difficult, your mind is often messy and numb. So leave important decisions where possible, until you are feeling more steady and balanced. If certain decisions must be made, ask for assistance from those you trust.
- Accept yourself as you are. Regardless of what feelings you might have about what you did or did not do before your loss, you need to find a way to love who you are. Feelings of guilt and anger are quite normal and often misguided. Our society puts a lot of pressure on all of us to be a certain way, a certain type of person. But we also put a lot of pressure on ourselves, and often don't meet those expectations. So be kind to yourself, accept yourself for who you are and your life will be much richer and you will be much healthier.
- This list might seem huge, but if you can find one or two things that assist you then that is where you start.
- 'A good laugh and a long sleep are the best cures in the doctor's

book' – Irish proverb.

#POINTS TO CONSIDER

- → Every death is a wake up call.
- → You have a duty to care for yourself first before you can look after others.
- → There are many support groups available to you.
- → Grief is not linear: sometimes it's three steps forward and two back.
- → Life won't be the same again, but it can still be a very good life and there will be a 'new normal'.
- → Love who you are, even if you have to work on who you are without that person in your life.

MY NOTES

MY NOTES

MY NOTES

CHAPTER 11

LIVING THE LEGACY

Man does not simply exist but always decides what his existence will be, what he will become the next moment. By the same token, every human being has the freedom to change at any instant.
— Victor Frankl

I do believe that most people care about what legacy they leave behind when they die. For me it is knowing that my children have a sense of community, a sense of knowing who they are, a sense of worthiness, a sense of compassion, justice, love and consideration.

I learnt from my extended family about:

- open-mindedness;
- trust;
- modesty;
- empathy;
- kindness;
- respect: for one's self, for others, for the environment and for possessions;
- honour;
- determination;
- hard work.

We have the opportunity in our life to make a difference in so many ways - some are obvious, some less so. I also learnt from my grandparents about passing on skills and how deep a love for family can be.

One of my passions in life is being able to assist others in living a life that fulfils their goals and dreams: to 'live the legacy they hope to leave'. Since the age of fourteen I've been fortunate to teach in many areas of my life, be it music, business, IT, marketing, public relations and, more recently, celebrancy, and this has allowed me to assist many people to live their dreams.

This book has allowed me to leave behind a part of me that I hope will live on for some time after my death, so I would like to leave you with a couple of questions to ponder.

What legacy will you leave behind? Legacy is defined as "something received from an ancestor or predecessor or from the past" (Webster). It also means how someone is remembered, and what contributions they made while they were alive.

I believe in the premise that most people live in hope of leaving a memory. When you die, everything you did or owned is rendered meaningless if it didn't bring value and joy to yourself and others.

◑ DID YOU KNOW?
Your legacy matters. Many people believe that it's the one and only thing that lives on once you're gone. Creating a legacy of joy and value is not necessarily a difficult task, but in the busy lives we lead, it is easy to forget to live life to the fullest without regret. Don't wait until it's too late for you to enjoy it. And, please don't blame others for not being able to achieve things in life.

Life can be hard. I was brought up in a very turbulent family, with a violent, alcoholic mother. At times I wondered whether I would reach adulthood. Many times I prayed that I wouldn't. As I grew and came to understand more about genetics, I even feared I might turn into my mother, that the 'cell memory' from my mother would somehow invade every part of my being. I was very angry that I had been born into a family where violence occurred on more occasions than it did not. I survived and I am a survivor of family violence.

I believe that we have a choice, a choice in our attitude. We can choose to be a victim, or we can choose not to allow our history to govern how our life unfolds.

I was conditioned to believe that if you worked hard and reached the pinnacle of your career then you were successful. When I hit the age of forty I realised this is a myth, that success has nothing to do with your career at all. I climbed the corporate ladder and was a successful CEO of a national communications agency but it did not make me feel any better about myself or what I was contributing to society. At that late age I finally realised that 'success' was about relationships and was a result of those relationships; of how you will be remembered. No one will remember in fifty years time if I was good at my work or the role I had. But hopefully someone will remember if I was a good person and that the skills I learned had been passed on to someone else, who in turn passed them onto another. I love the adage of 'passing down your value not your money'. Your legacy is about far more than material things.

Steve Krupp, who leads the executive talent management business Oliver Wyman-Delta Organization and Leadership, said: "Great leaders ... leave a legacy that transcends them and cements their contribution to the growth and transformation of their organisation."

And it's the same with your personal life: the legacy you leave should outlast you and cement your contribution to the growth of others.

As a celebrant I conduct funerals for many people who die much younger than you'd expect and in nearly every case the family told me that the deceased and the people left behind had regrets that they had not achieved their goals in life; yet. They were just starting to plan their life. Well, don't let life get so busy that the planning might happen but the living doesn't start until it's too late.

What about your life?

Are you ready if today was your last day? Are you living the life you want to live? Are you the person you want to be? If we accept the fact that we can die at any time any day then we might live our lives differently. So don't put off every day the things closest to your heart.

- Let's talk about success. What is it for you?
- Where are you are in your life now? How does it feel? Are you living the life you want to live?
- If money was not an issue, what would you be doing in your life?
- You never know what small action of yours might bring about a big change in someone else's life.
- How have you made this a better world to live in?
- Dream big, think big, and aim for bigger and better things in life, not necessarily material things.
- Think about small things you could do that might change someone else's the life.
- Set goals to achieve what you want out of life. Be proud of those achievements and celebrate them, no matter how small or large they might be.
- What kind of legacy do you want to leave? Plan what you are going to do with your life to leave a legacy you are proud of.
- How will your story be passed on?

Make today count towards the legacy that you will leave behind. The choices we make in our life and the way we live our life will determine the kinds of legacies we leave behind. What action can you take in the next four weeks that will make a difference to the legacy you will leave behind?

I will leave you with the beautiful message from Scarlett Lewis after the death of her son, Jesse, at the Sandy Hook shoot-out. She learned that love was indeed the essential element necessary to move forward and that taking that path of love is a choice.

'We can live in anger and resentment, or we can choose love and forgiveness'.

For me, choosing love was the key to creating a healthy, safe and happy world.

MY NOTES

MY NOTES

MY NOTES

APPENDICES

CEREMONIES AND RITUAL: WRITING 'THEIR STORY'

Your story is the greatest legacy that you will leave to your friends. It's the longest-lasting legacy you will leave to your heirs.
— Steve Saint

The passing on of stories from one generation to the next is a tradition that seems to be disappearing from our world. Storytelling used to be a very important part of life for most cultures. Some cultures still do it well and stories are passed down through the ages. With the new technological age we are losing the desire or the time to talk with each other at any great length. Much is done through social media and not much time is spent sitting around a table, or campfire and just talking. In everyone's busy life spending lengthy periods of time together seems more and more difficult. Unless one makes a conscious decision to do this it simply won't happen. Such times give us the opportunity to sit and have an ongoing dialogue with each other that is meaningful, because we are not rushing and continually worrying about work or other stresses.

The importance of spending time together to share and enjoy each other's company cannot be underrated. For most busy families this is something that has to be planned and honoured to ensure it takes place as a focus within a family.

Storytelling

In 2011 I received a call from a young lady whose wedding I had conducted a few years earlier. She wanted to talk to me about conducting her grandmother's funeral. Her grandmother was Albanian and a Muslim and I knew that it would be very unusual for her family to have a civil funeral ceremony. I enquired as to why the family had chosen a civil ceremony and she told me that her Nona (grandmother) had loved her wedding that I had conducted and loved hearing the story of how the couple met and what was important to them in their relationship. On hearing their ceremony she had mentioned to her family that on her death she wanted me to 'retell her story about how she immigrated to Australia'. They had considered their options carefully and asked me if their Imam could come in at the end of the civil ceremony and perform a simple blessing, to satisfy those who might find a civil ceremony unusual. Naturally I was delighted. I had never had the opportunity to work with an Imam and was excited about the prospect, along with the opportunity to tell this women's story.

It was a wonderful experience, although the pressure was somewhat daunting. The funeral had to happen very quickly and gave me very little time to work with the family to gather the information for the ceremony. They knew many of their friends might question their decision about having a civil ceremony, but the family was adamant about following their grandmother's wishes. It was a wonderful experience that will stay with me for a long time. Muslims go through a detailed washing ritual to prepare the body and people of the same sex as the deceased always do this. Another important detail for this family was how the body was to be wrapped in a shroud. For women, the wrappings are much more intricate than they are for a man. These cultural rituals that the family wanted to honour were met before and during the funeral and at the burial. The funeral company they engaged was very helpful and flexible with the family in meeting these matters.

One of the most profound elements of that funeral was when I introduced the Imam to come forward at the end of the ceremony, and the first thing he spoke about was how privileged he was to have heard her story and turned to me and thanked me for re-telling it. He said he had been unsure about being involved outside his mosque and was somewhat nervous about his involvement, but was pleasantly surprised how the ceremony unfolded.

I thanked him greatly afterwards because that meant a great deal to the family and myself.

> Bobby Symons, a funeral celebrant and a student of mine, says: "Our lives are a story to be told and shared". There is no distinction between great and small. We are all important, our lives all have meaning and purpose and the lessons learned need to be passed on down through the generations, sadly far too many families have little knowledge of the life and successes, the pain and the losses of a departed loved one. Story telling at a funeral adds dimension, purpose and meaning to the life journey of the deceased it also helps to bring closure and meaning, and I would add it needs to be told well with flair, enthusiasm and mirth.

There are many ways to go about writing someone's story. If possible, working with the person before they die is wonderful. So having time can be very helpful. If you can get together over a series of meetings then it seems to work best as this gives you both time to consider what you have discussed and decide what is important. Also, hearing their story firsthand is far more authentic and accurate than hearing it from others. Naturally, there may be a lot of information and only some of it might be used for a funeral. However, it will mean the family has that 'story' to keep and pass on to future generations.

After my father died I spoke to my brother Jim about how distressed I was that we no longer had anyone to go to, to tell us stories of our parents and our early life. What we knew collectively was all we had. It was a stark reminder for me and it continues to grieve me at certain times when I cannot remember facts or memories clearly. Very little was written down about my parents, especially my mother's early life, and I'm certain that our memories fade over time. So if the stories are written down and kept then this is a way that they can keep being re-told to generations to come. Work done when planning for a funeral can leave behind a very valuable document. Most of which probably won't be used at the funeral but will be available for future generations to read.

To start this process I suggest you create a list of questions to ask and give the person plenty of time to consider their answers. If the person is unwell then gathering information may need to be done over a number of very short sessions as they might be able to converse with you for only ten minutes at a time. Sometimes it will be weeks or months before the answer is given, and sometimes recalling some of their past will be difficult, emotional and stressful, so please be mindful of that. However, it can also be a very cathartic experience.

The type of questions would differ for each person but I hope the following examples of possible questions you might start with is helpful:

- What are your first memories as a child?
- What do you remember about your childhood?
- Where did you grow up?
- What schools did you attend?
- What did you enjoy at school?
- Tell me about your teenage years.
- Tell me about your family, your siblings, and your extended family.
- What was your first job? And subsequent roles or positions.
- What was your favourite job and why?
- How did you meet your wife or husband? Tell me about that experience and why you chose her or him.
- Children and grandchildren?

Ceremonies and Ritual: Writing 'Their story'

- Places you lived?
- Places you travelled?
- Favourite people in your life and why?
- Hobbies and activities that you enjoy.
- When in your life have you been the most settled and why?
- What is your favourite time of day?
- What annoys you?
- What excites you?
- What is important to you?
- What are you most proud of?
- What legacy do you leave behind?
- Do you have any regrets?
- Who would you like to thank?
- What are the most important changes you have witnessed in history? (Radio, technology, the internet for example).

If the person is not well enough to answer these questions, or has already died and this information has not been gathered, then the family will have to re-construct their story. A good place to start is to check if there is a family member who might have been writing the family history.

A person's life story is a composite of many elements: personal memories, anecdotes and relationships. The facts are usually easier to gather and constitute what I refer to as the eulogy. The various stories give insight into what is effectively the essence of the person. This is what people want to hear and what they will gain most from. A eulogy of facts is often quite boring for people to listen to, but the anecdotal stories never are. This may sound harsh but the reality is most people know many facts about the person but the stories are personal and real and often give a light-hearted feel to the ceremony, which most mourners are very thankful for. Yes you can have humour in a funeral ceremony. Most people will be thankful for this element. Clearly the best ceremonies are those that are balanced with light and shade.

When writing someone's story, naturally the more input you have from family and friends the more rounded and richer the story will be. Getting input from all family members where possible is best, as everyone has a different perspective. How each family member remembers the deceased will differ. Once everyone has had his or her input then someone can compile the information and put it into a final draft.

This document might be lengthy and a decision on what is important to be included in a funeral will need to be made. If the full document will be used for the funeral then you need to consider if a celebrant will use the information or if the family will have someone else read it. In my experience when the celebrant reads the eulogy and the family reads the stories and tributes then we have the best outcome for most families and for the mourners. It is often easier for family members to tell the stories, including some humour, and leave the eulogy to the celebrant. This arrangement has worked for most of my families for many years. I suggest that the speakers are spread through the entire ceremony and are invited up to speak at the most appropriate time in that person's life. For instance, if a sibling were speaking then I would talk about the person's life as a child and then ask that speaker up. It seems to make sense to the mourners and it is easier for them to follow along. It is also important to inform the guests of the speaker's relationship to the deceased, before the person reaches the lectern. Otherwise the mourners will be wondering who this person is while the person has already started speaking.

#POINTS TO CONSIDER

- → Stories get lost unless they are passed down.
- → Try to spend extended time together as a family so that the stories and narratives can be known and shared.
- → Involve others if the family members you meet with do not know facts. Sometimes another family member who is not able to meet with you may have that information available for you.

Creating a ritual

This is what rituals are for. We do spiritual ceremonies as human beings in order to create a safe resting place for our most complicated feelings of joy or trauma, so that we don't have to haul those feelings around with us forever, weighing us down. We all need such places of ritual safekeeping. And I do believe that if your culture or tradition doesn't have the specific ritual you are craving, then you are absolutely permitted to make up a ceremony of your own devising, fixing your own broken down emotional systems with all the do-it-yourself resourcefulness of a generous plumber/poet.

Elizabeth Gilbert, *Eat, Pray, Love*

Ritual is a very natural and innate part of some people's lives, but I am aware that for some it is quite foreign and may conjure up variety of sometimes weird images!

In this chapter I hope you will be open minded and understand that our daily lives are full of ritual; from the first cup of coffee in the morning to turning out the lights at night before bed. If you can be receptive to the new and different idea that ritual can be quite simple and very informal then you can understand how ritual can assist at a time of loss. A ritual can be very simple, such as lighting a candle each night to honour the person you have lost.

In my experience you can best honour life's transition by using ritual as the vehicle. When you experience loss you can address your feelings and the changes in your life with ritual. And the ritual does not have to be a large event. I have created many where only one or two people participate.

The best place to start is to have a clear plan of what you want to achieve and decide on an outcome. Once you've done that (along with others who can assist) you can then create the ritual that is best suited to your needs. If there are a lot of people to cater for, this can make the planning quite complex, nonetheless it doesn't have to be difficult.

The funeral ceremony is a traditional ritual that reflects our beliefs, thoughts and feelings about the death of a loved one. Death rituals are more than private occasions, they are social events which throw "into relief the most important cultural values by which people live their lives and evaluate their experiences ...[and] fundamental social and cultural issues are revealed" (Metcalf & Huntington, 1991, p. 25). Rich in history and symbolism, the funeral ceremony helps us acknowledge the reality of the death. It gives testimony to the life of the deceased. It encourages the expression of grief in a way consistent with the person's values. It provides emotional support for mourners. In essence, the funeral reflects our thoughts about life and death and offers continuity and hope for the living.

I think it is important at this point to look at the derivation of the word ritual and its meaning. The word comes from the Sanskrit *rita*, which refers to both art and order. "Like all real art, rituals provide organic order, a pattern of dynamic expression", says Jean Houston, in her book, *The Search for the Beloved*.

I believe that rituals do not have to be stereotyped, nor do they have to necessarily be influenced by any religious creed. They can be the complete opposite. Ritual can be informal and non-traditional, with no rules other than being safe and respectful.

Karla Helbert, a licensed psychotherapist, in an article on ritual and grief, says that we humans don't like change and prefer to stick with what we know. When a death occurs in our life we are left floundering, and the depth of that grief will depend greatly on how we were connected to that person. The closer we were with that person the greater the grief we experience over their death. She goes on to say that: 'Rituals are made up of actions that represent ideas, thoughts, myths, or beliefs about a particular thing. Rituals give purpose to action and always serve to connect us to something else, generally something greater than our own solitary selves. We may engage in ritual as we seek peace, clarity of mind, or to become more grounded. We may seek connectedness to family, a particular person, our culture, society, traditions, ancestors, or even to our own selves.'

Our lives are filled with daily ritual, from coffee first thing in the morning to the particular way we end a conversation, or send an email or a text to a family member or loved one.

Karla says: "Whether small or elaborate, the rituals we engage in tell stories about who we are, who we want to be, and what is important to us in our lives. Your own rituals may be derived from your family, culture, ethnicity, or a particular religious or spiritual tradition. No matter what stories they tell, rituals always provide structure, meaning, and connectedness."

It is apparent that ritual in many ways creates order to what might be considered the confusion and chaos in our lives. And then when our lives are thrown into chaos, as they are when a death occurs, then this is the time when we most appreciate and need ritual. In our culture there are few rituals to do with death and dying, unlike many other cultures whose lives are full of ritual during such times.

Planning a ceremony or ritual

When planning a ritual, it is important to sit down as a family and decide what is important to you as a group. This can be stressful and cause some anxiety, as not all family members are likely to agree. It is even more complex now that the traditional nuclear family is no longer necessarily the norm. Family structures have changed considerably over the last ten or so years and there may be a previous family as well as the current one. This means the dynamics of this wider group can be quite complex and not always amicable. Where humanly possible we must consider the children from a previous marriage, even if we are unable to include an ex-wife or ex-husband. I love the terminology of working with 'Family Forests' rather than the typical 'Family Tree' as was the norm years ago. It speaks a thousand words about the complexity of many of today's family dynamics.

It is imperative to always remember what would have been important to the person who died. I do challenge families if they are having a civil ceremony when the person who died was religious and had a strong faith. I would hope the family would put their needs after those of the deceased. And I do believe that if the person was religious and the family is not, then they can usually find a clergy who would be happy to adapt their 'standard prescribed script' to meet the needs of the family. Or at the very least use a civil celebrant happy to include some religious elements, maybe even alongside a clergy.

What does a ritual look like?

A ritual can be or look like anything you want it to. A simple gathering of people talking about the person or about their grief might be what is needed, rather than a full structured ceremony.

Here are a few examples which illustrate how different and varied rituals can be, unique to the occasion.

1. When my father died many people attended his funeral as he was well respected in our wider community, especially in the sporting arena. I was quite upset about what occurred, or rather what didn't occur at his funeral. Because I was not given a chance to be involved or make any decisions about the planning my needs were not met. So my brother, myself and another friend decided

to have our own meeting down by the Yarra River and conduct our own informal ceremony. We planted a tree, said a few words, cried a lot and then played one of my father's favourite songs on a portable player. This ritual gave me an opportunity to say what I wanted and was extremely helpful in allowing me to grieve without the anger surrounding his more formal, very large, public funeral. I think about this simple ritual often and am so grateful that we took the time to share in it. I needed this desperately, because my personal needs were not met at the funeral and so I was stuck in anger which I needed to be rid of. By performing this small ceremony, which I will always cherish and that will stay with me forever, I was able to move on.

2. I created a very informal ceremony for a woman who was told that her father had died three months earlier. For reasons unknown to me her mother chose not to tell any of the family about the death. My client found out through other sources that her father had died, his body had been cremated and his possessions packed up. Understandably there was much anger and frustration when this came to light, but to her credit my client (the daughter of the deceased) knew she had to honour her father's life in a way that would assist her grieving. So I conducted a very small memorial service for her and her best friend in a local park where she had many wonderful memories as a child. This small ceremony only lasted about twenty minutes and included the playing of a special song, but it will be a lasting memory for his daughter. She had finally had the opportunity to honour her father and her relationship with him.

3. One lady wanted to spread the ashes of her husband and their fourteen-year-old son out on the bay. I had previously conducted a large-scale funeral for her husband twelve months previously. For the purpose of spreading the ashes I assisted her in creating a ritual where she, her two remaining children and her parents, could go out on the boat, throw the two pods containing her husband and their son's ashes overboard, and have their own private

mini ceremony or ritual. Although I was happy to attend and facilitate this happening, I encouraged her to manage this on her own, with my guidance, if they wanted and ultimately she elected to keep it as a private family affair. They did not require I attend but I was thrilled to later find a huge bunch of flowers on my front door step, with a note that will stay with me forever. It simply said: "Sally, you have no idea how much you have assisted us in our grieving. Every day that we re-read the ceremony from the funeral a little more grieving gets done."

4. When my close friend and fellow celebrant, Ginny Bydder, mentioned earlier, died, she was adamant that she did not want a funeral. She had completely organised the 'direct to cremation' service prior to her death. She had even chosen the spot which she could see from her bedroom window, for the burial of her ashes. We had expressed to her the implication of her decision and that her husband and others would have preferred to have been able to gather at a funeral and celebrate her life, but of course we honoured her wishes. Those closest to her had needs of their own, and she understood this so we came up with a compromise. We had a ritual in her back yard a few days after her death where five of us surrounded by her enquiring dogs, buried her ashes in her backyard. Whilst we did this each of us read a piece we had prepared and grieved together at the loss of this amazing woman. Conducting this small informal ritual enabled us to grieve in a way that was meaningful and healthy.

Location

A choice of place for a ritual can be somewhere very simple. For example, meeting up with a few friends at home or in a park or some meaningful or significant place, and all saying a few words, either about the deceased or about one's owns memories and feelings, can be very cathartic. If you choose an outside venue there may be local by-laws that have restrictions on coffins and formal gatherings so best to check on the relevant local laws or conditions during the planning stage.

Timing

You can take as much time as you want. However, it is worth keeping in mind that most people nowadays do not have an ability to engage for lengthy periods of time, so I would be inclined not to make any ceremony or ritual too long.

Privacy

This may be very important to you so you need to choose a location or venue where you feel comfortable and where you will be undisturbed. Who can see you? Neighbours you have a good relationship with, or someone who has been looking for an excuse to make trouble for you? If you're working with other people, do they feel comfortable if someone notices what you are doing together? How much noise and distraction will there be? These are all factors you need to consider if you are going to hold the ceremony outside.

Safety

At all times safety considerations need to be taken into, account, both your safety and the safety of others attending. Those who are grieving often have confused and muddled thinking so I would suggest it best to get someone else's opinion if you are the grieving one, and you are uncertain about this issue.

Structure of a larger ritual or ceremony

If you are looking at creating a large-scale ritual or ceremony it is wise to have some structure to work with. While there is no set agenda to a civil ceremony, there are usually some common aspects. Music is usually included in such ceremonies, and while it certainly does not need to be funereal most families would agree that it should be respectful of the occasion. A welcome message is usually spoken, often by a celebrant, MC or member of the family, followed by one or more readings, whether they are from a published novel or a poem or a prayer.

A period of quiet thought or reflection is also usually observed at ceremonies, as it is an opportunity for others who may not have been directly involved up to now, to just sit and reflect. Such ceremonies often end with words of thanks from the family or a formal farewell.

Although the planning should be flexible, it does help to have some idea or framework of how the ceremony might look.

Welcoming music

Welcome and introduction

Any housekeeping that may be necessary, such as signing of memorial books, donation envelopes, gathering afterwards for refreshments and sharing of memories.

Setting the tone for the ceremony.

Acknowledging and honouring the feelings of those who are in attendance.

Explaining the meaning of the ceremony and include people who could not be present.

General thoughts of life, death and relationships (making sure that it is relevant to the family).

The eulogy and tribute

Speaking on behalf of family who may not be able to speak for themselves.

Honouring and remembering the person who has died.

Personal remarks and stories from family, friends and colleagues.

Time for reflection

Could be accompanied by music.

The Committal

Closing words invoke a spirit of gratitude, healing and love and also as an inspiration for those who live. If appropriate, I love to send someone off with a 'rowdy applause'!

Closing music

Tributes and stories should be spread throughout the ceremony rather than clumped all together, unless there is a good reason to do so.

The above sample structure is just a guide, hopefully with some helpful suggestions. Over the years I have created many different types of funeral rituals, some of which involved just a few people. This can occur when some individuals feel their needs have not been met either because there was no ceremony at all, or because the ceremony held did not satisfy their personal needs.

Naturally, families of well known notable public figures in the community often struggle when deciding whether to have a public or private gathering, or both. Many times the decision is made to have both. This can cause some difficulty with logistics, when you have to consider at which funeral burial or cremation will take place, and whether the private funeral may come first, especially if this will include a burial. A public memorial without the coffin then can follow. Some friends and members of the wider community might find this hard to accept and may even find it difficult to grieve if the coffin is not in attendance at the second ceremony. In such instances families need to consider the options carefully and take the time to work out what suits them best.

The informal ritual or ceremony

A smaller more informal gathering can take any form you wish. If sitting around in a park or by a river and just talking appeals, then do that. Work out what you would like to accomplish and work towards making it happen.

Once you have determined what will be done for your ritual you then need to decide on who does what. Sharing around the tasks often works best, but each family will have their own ideas on this. It is not uncommon for families to be very clear that certain members of the family will not be allowed to speak. This needs to be addressed prior to the day to avoid any public humiliation or confusion on the day. A celebrant can't get involved in these matters but we do need to be aware that the possibility of a family member trying to speak is there, and that the appropriate contingencies are put in place just in case.

When planning the ritual you will probably be feeling quite overwhelmed by other things that are happening to do with the death. Your natural and necessary feelings of grief make these tasks even more difficult. I've observed that people often have 'messy thinking' when grieving, so it's important to slow down, take a deep breath, and focus on what is really important, what is essential about the funeral you are planning. There is no rush so taking your time is the means to achieving a great outcome. To honour that unique life, the funeral must also be unique and authentic. Families frequently tell me that the best funerals are those that are personalised. Give yourself licence to be as creative as you can. Together with your family, friends and the person who will lead the service, brainstorm how best to remember and honour this special person.

There is no right or wrong, as long as it is safe, respectful, authentic and meets your needs. Take a blank canvas and be creative, think outside the square and have the ritual you want that meets your needs. We often get caught up in what we think other people think we should do; as I mentioned earlier in this book, Abigail Carter had this continuously thrown at her after the death of her husband in the World Trade Center tragedy. Everyone else had his or her own ideas on how she should honour Arron's life. She slowed everything down and took her time to work out what was right for her. It wasn't easy for her because it was not necessarily meeting the needs of his extended family, but at the end of the day she was his wife and the mother of their children. Once again, this might require a couple of rituals to ensure all needs are met.

Bobbie's story

This is the story of my close friend and fellow celebrant Bobbie Symons. It is with grateful thanks to her that I would like to share the details of an event that took place in 2012 close friend of hers died. These are Bobbie's words.

> My beautiful young friend of many years was diagnosed with bladder cancer during 2011. It was devastating news for her and her husband and family.
>
> It took some weeks to correctly diagnose and the advice given was 'remove the bladder' as quickly as possible. This was a serious decision which needed no second thoughts and surgery was scheduled.

Unfortunately the cancer was not contained and had spread to the bowel and more surgery saw my amazing friend now wearing two bags. All through the ensuing months she remained bright, bubbly and cheerful and held the belief that all would be well. She endured chemotherapy for many weeks but the cancer continued to spread and a few months later scans showed the tumours had attached themselves to her pelvis and many other parts of her body. She still remained optimistic until the hard reality of truth had to be faced and she realised her death was imminent. Accepting the prognosis she began to plan her own funeral as well as her fiftieth birthday party.

Many friends arrived for the bash. It was a fabulous night. My friend was seated in her decorated wheel chair which her grand babies (as she called her grandchildren) had decorated with lights, streamers and a honking horn. We all gathered around reminiscing about the wonderful times we had shared with her over the years and much affection was shown. Many friends spoke of their love and affection for her and we sang Happy Birthday as she cut the cake. During her thank you speech she broke down and cried over what she was going to be leaving behind: her wonderful husband and best friend, her daughter and her stepdaughters and all the little ones and the many friends who loved her so much.

Earlier in the night she had asked me if I would officiate at her funeral. I told my friend that I would feel extremely honoured and privileged to preside at her last rite of passage. She had it all planned and told me her last wishes and requests and was adamant about the songs that she wanted played. I gave her my word that her wishes would be carried out. She asked what funeral director should she call and I gave her the name and advised which funeral chapel would be best to hold such a large number of people who would attend. We made a date for five nights later for me to go to her home and meet with the funeral director and record her requests. She said she would call me and confirm.

Sadly the call never came as she was admitted into hospital four days later for pain management, she slipped into a coma and a few days later passed away.

Things didn't go according to plan and her last wishes suddenly were going in another direction. I was informed that her service was going to take place in a Catholic church and that she was under the influence of morphine when she told myself and many others of her final wishes.

I was devastated, I knew what my happy and organised friend wanted and there was nothing I could do. I didn't sleep well that night. I was not the only one suffering because she had asked another close friend to speak during the eulogy and now he was being told he couldn't.

It was a shattering experience knowing what she wanted and knowing it was out of our hands and there was nothing we could do about it. It wasn't about me, it was the fact that her wishes as we knew them weren't being considered.

I felt overwhelmed with grief on both fronts. I needed closure, I needed to know that maybe she had changed her mind after speaking with me that night, and if I knew that then I could be consoled and move forward. I knew I could not officiate in a Catholic church.

At five o'clock the night before her funeral her husband phoned me and we shared some small talk. I asked him how he was coping because I knew that he was in a terrible place as they were such a devoted couple. He told me that he had just been with the priest who was going to officiate the next morning.

None of us knew she was a baptised non-practising Catholic but we knew that this was a second marriage for both of them.

He told me that I was listed as one of four speakers during the eulogy. I responded that I didn't know that and he said "Haven't you been told?" I replied that I hadn't, the only thing I was aware of was what I was asked to do on the night of her birthday. He went quiet and said that she was under heavy sedation when she made her requests and didn't know what she was asking.

I agreed to speak and he asked if I could email the content to the priest so he could have a look at it. I agreed, then panicked as it was now 5.30 pm and I had two more interviews with clients before I could get my head around what I was going to say and the subject I had chosen to speak on.

At 9.30 that night I emailed a few pages to the priest for his consideration.

I hardly slept. On arriving at the church the next morning I was met by a woman I didn't know but it was obvious she knew who I was. She took my arm and hand and told me that Father wanted to speak with me. I gulped because I had written the word 'Bloody' in the script and I felt I was about to be admonished. Things have changed dramatically within the Church since the passing of Pope John Paul II. The church has closed ranks and her all-embracing arms are no more welcoming.

My beautiful friend wanted to be carried out to the Tina and Ike Turner song *Nut Bush City Limits*. A rebellious streak in me had given considerable thought to taking my own PA system and playing it for her outside the church! But professional reasoning won out thank goodness.

The priest held out his hand and took mine in a warm gesture and he asked if he could speak with me in private and steered me toward the church sacristy. Once inside he took both my hands and said: 'I know and understand what has been asked of you by your friend and I'm putting my neck on the line here, would you please join me on the altar beside the Paschal candle for the final commendation. After I sprinkle the coffin with holy water and incense I want you to read part of the commendation with me.'

I was overwhelmed with the magnitude of what he was about to do and I also knew what this meant and the honour it carried. I was speechless and tears ran down my cheeks he gave me a hug.

When the time arrived I walked up and stood beside him on the altar steps at the head of the coffin. He placed his hand on my arm and announced that: "I was a close friend of the deceased and that I was also a celebrant who had been invited to officiate for her", and he added "but this is the Catholic Church so you got me. However, Bobbie shall join me in the prayers of the final commendation".

When the ritual was completed Father invited me to lead the coffin out with him and throughout the church the sound of Tina and Ike Turner singing *Nut Bush City Limits* reverberated. The mourners started clapping in time it was a profound moment. Father also invited me to join him at the cemetery for the final prayers, which I also read.

I am still feeling humble, overwhelmed and tearful. This beautiful, humane, and considerate man of God showed immense compassion, courage, strength of character, understanding, warmth and great common sense that the final wishes of the departed be followed as far as he was able. For me it was a moment of great blessing, and grace, which gave a peaceful closure.

After the ceremony, I spoke with the funeral director who told me that the family had asked him if I could officiate and he had to tell them as much as he loved me this could not happen as it was against Catholic law.

The funeral director also added that he in all his time in this industry had never seen anything like what the priest did that day. He said it just doesn't happen.

Bobbie had phoned me prior to the funeral and was quite angry with the family's decision (remember she was not only a celebrant but a very close friend of the woman who died), but as we both agreed this is something that we, as celebrants, cannot get involved in. When a family makes a decision like this we must abide by it even though we may feel that justice has not prevailed.

After the ceremony Bobbie rang me and we cried together as she told me what had happened. I commend this priest for going out on a limb to ensure the wishes of the deceased were followed. He went beyond what his role really permitted, including risking his job, to ensure the deceased's wishes were followed. All blessings to that man.

#POINTS TO CONSIDER

- → Rituals can take many shapes and forms.
- → Our daily lives are full of rituals.
- → Don't be afraid of the word 'ritual'.
- → Creating a ritual can be done with just one person or one thousand.

- → Regardless of the wishes of the deceased or their family, you can choose to have your own ritual if that is what you need.
- → Take your time and work out what ritual best suits your needs.
- → Obtain the assistance of someone who can help to put the appropriate ritual together.
- → Rituals should always be safe and respectful.

Examples of Ceremonies

I have set out below a number of scripts by different celebrants and of various ceremonies. These examples show the different kinds of structures you can choose and are a guide to what you can include in a ceremony. Every funeral should be about the deceased and the relationships they had in their life. It should be authentic and leave no one in doubt as to whose funeral he or she has attended. As celebrants we are fortunate to have a role living and working with meaning and purpose as we serve our communities.

Ceremony for Nicholas Jonathan Pryce

Funeral written and conducted by Sally Cant

Entrance song to commence the ceremony
Hallelujah – by Jeff Buckley

I welcome you to this ceremony to celebrate the life of Nick Pryce. My name is Sally Cant and I am a celebrant, and I am honoured to have been asked to conduct this ceremony for you all today. Nick's family thank you for gathering today to share this time with them; to remember the character that he was with stories and music from his family and friends.

Nick would not to want us to mark his passing with grief and sadness. Of course we cannot be without these feelings when we lose someone much loved, but the music sets the tone to encourage you to think of Nick as he lived, and help you to remember him with a smile, when the feelings of loss overcome you.

I would like to take a moment to read a quote that speaks to me about life and death by an American comedian and actress Gilda Radner

> *I wanted a perfect ending. Now I've learned the hard way that some poems don't rhyme, and some stories don't have a clear beginning, middle and end. Life is about not knowing, having to change, taking the moment and making the best of it without knowing what's going to happen next. Delicious ambiguity.*

For me that poem sums up life: that there is not a reason for everything, that we are not always in control of everything that happens. So then the challenge is to somehow, out of these often difficult tests in life, to make the best of it.

Today we are here to share our stories and support each other as we come to terms with Nick's premature death, which I know grieves you all deeply. Nick's family are comforted by your attendance today and the kind support expressed in thoughtful ways since his death.

There are few words that can cushion the shock experienced when we are faced with sudden and unexpected death, especially in someone who you would have hoped had many, many more years still with us. Today, in remembering and thinking about Nick we have a choice; we can choose to concentrate on all the questions that lie in the back of our minds, or as a group of family and friends, we can remember him with love and cherish the shared years, days or hours in his company. We can choose to celebrate his life. The family is comforted in knowing that even though Nick was 'a troubled soul', his life ended peacefully at his home in his own bed and it was not an intentional death. Each of you will possess your own memories of him because he was not exactly the same person to any two people here. Nor was he the same throughout his years with you; because he grew and changed, just as we all do.

We know that no two human relationships are the same and we invite you to share your memories of Nick with his family and one another when refreshments are served at the conclusion of this ceremony. And please try and sign the memorial book that is available, if you haven't already done so on your way in this morning.

We have also made available today donation envelopes for Lifeline. So please consider making a donation today in lieu of flowers.

We come together from the diversity of our grieving to gather in the warmth of this community, giving witness to our belief that in times of sadness there is room for laughter. In times of darkness there always will be light. May we hold fast to the conviction that what we do with our lives matters and that a caring world is what we are all working towards.

Coming to this ceremony is important. And continuing to care is imperative for the health and well-being of you all. Please be there particularly for Amanda, Allan, James, Michelle and Sophie and his closest friends, in the painful times that are ahead as they slowly reconcile the loss of a precious son, brother and friend.

Your love of Nick is the cause of your grief today and if you ponder for a moment you will find that you would not have it any other way. For the grief will subside over time, your love on the other hand will not wain a bit. So don't think ill of the grief, use it as a barometer of your love and a catalyst for all the loving memories that we all possess.

Nick, you have chiselled your spirit into the hearts of those you loved. Even through all your troubles you touched the lives of those you met on your too short journey. Today we will speak of you. We remember your love of music, footy, particularly the Melbourne Football club, your enjoyment of finding a bargain, your enjoyment in other's achievements, your sense of humour, how fearless and energetic you were, how you tried to always 'push the envelope', how you could 'talk yourself out of any trouble you got into', and how you had 'the gift of the gab'.

I was listening with interest on a Sunday afternoon to an interview on the ABC with Rosemary Dobson who is a wonderful Australian poet and author of many books, to hear her talk about death as an 'Ordinary Tragedy'. And I suppose it is, because of its inevitability. Nonetheless it is something that is quite difficult for most of us to deal with.

When death comes to someone as young as Nick our grief is one of deep sadness. We all know that death is inevitable and most of the time we can accept death as part of the biological chain of generations. But when death becomes personal through someone we have known and loved, it comes in a variety of guises and triggers varying emotions.

Death is a very personal matter for those who know it in someone close to them. But we are all concerned directly or indirectly, with the death of an individual, for we are all members of one human community and no one of us is independent and separate. Though some of the links are strong and some are tenuous, each of us is joined to all the others by links of kinship, love, friendship, by living in the same neighbourhood or town or country, or simple by our own common humanity.

For those of us who do not have a religious faith and who believe that death brings the end of individual existence, life's significance lies in the experiences and satisfactions we achieve in that span of time, its permanence lies in the memories of those who knew us, and in any influence we have left behind.

Let us now look back over some of Nick's life.

Eulogy – Lead by Sally

Nick was born in Melbourne on the 3rd November 1984 and named Nicholas Jonathan Pryce. He was a much anticipated part of a new adventure in Australia for his parents Amanda and Allan, who had arrived from England some months earlier. As a baby and young child Nick was out and about with his parents as they explored Melbourne and its surrounds. Nick was much loved but at the same time, a restless and challenging baby, characteristics that were to remain part of Nick throughout his life.

When Nick was four, younger brother James arrived and a year later the family moved to Traralgon where Nick went to Kindergarten and then began school at Kosciusko Primary School. He was always quite a capable student.

Nick was an active child and his childhood in Traralgon was filled with outdoor activities. Riding bikes, playing on the trampoline, rollerblading and going to the park were some of the activities Nick enjoyed. Weekends were spent at Traralgon South and later at Tyers with Dad Allan and his partner Michelle and daughter Sophie, where Nick and James enjoyed the bush surroundings

Family tributes – Amanda (Nick's mother)

Nick was born on November 3rd which made him a Scorpio and to quote the opening sentence of a popular astrology text *"those born on the 3rd of November are fighters with the stamina and endurance to hang in there, no matter what"*.

And Nick was a fighter. He fought many internal battles and struggled with many inner conflicts over the last few years. It wasn't easy for him, yet he somehow found the strength to keep going

He was burdened with regrets and plagued with thoughts of what could have been, but his personal traits created challenges in all directions and in many ways he was a victim of his own nature.

Fighting depression and self-destructive impulses wearied him and took their toll over many years. He could have succumbed on many an occasion yet he endured and struggled through periods of his life where a weaker person would not.

As I said Nick was a fighter and he continued to put up a fight until the very end.

I know that he would have loved to have slain his demons and help other people similarly afflicted. He spoke often of doing a Community Development course and working for a welfare agency, getting his life back on track and helping others to do the same.

But in the end, battle weary and momentarily distracted, he took the final shot.

I'm going to finish with the words with which I would always reply to his ....

"Love you too Nick"

Nick always had one or two close friends and as he always enjoyed company, most weekends you would find him with friends as they stayed over or he stayed over with them. Nick tried a variety of sports over the years and particularly enjoyed Little Athletics.

As a teenager Nick, James and Amanda often went to the movies or to Melbourne to watch the Demons play. Nick also particularly enjoyed camping with mates. Once he had his licence and a car, Coopers Creek was a favourite place to go.

Nick was a strong minded and persuasive person. As a teenager he brought home a kitten despite strong opposition 'just to mind over the holidays'. Of course Sasha became a much loved family member. Nick was quite family minded in many ways and he loved the depiction of family life in the movie *The Castle*.

Nick attended Traralgon Secondary College where he successfully completed VCE and gained entry into the Outdoor Education course at Monash Gippsland. He completed a semester but wanted a break from the rigours of study.

Nick was then keen to join the Army. He passed the required physical, but needed to improve his maths results to be accepted. He followed a friend to Wagga Wagga, where he stayed for more than a year, working in a number of jobs, including a call centre, whilst attempting to complete a maths course at TAFE. Ultimately it didn't work out and he returned home. Nick had also thought about Nursing as a career. He commenced a Nursing Course through RMIT, which was being run in Sale, but decided it wasn't really for him. In recent years Nick worked in a number of jobs. For some time he worked for a Landscape Designer and was quite enthusiastic in showing his mother Amanda the gardens he had worked on. Landscape Design was something Nick had shown interest in while at school, after completing work experience in that area. Ultimately however, in terms of a career, Nick was still searching for his pathway in life.

I'd now like to share with you the tribute written by Allan and Michelle

Nick was a thrill seeker and risk taker from a very young age. The cuts, bruises and on one occasion a broken arm attested to that. "I can jump from there" became an all too frequent shout from Nick. From trees, from electricity poles and on one memorable day from the house roof itself. Most times Nick managed to get away with these feats unscathed.

We think that Nick went through later life in much the same way, believing that he was invincible regardless of the activities he pursued. Nick was a confident young boy.

A work colleague recently recounted his first memory of Nick from some 24 years ago. It was Nick's first day of kindergarten. On entering, he marches confidently to the centre of the room and announces to all and sundry "Hi I'm Nick!!" Almost as if to say "OK I'm here. Now we can get down to business".

While at primary School Nick took part in the statewide athletic championships. Some people might say that his ability to outrun people was a benefit to him in later years!!

He loved the outdoors and when younger spent much of his time camping with mates and building bush huts on our block in Koornalla (quite how he avoided snakebites is still a mystery to us).

Nick had a very special relationship with Michelle's father (known to everyone as "Pa") and despite numerous injuries inflicted upon Nick by "Pa" (accidentally of course!!!) we would like to believe that somewhere they are bickering and enjoying a cold beer together.

Nick was so very proud of James and Sophie, although like all siblings they knew how to have some mighty disagreements

Throughout his life despite what was happening around him he always retained his sense of humour.

Just an observation about Nick's sense of humour, on occasion one look or one word could top anything else said. He had a unique gift for not only being able to make us laugh but also to make us cry (sometimes simultaneously).

Over the years we had some mighty fine disagreements, in that we were no different to any other family. However on the last day we saw Nick it was different. We had a great day and loads of laughs. He polished off most of the BBQ and took more home! He indulged in his BBQ speciality, introducing us to the delights of BBQ'd Dim Sims (without food poisoning). Nick also had the opportunity to check out Sophie's boyfriend, Jesse, and grant his big brother approval.

In later years Nick's choices sometimes made it very hard for everyone, especially Nick.

But he was a son and big brother and we will never stop loving him.
May God bless and keep you always
May your wishes all come true
May you build a ladder to the stars
And climb on every rung
May you stay forever young
Grief is not forever - but love is.

I will now like to ask James to share with us what he has written for this occasion.

My brother, growing up with you was interesting to say the least. There was never a dull moment when you were around. If it was you making me cry or making me cry with laughter, it was like riding a roller coaster with you. We had some great times and some shitty times, but I wouldn't have wanted it any other way. I'll never forget the days when we would sit for hours playing the computer and listening to Nirvana on repeat.

Or the endless summer nights of backyard cricket where the game got so competitive and intense it would generally end up with us scrapping on in the backyard to determine the winner, which was generally always you. I always find it funny we stopped fighting the day I grew and got bigger than you. Coincidence? I think not big brother. You're not as silly as some may think!

I know you were proud of me, and the truth is I wouldn't be the person I am today without you. And I have you to thank. You walked a hard road and sometimes made the wrong decisions. But you were always there to make sure I didn't make those same mistakes and guided me in the right direction to where I am now. You made my life easier; you walked the hard road and ensured I never had to. You were very persuasive and a massive influence on my life. Who else could have convinced me to support the Melbourne Football Club? I guess that was one of your mistakes I didn't learn from. I love you my big brother, until next time.

And from Sophie

Nick and James (or Mick and Bay-mie as they were affectionately titled when I was little) were always there for me no matter what. Despite the fact they were the cause of many a temper tantrum I couldn't have asked for two more amazing brothers to grow up with. From feeding me hot English mustard and donkey poo to hanging me on the clothes line the boys were never short of entertainment. Nick, I still can't bring myself to believe you're gone but I know you're watching over us and you'll be in my heart forever. You've helped shape me into the person I am today. I'll miss you being able to make me laugh with a single look, I'll miss the constant bickering, but most of all I'll just miss having you around. Rest in peace Nick, my incredible big brother, I love you to bits.

Now I'd like to ask Lynne Jansen to come forward to say a few words. Lynne has been a friend of the Pryce family for many years.

We met Amanda and the boys when we first moved to Traralgon in 1991. Nick was six and James was two. Phillip was four and Timmy was one. The boys played very happily together and before long, Amanda and the boys became regular visitors. Nick was always polite and well mannered and easy to have around. The boys spent their time playing in the sandpit, making cubbies, playing with Duplo and later Lego, riding bikes and playing in nearby parks.

As the four boys grew older, we started going on day trips to the bush, to the beach and to various parks with Amanda and the boys. Nick often had a friend with him and sometimes we had two extra boys in tow. We became experts at packing sandwiches or sausages into a bag with cordial, snacks and some fruit before heading off for the day. We ranged far and wide, from exploring ferny paths and creeks at Tarra Valley to playing in the snow at St Gwinear. Over the years we made visits to Wirilda Park at Tyers, Moondarra Weir, Rintoull's Creek, and Walhalla amongst others. We also made day trips to Puffing Billy and Coal Creek at Korumburra.

In the summer, Inverloch became our favourite destination and we spent countless happy days there, with the boys playing in the shallows and the surf, building sandcastles, exploring rock pools and jumping off sand dunes.

We also went on holidays together on many occasions, including trips to Inverloch, Phillip Island, Lakes Entrance, Mallacoota, and to Mt Kosciusko. The boys played very harmoniously together and I can't recall many cross words between them in all the years they spent together, although I am sure that there must have been the odd altercation.

Nick was quite adventurous and loved to climb, so we got to know all the interesting playgrounds for miles around from Heyfield to Mirboo North. At Inverloch I remember Nick scaling the heights of Eagle's Nest rock, which was quite a challenging feat, while his Mum looked on anxiously from below.

In all the years, the only injury Nick sustained was a broken arm caused by trying to leap into a tree from a new power pole lying on the nature strip ready to be put up. He later explained that he was just trying to fly like Superman. As Nick grew older, it was the TV character, secret agent MacGyver who became a bit of a hero for him. Nick particularly enjoyed the way in which MacGyver managed to find creative ways of escaping from sticky situations.

Once Nick and Phillip hit their teenage years they understandably preferred to spend time with their mates rather their mums, so they stopped coming on daytrips. But with Nick's enjoyment of spending time in nature, it came as no surprise when he explored various career options involving the outdoors.

So, thanks Nick for being part of so many happy, sun filled days, in so many lovely places.

DVD of images from Nick's life

Music – My hero by the Foo Fighters

Let's enjoy watching a snapshot of Nick's life in the photos put together by his family.

We are now going to pause for a few moments and reflect on what Nick meant to each of you and how he touched your lives. You might like to give thanks; or just acknowledge the good times and the hard times and all the times in between. Think of the road you have walked together throughout the years and the multitude of experiences you shared; moments of joy and pleasure and moments of sadness and disappointment at various times of his life; remember him just as he was, no more or no less. While we do this we will listen to **Cat Stevens singing – Oh Very Young.**

Sally - Current days

Over the last few years, Nick experienced some quite low times in which he was supported by family, his girlfriend Nicole and many others including professional assistance by organisations like the local Mental Health Services, Mind Aust another leading provider of community mental health services and Lifeline. However, in the last week of his life, Nick was in good spirits. He had visited his Dad Allan, Michelle and Sophie at Tyers for a BBQ and had offered to help his Dad with some projects. Nick had also visited his Mum at Yallourn North, where he regularly spent time staying there with her.

After speaking with the family I think Nick may have turned a significant corner in his life in that last week. For the first time he voiced his concern to others, especially his family, about what he had done in his life, the regrets he had, and what he could have achieved. So there was some level of self-reflection and a growing in wisdom, so I think in acknowledging this Nick was in a good place. But sadly life left him on the morning of the 9th November.

The family is very grateful for the assistance given to Nick by the Mental Health Services, Lifeline, the Emergency Department staff and the ambulance officers for their efforts when they attended to Nick on numerous occasions.

It also needs to be said that Nick got so much support from many people and everything that could have been done to assist him was done, so please know that you all did your best to be there for him. Together, let us farewell Nick at the end of his journey here on Earth;

His earthly body could never hold all that is Nick but was a place for his brief earthly journey and is to be respected and honoured, because it gave us a glimpse of this loved man.

This ceremony has provided, for a while, a time and space for healing, a time for celebration and for mourning and time to acknowledge, honour, and say farewell to Nick.

NICK - We will always wish you had stayed much longer with us, but we will now set you free as you travel on into a new day. You will always remember Nick and you will value who he was to you. Eventually in time you will find some solace and things will get a little easier, whilst never ever forgetting Nick, but rather taking comfort in knowing he is now at peace.

In sadness for his death, but with great appreciation for his life we remember Nick Pryce, let us remember the words of C. Day Lewis; *His laughter was better than birds in the morning, his smile turned the edge of the wind, his memory disarms death and charms the surly grave. Early he went to bed, too early we saw his light put out, yet we could not grieve more than a little while. For he lives in the earth around us, and laughs from the sky.*

It is at a time like this that we need to focus on our own relationships and be there in support and love for each other. Now we must return to living our own lives, enriched by these memories. It is always an opportunity at a time like this to please take a moment to remember how fragile life can be. And those around you may not always be here, so take the time to say "I love you" to those close, or pick up that phone and call someone whom you may have not kept in touch with. Life is short, make the most of it by doing things that have meaning to you.

Before we go I'd like to take this opportunity on behalf of his family to thank you for coming and for all the warmth, support and love you have given them. Please stay with us as we share in 'a cuppa' afterwards, where your memories and stories can continue to be told.

Don't hold back from offering your support, or simply a phone call to check in with each other. People often worry that they might say the wrong thing to a grieving person, just be there and be yourself. Remember there is great comfort in just telling someone close to Nick that he's not forgotten and just asking how they are?

Nick would not want us to dwell on the sadness or on the years you won't have with him, instead this morning he would want us to remember him just as he was, reflect on the times you had with him and say farewell, but most importantly rejoice with everyone here today for having Nick in your lives for the time you did, regardless of how difficult some of those times might have been.

I remember the words James shared with me last week: that he looked up to Nick, that Nick taught him lessons in life, and that Nick always 'had his back'.

I believe that every relationship that we have in our life, our contact with each person, place and event, serves a very special if yet to be realised purpose; they are a mirror that can serve to show us things about ourselves that can be realised in no other way. So always think of the times with Nick as positives. Don't let the memories get lost, share them around and enjoy recalling them.

Committal:

I'd like to ask you to stand now, as we conclude this service with a final farewell.

I'd like to close this ceremony with these words:

When things go wrong in life, don't waste your time looking back to what you have lost, for the road of life was never meant to be travelled backwards.

It was Elisabeth Kubler Ross who wrote, *"The most beautiful people we have known are those who have known defeat, known suffering, known struggle, known loss, and have found their way out of the depths. These people have an appreciation, sensitivity, and an understanding of life that fills them with compassion, gentleness, and a deep loving concern. Beautiful people do not just happen."*

Nick. We all want to tell you that despite what happened in your life you are forgiven and that we are all comforted that you are now in peace.

> Those we love don't go away,
>
> They walk beside us every day,
>
> Unseen, unheard, but always near,
>
> Still loved, still missed and very dear.
>
> Farewell Nick

Music to recess out - Pete Murray singing *Opportunity*.

Ceremony for Baby Maya Anne Sonners

Funeral written and conducted by Jill Harper - Blackmans Bay Tasmania

Entrance song to commence the ceremony: *One Sweet Day* by Mariah Carey and Boyz II Men.

Hello everyone, my name is Jill Harper. I feel privileged to conduct this service for Leigh and Anita and on their behalf I thank you for being here with them as they say farewell to the physical presence of their precious baby daughter Maya.

Being together now with the people they love and know best is important to them. Their little baby was taken from them too soon; they feel their loss deeply and know how much they will need everyone's support and understanding in the days and weeks to come.

So much has happened for them this last week; it has been an overwhelming experience; the roller-coaster of emotions they have endured has been immense, as Anita says, "she wouldn't wish this on anyone".

Today, Leigh and Anita want you to know how special Maya was to them; they want you to know how much they loved her and wanted her in their lives. Even though the pregnancy was only twenty-three weeks gestation, Maya was already a part of their family circle, her birth was eagerly awaited. Now she has gone and they are heartbroken.

But, this morning we won't dwell on the sadness, instead we will remember that Maya was a perfect, tiny little girl and for the short time she was here in our world she brought hope and happiness into our lives.

Following the service Leigh and Anita invite you to join them here for refreshments – you will all be very welcome.

Could I remind you too of donations to the Hobart Private Hospital Special Care Nursery; a donation box will be available in the refreshment room.

Maya touched each of you in her own special way, as a precious daughter, a little sister of Brock, Matthew, Kristy and Jack; a precious granddaughter and a loved niece and cousin.

When we lose a little person so significant in our lives there is pain and grief, but when a baby dies there is a sadness that goes way beyond normal grief and, for the parents who have already formed a deep and everlasting connection with their baby, it is an intensely personal and overwhelming experience.

It takes time to accept that separation and loss, especially the loss of a future life with their child.

For grandparents too there is an overwhelming sense of loss. Maya's grandparents, Leigh and Anne, George and Nona wanted to love and care for her too; they wanted to be there for her on her journey as a toddler, a child and an adult. They are grieving for their own children now and if they could take some of their pain I am sure they would.

Leigh and Anita wanted the Lord's Prayer to be included in this service, perhaps now is just the right time for us to join together in reciting the words of this timeless and comforting prayer.

The Lord's Prayer is recited together.

A very simple, symbolic naming ceremony helps to heal just a little of the pain and grief of today. During these moments we will acknowledge the names Leigh and Anita chose for their baby and, recognise that even though Maya's life was so short she is a little baby who has a real identity within her family circle.

Leigh and Anita began the process of choosing a name for their baby. Maya was the name they liked a lot and the children also liked it; it's a name of English origin and they thought it would be just right for their little girl.

For Maya's second name it was always going to be Anne or maybe, Louise. Leigh and Anita chose Anne, it's a name that has been given throughout generations of both families.

Maya's last name, Sonners, is her dad's family name; it is the name of her heritage and it gives her place on the Sonners and Cargill family trees.

Leigh and Anita, you chose these names with thoughtfulness and love and you gave them to your daughter with pride. Would you like to light a candle for Maya Anne Sonners?

Leigh and Anita light a candle for Maya.

Lighting the candle symbolises the gift that Maya brought to your lives in the short time she was with you; it is symbolic too, of the light that will always shine for her and the love that you, her parents, will carry with you forever.

Leigh and Anita were pleased and excited when they knew that they were to welcome another little person into their lives.

The pregnancy progressed well for Anita; each step along the way played an important part in the bond between Leigh, Anita, Brock, Matthew, Kristy and Jack. Their baby had become a real little person and they began to wonder what she would look like, would she have lots of hair, or whose personality would she take on?

At about fourteen weeks into the pregnancy Anita and Leigh knew they were having a little girl! Anita remembers the moment well because she asked the doctor: 'What do I do with one of those?'

At twenty weeks Anita had a routine scan and everything was okay, their little baby was developing well, now they just wanted to get through the pregnancy!

But, three weeks later there were problems and Anita was admitted to hospital. She knew she would go early with this pregnancy but, not this soon, it was too early! The baby's heart was checked; it was beating strongly but it was a worrying time and everything was happening so quickly. Anita knew the outcome would not be good. When Anita and Leigh were told that their baby's heart had stopped beating they were shocked and devastated!

It was such a dreadful moment for them but they received amazing care and support from Anita's doctors, Lisa Turner and Bronwyn Fitzgerald, and from the Hobart Private Hospital midwives, Lorraine, Libby, Joanna and Rachel. Anita and Leigh say that they are all truly remarkable people, they were amazing and they are so thankful for their care, compassion and professionalism during the times they needed them the most.

Little Maya was born on Saturday 25th January 2014. She was a perfect little baby but she was so small and, very still. She weighed 580 grams (1.2 lb); she measured 29 cm long and her little head measured 21.5 cm; she had wispy dark hair and, Leigh could even see Jack in her.

Maya stayed with her mum and dad for a day and a half; they held her and cuddled her, there was nothing more they could do but be there with her, then the moment came for one last precious cuddle.

Leigh and Anita are so pleased that they could spend that precious time with Maya, it was a time when they shared something very special, a time that neither of them will forget. That night there was a brand new twinkle star in the sky!

This poem, by an unknown author says it all so well for Leigh and Anita:
>We couldn't wait to hold you
>And see your perfect face.
>To count your little fingers,
>And check your toes are in their place.
>It should have been the happiest day
>To remember all our life.
>But joy had turned to heartache,
>No breath, no beat, no life.
>We will never see you smile,
>Or hear your hearty cry.

> We will never be able to dry your tears,
> Or share your happy times.
> Our precious little Angel,
> We will always know your face.
> In our hearts and stars forever,
> You will always have a place.

Leigh and Anita, nothing has prepared you for what has happened. Understanding, acceptance and love are all so important for helping you get through the weeks and months ahead; you have each other and, you have your loved ones and your friends all there to support you.

Family and friends, let us take a moment now to be with our own thoughts and memories. During this time, if you would like to please come forward to scatter petals and say your own goodbye to little Maya.

Celine Dion sings *A Mother's Prayer*.

Leigh and Anita, Maya shared your lives fleetingly, now she has gone forever. But, she has left gentle footprints on your mind, your heart and your soul and because of this will always be with you and a part of your lives for as long as you live, you will always love your beautiful girl.

You chose the poem, *Silent Footprints* by Christie Michael because, again, the words are saying for you just what you want to say now.

Poem is recited.

We have come to the moment now when we brokenheartedly say a final farewell to little Maya.

Maya Anne Sonners, to your mummy and daddy you were precious and loved so very much "when tomorrow starts without you, you won't be far apart, for every time they will think of you, you'll be right there in their hearts', forever and ever.

We let you go now, your spirit is free to 'live among the angels ... and sleep beyond the shining stars ...".

Family and friends, in a moment or two when Leigh, Anita, Matthew, Kristy and Jack release balloons outside and we watch them climb to the sky we are symbolically letting go. But for now let us listen to the song that Leigh and Anita have chosen especially for this moment, *One More Day* by Rocket Club.

As the song is finishing please make your way from the chapel. Leigh and Anita will stay with Maya for a quiet moment to say their last goodbye, and then they will join everyone outside to release the balloons.

Leigh and Anita remain in the chapel then will join everyone outside in the courtyard to release the balloons.

Ceremony for Mary Moore

Funeral written and conducted by John Terry Moore – Geelong, Australia

Entrance song to commence the ceremony: Blue Danube Waltz

Introduction

My friends, good morning and thank you for your attendance as we celebrate the life of Mary Moore. And a celebration it shall be, because the very last thing that Mum would have wanted is for us to be downcast and sad at a moment such as this. So I therefore urge you all to adopt an attitude towards today's proceedings that Mary would expect of you.

Indeed, in her last few months, whilst retaining her strong opinions on a variety of subjects, Mum became very much at peace with herself.

She felt a sense of satisfaction, that she had lived a long and productive life; an interesting life full of challenges, but also full of triumphs, making the hardships finally seem insignificant.

As with all things living, there comes a part of the life cycle when it is time to go, and this was her time. Mary certainly understood her situation only too clearly; she didn't want sympathy, she was always far too independent for that.

Everything that could have been done for her has been done and done well.

She unselfishly prepared herself for the inevitable in a common sense manner, normalising the process by discussing it with her family; teaching by example to the very end.

She is now at peace, and she would hope that her family, her friends and all of those who cared for her on a regular basis over these last years of her life, can also find peace, knowing they always gave their best when it was required.

There is no doubt that she appreciated your efforts tremendously. Your attitude and your support for her during her lifetime has been exemplary.

No matter where you were, near or far, she knew you were thinking of her, and she knew your feelings for her.

And when she slipped quietly away she therefore felt loved and supported by everyone, and you should all feel very proud of your contribution as a consequence.

Reading

Ladies and gentlemen, the first reading could have been written for Mary, because it touches on the things in her life that really matter and offers some social commentary that would be very close to her heart.

It's called *The Dash*, by Linda Ellis and is presented by Robert.

Eulogy

Mum was born Mary Grace Coverdale, in Hobart, on September 21st 1918, eldest child of Fred and Nina Coverdale. Her younger sister Joan survives her.

Her family was typical of many Australian families at that time; there were never luxuries of any sort and times were very hard indeed. Her father was a well known oarsman, single sculler and later a coach of Tasmanian crews, and was a boat builder by trade. He worked for the Marine Board, and also with his brother Percy Coverdale, at his slip yard at Battery Point, before working from home building dinghies and small boats to order. So Mum's early life had a very interesting and rich background based on the waterfront and things marine. The Derwent and the Channel were like giant arteries in those days; in many cases the old steamers were the main form of transport.

She spoke lovingly of those times, of fishing trips and rowing trips, or just visiting relatives at New Norfolk. It was a much more gentle period of our history. Mary was educated at Princes Street Primary School, and Hobart High School, and it was during those years that her family, like many others, fell on hard times during the Great Depression. Fred lost his job, and went mining for osmiridium at Adamsfield, deep in the south west, sending home money when he could and hoping his little family survived. That period made a profound impression on Mary; she was only a fourteen-year-old at the height of the Depression in 1932, and it coloured many of her attitudes throughout her life. She could remember eating bread and dripping for tea on occasion and, as a result, was a hoarder of food all her life, never wasting anything and sadly never throwing anything out!

After leaving school, she went to work for Oldam, Beddome and Meredith, or OBMs as they are known, purveyors of books, stationery, sheet music and associated goods. She told such stories about her times there; and made friends at OBMs that she kept for life. She had a gay work mate, Alby Gallup, who appealed to her sense of humour. Among OBMs customers were three old nuns who were very disapproving of some of the modern sheet music. They would descend on the department like birds of prey, making inappropriate remarks about the new style of dance music which they obviously felt was most ungodly. Little did they know that the nice Mr Gallup was making obscene gestures behind their back at the expense of Mum, who was struggling to keep a straight face!

As the 1930s rolled on, the sheer poverty of the Depression gave way to the uncertainty and fear of yet another world war. About the only entertainment for young people were the local dances and she met our father at one such event, at Buckingham Rowing Club, in the late 1930s. It was instant attraction; love at first sight, and the beginning of a partnership lasting nearly fifty-seven years. Dad joined the RAAF and they were married a few days later, in June, 1940. He was eventually posted to Victoria, and was based at Sale, Nhill, Geelong and air force headquarters in Melbourne. He was there when the news came through that Darwin had been bombed, and together with every Australian, they felt real fear for the future. Mum fell pregnant, and she returned to her parents in Hobart for the last few months. Typically, I was well and truly overdue; Dad overstayed his leave and I finally arrived on January 13th 1943. And Dad was slapped in the brig for being AWOL. By 1944 the tide of the war had begun to turn for the better and Dad was discharged because, as a farmer, his service was regarded as essential.

They returned to Hillcot, their farm and home, and moved in with Dad's parents while they built their own home. Hillcot was in big trouble - our grandfather was an undischarged bankrupt, and whatever equity remained was in our grandmother's name. Dad and Mum put a proposition to the bank, which was accepted, and they began the long task of paying off the mountainous debt.

They grew vegetables, ran pigs, and finally planted raspberries. Hillcot was always a good sheep property. Our grandfather continued to be our 'sheep expert' for many years. Robert was born on June 5th 1948 and Fran on December 4th 1951. Together with a group of local growers they founded the Lachlan Cooperative Society, which effectively broke the price stranglehold of Henry Jones & Co. The Coop processed small fruit on Hillcot and sold the pulp directly to Cottee's. Mum was secretary of the Coop for many years, even after our family ceased growing fruit in our own right.

She served with distinction; she was involved with every aspect of the Coop's operations, including price negotiations, shipping and administration.

Her record of service to the industry also included a stint on the Soft Fruits Board, its only female member in those days, and she was thought of most highly by her fellow board members. I know she was most conscious of being on time for meetings and making sure that she paved the way for future participation of women in business. Terry and Mary made the transition from growing small fruit to hops and Hillcot prospered once again. They finally found the time to have some terrific holidays; they travelled to the UK, Europe and the United States, as well as catching up with friends regularly within Australia.

They added 300 acres with another property, running cattle as well as sheep.

After they retired from the hop business, they became involved with carpet wool sheep, and the carpet wool industry in Tasmania. Had they been a few years younger the overall industry outcome would no doubt have been quite different. They were leaders in their own right, always pushing the boundaries, and were horrified at the inertia from some of their fellow growers and from government who refused to invest time and money for the future.

But there was another life that both Terry and Mary invested their time in – the community. There was a common thread that ran through both individuals which made them great participators. They had a strong social conscience and were great lateral thinkers, born well before their time. They had strident political views which were well and truly left of centre, and were able to express themselves through the Labour Party, which gave them both a deep sense of personal satisfaction.

They were each awarded life membership of the ALP (Australian Labour Party), which was probably their proudest single possession. As we children grew up, Terry and Mary were active in the school parents and friends groups, the rowing club, and the hospital, to name but a few. Mum was deeply involved with the New Norfolk Hospital Women's Auxiliary and was a member of the Board of Review at Royal Derwent Hospital. She was sought out by government because she had the ability to use simple common sense in the decision making process, bringing some refreshing balance to the viewpoint of the academics. But it was her lifelong love of horses which was brought sharply into focus in the last thirty years of her life.

This was a case of where Mother took the initiative and Dad followed, giving many years of service between them to the New Norfolk Pacing Club.

Mum's fascination for horses went right back to her early years; back to Grandmother Coverdale, who rode side saddle around Hobart as a young woman, and who shared a love for all things equine with her granddaughter.

Mother often told the story of Grannie watching one of the local residents who always had at least one drink too many and would collapse into the back of his cart, and his faithful horse would take him home, completely unaided.

Grannie would say, "There you are my dear, a superior animal taking an inferior animal home".

Mum's horses became her life, and they became like an extended family to her. And the pacing fraternity also became extended family to her. She had an amazing ability to develop a network, from vets to trainers to farriers, fellow punters and bookmakers! One of the great friendships she and Dad made through the pacing industry was with the late Aub Wesley. Mum admired his gentle nature with horses and the similar connection he made with his fellow human beings. And the Wesley family contact with Mary has been maintained through the next generation, which she appreciated so much. Mum was a canny punter, she didn't place huge bets but there was seldom anyone who knew more about form than she did! She will be missed profoundly by the harness racing industry, for her participation at all levels.

Mary the person was quite a complex character in many ways. She was quite a gregarious person at times, yet she was also very private. She had a kind nature and was a most unselfish person. She was a natural mother who was denied the ten children she and Dad always wanted; but she was fiercely protective of we three. She had very good taste. Always a striking looking woman, she presented herself beautifully and set a wonderful example to us children, teaching us how to conduct ourselves in public, to use correct grammar, and she was a stern taskmaster with regard to table manners!

She also had the most marvellous descriptive sense of humour, I've ever heard. Many of her expressions came from her father and were so 'homespun' in nature, and described the people she was referring to so well. She always saw the funny side of everything and that gave her personality a terrific balance. She had societal views that were quite opposed to her original family background.

She was proud of the journey she had made from the conservative far right to the bosom of the Labour Party, and was totally one eyed when she got there.

There was no room for any other opinion, she didn't take prisoners but, in fairness, she did call in favours from time to time when she thought government became too remote from the voter base. She continually fought for the local district until very recently, particularly the New Norfolk Hospital.

She was awarded the Centenary Medal for her service to the community.

Robert and I were very proud of her when she promoted the issue of same sex legislation, making sure that the electorate was heard.

She was delighted when that legislation succeeded, and Tasmania, from a poor last in the Commonwealth, suddenly leapt to the forefront of international social attitudes, bringing with it of course a substantial financial spin-off for the state.

As you all know, Dad was always a difficult person to live with; he couldn't help being so, because he suffered from an inherited depressive illness.

As he grew older he became even more difficult for Mum to handle.

Regardless of that particular period of her life, she gradually grew more forgiving and, if she were amongst us now, she would have to admit that the most important thing in her life was the partnership she shared with Dad for nearly sixty years. Ladies and gentlemen, more than ever, this society's very foundations rely not on individuals but on partnerships such as Mary and Terry's. It is obvious that their personalities complemented each other - what one may have lacked the other had in abundance, a true meeting of minds.

They worked together, supporting each other yet allowing each other space to do their own things. As they grew older, many of their projects such as harness racing became mutually inclusive, proving they could still work together as a team.

Mum helped raise her family by using three basic ingredients; example, example and example. She set a wonderful example and right up to her final moments, she believed in the strength of environment over genetics.

She truly believed that a child from an underprivileged or genetically challenged background simply needed love, attention and a good example to overcome their difficulties! Teaching by example and working together with Dad has produced a unique result, not just in we three kids, but in their three grandchildren and now three great grandchildren as well. Mary was understandably very proud of us all, and we of her.

Reflection

Music: *We'll meet Again* – Vera Lynn in background

Friends and family, we come to the part of today's ceremony where your participation is welcomed. In paying tribute to Mary's memory, may I ask everyone present to observe a short period of reflection. Please take this time to reflect on the meaning that her life had for you. Knowing that she would want no fuss, just a quiet space to ensure those of us remaining keep our priorities right and to support and love those dear to her that are left behind, particularly the younger generations of the family. So remember Mary as we listen to music from another era. Thank you everyone.

Reading

My friends, wiser people than I have written much about the grieving process over the centuries, and all are basically focused on the one subject - healing.

Healing from the release of bereavement, so that life can continue.

Healing by remembering the past with fondness, whilst taking responsibility for the future, particularly the care and love of our younger generation.

Fran will present this little piece, *You can shed tears that she is gone*, by David Harkins.

Family statement

Family and friends, there is an old and true saying that we only get out of life what we put into it. For every kind and generous deed there is another made in return. Because Mary was such a contributor to humanity, it is obvious that humanity has already returned some of that contribution during the last years of her life. That is the nature of things; sometimes at the end of a life the true nobility of the human spirit emerges, and this is such a time. In her final difficult years, the medical professionals (particularly Dr Sweet), Tony, Rose, Mandy and Ken, and just ordinary people have been marvellous to Mum, and we are most grateful. We feel uplifted because of the experience, and our faith in humanity is strengthened as a result. We thank you for your attendance today and we would be pleased to have your company for a light lunch immediately after today's ceremony.

Committal

Family and friends, from time immemorial humanity has struggled to define an afterlife. A very human reaction because we naturally care deeply about our loved ones who pass on. Have the courage to simply trust our own family members and your fellow human beings.

To place your trust in the people and things of which you can be certain.

Because there is always room to understand simple human spirituality, particularly through the eyes of Mum's descendants. Mary will always be with us as long as her descendants are with us. So to our family members, Gran is ever present because in the process of renewal there is part of her with you always. Think carefully about this; as her direct descendants you each have part of her flowing through your veins.

Feel good about yourselves, because over time the family tree has borne a rich harvest of kind, loving and warm human beings. People who are resourceful, hard working, who have a positive mental attitude, who work hard for their community and who get on with life. She will always be with you because she is part of you. When you least expect it you will recognise, in your children and their children, many of the fine qualities she brought to this world that will reach down through the generations ahead and remind you of her presence.

She is not taking those qualities with her; those qualities remain with you as an expression of her love and her concern for you all.

Would everyone please stand?

They are not dead, who leave us this great heritage
Of remembered joy.
They still live in our hearts, in the happiness we knew
In the dreams we shared.
They still breathe in the lingering fragrance
Windblown from their favourite flowers.
They still smile in the moonlight's silver and laugh
In the sunlight's sparkling gold.
They still speak in the echoes of words we've heard them say,
Again and again.
They still move in the rhythm of waving grasses,
In the dance of the tossing branches.
They are not dead;
Their memory is warm in our hearts,
Comfort in our sorrow.
They are not apart from us, but a part of us.
For love is eternal, and those we love shall be with us
Throughout all eternity.
(Adapted from the poem *The Heritage* – author unknown)

Thoughtfully, and with the remembrance and appreciation of a life well lived, we say our final farewell to Mary and finally commit her mortal remains to Mother Earth, from whom we all came and to whom we all return. We acknowledge her contribution to our lives, and to our society and we remember her example, with a smile in our hearts and hope for the road ahead.

Music: *In The Mood* Glenn Miller

Ceremony for Kathleen Reekie

Funeral written and conducted by Bobbie Symons – Traralgon, Australia

Because of you (author unknown)
Because of you
The world is a much nicer place
Because of you,
We have faith in the human race.
Because of you,
We know what it means to love unconditionally.
Because of you,
We know what it means to give unselfishly
Because of you,
We believe in magic and mystery and worlds unseen.
Because of you,
There is joy - wherever you are or have been
And it's all because of you Kathleen.

Good afternoon family and friends, on behalf of Kathleen's daughters Joanna, Rhoda, Kathryn, Amy, and their families, I warmly welcome you and thank you for coming to this thanksgiving and celebration service for their beautiful mum. A lady who was a much loved daughter, sister, niece, wife, mother, aunt, a grandmother and a great-grandmother, a lady who we all knew loved and respected: Kathleen Reekie.

My name is Bobbie Symons I am a civil celebrant and a funeral celebrant.

And I feel especially honoured to be here in this role this afternoon and I thank Kathleen and her family for this great privilege. I sincerely thank my colleagues from Latrobe Valley Funeral for their care and dedicated professional assistance given to Kathleen's family during these past few days.

I would also take this opportunity to remind you to please make sure you have your mobile phones switched off during this service. Thank you. After the conclusion of this afternoon's chapel service Kathleen's family warmly invite you to join them for refreshments at the Morwell Italian Club, a place that Kathleen loved to visit with her family and friends. I thank you all most sincerely for the cards, floral tributes and the many words of condolences offered and given to Kathleen's family as they come to terms with their sad loss, your thoughtfulness means so much to them and is greatly appreciated. The family has also requested that in lieu of flowers you may wish to kindly donate to the Cancer Care Unit at the Latrobe Regional Hospital, Traralgon, to help with the valuable research they are carrying out in their ongoing battle to find a cure for a rampant disease that has no respect for age or gender. The present statistics are that one in every three will suffer from some form of cancer.

This afternoon, we have gathered together to give thanks for the gift that Kathleen was for all of us, she lit up our world with fun and laughter and we are here to celebrate her life, she was such a rich and valuable part of our personal world for eighty-three years and we celebrate the vital and integral link that she was to our past, our present and she was the threshold into her families generational future.

Candle of life

On the 18th of February this year we lit a candle in honour of Kathleen's husband Bob Reekie and this afternoon his candle burns brightly, and beside his beacon of light is a new candle for his beloved wife Kathleen.

I would like to invite Kathleen's daughters to come and light their lovely mum's celebration candle. Kathleen, the candle is now lit and today we are here to honour you, we are here to celebrate you, and we are here to give thanks for you. From this day forward whenever we light a candle we will think of you and all that you have meant to us. We will remember the happy times and the fun times and the magic of your laughter the twinkle and mischief in your pretty eyes.

Last Monday week I had the very humbling privilege of spending a few hours with Kathleen. Her daughters had invited me at Kathleen's request to visit her in the Tanjil Ward of the Latrobe Regional Hospital. Kathleen wanted to organise her going away farewell. She was bright, lucid, fun and definite about her final wishes. She was ready to leave this world, she wasn't afraid. Kathleen knew her time to depart was imminent and she faced death with a fearless strength of character and composure that she had displayed all through her life.

I have spent a lot of time these past few days thinking about Kathleen and her beautiful daughters and granddaughter Lisa since that afternoon. For Kathleen, her work here on earth had been done, she was signing off, punching in her work card. She had carried out her career as a wife, a mum, grandmother and great grandmother admirably. She had fulfilled her marriage vows of loving her Bobby in sickness and in health until death us do part. She had raised her beautiful daughters to be responsible, loving, caring adults, wives and mothers in their own right and she had guided and nurtured them in the ways of this world, embracing their husbands and rejoicing in the births of her grandchildren and great-grandchildren. In those last few days of her life she gathered her girls around her, like a mother hen loving them as only a mother could, as she prepared them to release her and give her the permission she needed to leave the nest and fly on, up and out into the unknown. Her girls kept watch, providing loving comfort and security as they all reminisced about the past and the present. A bonded family to the very end, they remained faithful to their promise to their mum that she wouldn't be alone; they were true to their word, remaining by her side whispering their heartfelt messages of love, comfort and support to her as she was preparing for her last rite of passage we know and call death. Her girls gave her comfort and courage for her journey into the unknown and Kathleen comforted her girls. When Kathleen released herself from this mortal world at 6.10 am last Thursday the 28th of November it was peaceful and beautiful.

The ebb and flow of life continues on to write its own history for the generations to follow in the lineage of Kathleen Reekie.

This afternoon we are going to relive and reflect on Kathleen's life. There is stored within each one of us a treasure box. It's a place we can visit anytime and anyplace. It's a magical box something like a filing system where we store images and sounds and pictures and thoughts. It's our memory. Our creator created such a place for he knew that when a loved one passed away we would need to open our memory box for comfort and security. Memories are tears that roll down our cheeks as we remember and relive special moments, special places and special people.

Today we shall allow those memories to roll down our cheeks as we journey back in time to revisit Kathleen's life as she journeyed from birth to death.

We shall laugh together and cry together and it's quite okay to do both. We are family and we are friends.

I shall begin Kathleen's eulogy and time line and her family members shall share more intimate stories of their beloved Kathleen.

Eulogy

Kathleen Reekie was born on the 16th of March in the year 1930 in Tayport Scotland. Kathleen was the sixth and youngest born child of Pasquale and Trofemina Taiano. To keep it simple they called themselves Peter and Amy.

Kathleen's siblings in right pecking order were Bridget, Freddie (deceased) Amy, Percy, and Andrew Her father and mother were Italian, both immigrating to England in the 1900s, meeting one another when they were both eighteen years of age. They married in London.

Her dad was an enterprising man. He sold vegetables from a wheelbarrow and ran chickens on the common, selling them in the villages. Hence the term free range hens. They lived in a small cottage and Peter ran a takeaway fish and chip shop next door to the cottage, later selling ice creams to put a few more coins into the family's financial fund.

Kathleen's eldest daughter Joanna tells the story that her grandfather Peter propagated a pear tree from a seed and planted it beside the family cottage. The cottage is now well gone but the pear tree still stands proud and tall, still bearing good healthy fruit in season.

With so many children to raise their mother Amy kept the cottage home fires burning, cooking and cleaning for her young brood and looking after her husband.

Kathleen's dad was a strict hard man; he and his wife did their utmost to blend their children into the ways of their new country.

After the birth of their fourth child Percy, Peter moved his young family to live in Scotland where they settled in the village of Tayport on the river Tay.

It was in Tayport that they extended their family with the births of Andrew and Kathleen.

Little Kathleen began her schooling education at the age of five attending the Tayport primary school, which educated the local village children to grade eight.

When Kathleen had completed her schooling she began working in the office of R&G Simpson's in Dundee. The company made copper boilers.

In those days there was no such thing as a washing machine as we know them today. The washing was put into large coppers with a fire built underneath and when the water boiled the washing was loaded and poked around with a stick which was the way of agitating the clothes to release the dirt.

It was hard tough work. I watched my own nanna in the outhouse as the outside laundry was referred to in those days ... as she toiled over a bubbling copper boiler, and as a young bride I was subject to the same washing methods ... but not for long.

Kathleen would travel to and from Tayport to Dundee by train four times a day. It was only a short distance so she would go home daily for her lunch.

When she was fourteen years of age she formed a permanent crush on a handsome young man in the village. His name was Bob Reekie. Bob lived with his aunt and uncle in the village of Tayport. Kathleen was friendly with his cousin Joy and she didn't go unnoticed by the young man who unbeknown to him had won her girlish affections.

She was a very tiny and pretty young lassie who was both a bundle of charm and sweetness. Despite his shyness he invited Kathleen to go to a dance one night with him, she was nineteen years of age and he was twenty-one. She didn't need to be asked twice. Bob and his sweet lassie loved the big swing bands of Glenn Miller and the like and that night was the beginning of many more such nights of dancing together for many years to come.

In 1949 Kathleen's dad passed away, Kathleen's siblings had all moved on in their lives. Her closest brother, Andrew, being eleven years older than her, had long gone to discover the world around him.

Kathleen had become accustomed to living with difficulties in her life for she had grown up in the war years and times were extremely difficult. Food was rationed and jobs and money were as scarce as hen's teeth. Many a night her family ate porridge for dinner and there was a shortage of sugar. Only those well off enjoyed the pleasure of the luxury of rationed sugar. Kathleen never forgot those years and in later life to the present insisted that there were always a few bags of sugar in her pantry.

Love blossomed between Kathleen and Bob they were married on the 8th of December in the year 1950 in the minister's manse in the village of Tayport. Kathleen was twenty-one and her Bobby was twenty-three years old. After the wedding they moved into a wee cottage in Nelson Street Tayport. As soon as Kathleen was married she lost her job as the firm she worked for didn't tolerate married women. While living in Nelson Street Kathleen and Bob welcomed with much love a little daughter and named her Joanna.

They moved to a new address in the Cow-Gate and were happy there for the next eighteen months. It was where they welcomed their second little daughter and named her Rhoda. Kathleen would visit her Mum every day. She had a very large English pram, which was almost too big to get into the small dwelling where her Mum was living. The Italians are a very superstitious race and it was considered very bad karma to wheel the child feet first over the threshold so the tiny little Kathleen would struggle against all odds to negotiate and push the over large pram head first into the very narrow passage way and get it out again head first in order to protect the household and her babies from evil doings.

Then Bob moved his family again this time to a new council house in Banknowe Drive, Tayport, and once again they celebrated the safe arrival of another cute little daughter and named her Kathryn.

When Kathryn was two years old and on the 17th of January 1966, Bob and his family left Scotland aboard the ocean liner SS Canberra, seeking a new and better life in Australia.

It was a three-week voyage at sea and a totally new learning experience for Bob's kids, especially as they sat down to dinner each night in the large ship's dining room. It was huge and with such a large array of silver cutlery lined up on either side of their plates confused them considerably.

The family's first port of call in Australia was the port of Fremantle, Western Australia, where their ship was docked for a day and night. A friend of Bob's who had migrated to the big island at the bottom of the world earlier was possibly responsible for Bob's serious thinking and final decision of coming to a new country. He met Bob and his young family at the wharf and took them around Perth for the day.

The next day the ship sailed for Melbourne in Victoria and what a grand sight it was when they docked. The family had a case, a trunk and ninety pounds in old currency to begin a better life and greater opportunities for each other and their daughters.

Kathleen's brother who had emigrated earlier met them at the wharf and drove them back to the township of Morwell where Bob and his family settled into number 9 Jill Street. During 1967 Kathleen announced to Bob that he was going to be a father again so he moved his family into 26 Haywood Street, Morwell across from the technical school. Amy, their fourth daughter and a little Aussie blessing, safely entered the world. Bob now had five females under one roof to contend with. On his arrival in the valley Bob took up employment at the Highway Joinery Works situated in Davey Street, Morwell.

Kathleen loved her role as both a wife and a mother. Her girls tell the story that she was deaf from a very early age but in spite of her deafness she never missed a beat. She always knew what her daughters were up too because she had learned to lip-read. The only thing that threw her was when someone spoke in another language!

I wish to introduce Kathleen's youngest daughter, Amy Campbell, and I invite her to share with us on behalf of her sisters some fond memories of their beautiful mum.

Kathleen's daughter Kathryn has written a tribute to honour her lovely mum.

> Mum, what times we have shared! We have bolstered each other up through the sad times and shared so many happy times. Oh what fun we have had!
>
> Shopping with the pink card was definitely one of your favourite things to do. I will never forget, on one of our many shopping trips, driving dad's car while holding your hand, both of us laughing like schoolgirls because neither of us knew what day it was and neither of us cared.
>
> The many days we were lucky enough to spend together, sitting in your room, feasting on bread and cheese, watching DVDs, peeping out your window to see the latest comings and goings at the Manor, gossiping and sharing secrets over a cuppa or two.
>
> Some days, when you were tired and not feeling well I would sit quietly and watch you sleep. My brave, strong, beautiful Mum. When I grow up I want to be just like you, 'cos we're mates always!

I now wish to invite Kathleen's granddaughter Lisa to share some of her fond memories of her unforgettable grandma.

Kathleen's daughter Rhoda would like to read a verse on behalf of Rosemary, a family friend from England.

Kathleen,
I truly wish I could have come
So that I could have seen you one more time
To give you one more gentle hug
And put your hand in mine

We could have talked of times long gone
In our little Scottish town
When I was just a little girl
And you never let me down.

But I couldn't come.
And you've slipped away
And I haven't said goodbye
But I'll never, ever forget you Kath
Until the day I die.
Rosemary.
Poem read by Lisa, Kathleen's granddaughter
My Granma
Precious memories that I will cherish
Caring
Loving
Looking after me when mum was sick in hospital
Happy
Generous
School holiday sleep over's, bus rides, cafe lunches, shopping trips, swap cards from the toy shop, gifts
Kind
Thoughtful
Peeling carrots, making porridge with milk, cream and sugar, preparing the breakfast table the night before, spaghetti bolognaise
Naughty
Always something yummy to eat in the larder, cups of tea
Cheeky

Funny
Everyone has had a backhand from her a time or two, even my children
Honest
One of a kind
Sharing
Reading, sewing, crossword puzzles
Strong
Dependable
Always there when you needed her even when you thought you didn't, spoiled you rotten, made you feel special and loved
Special
Loyal
Our 'Queen', yes indeed who will wear that crown now?
You are a wonderful and beautiful person, I am honoured that you are my Grandmother. I feel privileged that I've been able to share so much of my life with you. I know you will always be with us.
I hope Grandad was there to greet you, arms outstretched and those lips puckered up to kiss you.
Together again
Peaceful
While we thought we held you high, I think that in fact you held us highest.
I love you
My Granma, My Angel

Family and friends, Kathleen's family have put together a number of photos of her and now wish to present a photo tribute to honour her. The background music to accompany this tribute is reminiscent of the days she and Bob tripped the light fantastic. I invite you all to relax and enjoy this collage of wonderful memories accompanied by the Glenn Miller's Big Band playing *In the Mood*.

Photo tribute

Prepared with love

Music: *In The Mood* Glenn Miller

Eulogy continued

Kathleen absolutely adored and lived for her family; she was extremely proud of you, her beautiful daughters and your families. Kathleen and her Bobby shared sixty-two happy years of married life together, knowing each other for sixty-six years, and she said that "her Bob made the best cup of tea imaginable and he brought it to her in bed every morning".

After he passed away in February this year Kathleen mourned him deeply.

She herself had been diagnosed with cancer in 2010. She battled with Bob's early dementia and her own serious illness. Her desire to look after her Bobby was greater than caring for her own illness, so she put that on the back burner to concentrate all her efforts on her beloved husband, her beautiful Bobby.

During September 2012 Bob went into permanent care and Kathleen was deeply upset, but the reality was that she just couldn't continue caring for him. She was devastated that she couldn't care for him in the way that was needed, such was her devotion and love for him. She stayed on in their family home in Kingsborough Court, Traralgon.

It was during December 2012 that Kathleen's daughter Joanna realised that her lovely mum needed care herself and that she couldn't be on her own anymore, so in January this year Kathleen moved in to live with her daughter Rhoda and son-in-law Hoss.

Kathleen's health deteriorated even further due to the ongoing chemotherapy she was receiving for her cancer, so she was admitted into Maryvale Private Hospital for a time and on her discharge on the fourth of February Kathleen was placed in Heritage Manor for respite. Seven days later her Bobby passed away.

Kathleen's health was such that she needed to stay in Heritage Manor and true to form she started mothering the inmates as she called them. Her new friend Mary Ann was the longest inmate and Kathleen's other 'besties' were Reenie and Dorothy Ann who resided just up the corridor.

You all heard earlier in this ceremony that Kathleen was mischievous and naughty at times. Well, she kept up the standard she had set in life while still in residence at Heritage Manor and on her recent admission to the hospital. She was strong willed and determined, as Amy has said. If she didn't want to take her medication, and she really did have problems at times swallowing the horrible little pills, she would wrap them up in tissue and hide them in her bedside drawer, or her pocket, or wriggle them down between the arms of the chairs or just throw them minus the tissue into the lolly jar.

Kathleen won hearts wherever she went. She had a charisma about her that shone and sparkled, you just couldn't help yourself. There was something so special about her, she just drew you to her, beautiful, unforgettable.

To Kathleen's family we offer you our deepest heartfelt condolences. You grieve today because you are parting with someone who you have known and loved, and who has now permanently departed from your midst. Please take comfort in the love that you hold for one another and the love of your many friends that surround you, and in the knowledge that, in you, a part of your beautiful Kathleen remains and always will, for you carry within you a part of her, a part of her personality, her mannerisms, her laughter and her mischievous spirit. She will never leave you. Please remember that from this day forward you will carry her in your hearts. You have such beautiful memories that nobody can ever take from you. In the pudding bowl mix of life she was the well-blended mix of ingredients needed to guarantee that the recipe of life would be a success.

Now it is time to prepare ourselves to say goodbye to the presence of Kathleen in our lives.

I wish to read to you a verse titled *Together Again* written by an unknown author. Bobby's ashes are with Kathleen today. As I read this piece I shall be accompanied by Danny Boothman playing his mandolin.

Together Again
A reunion will occur in Heaven this week
Of the sweetest and most joyful kind;
As Kathleen's spirit moves beyond this earth,
Released from this mortal life.
And what a reunion it will be!
A joy beyond our conceiving,
When Bobby meets his Kathleen in Heaven again;
Ending months of dignified grieving.
And we are certain that Bobby will be holding his Kathleen's hand,
While he cherishes each moment by her side;
And they'll experience the joy of being together again,
Catching up on the months they were denied.
We are confident they'll be looking over us,
Hoping their happiness will lesson our pain;
As we contemplate the joy that they finally feel,
Being together again.
And though we'll miss them terribly,
And will long for them with deepest grief;
We are reminded that love is more powerful than death
And this knowledge gives us comfort and peace.

We can still feel their love surround us
Giving us a desire to continue on;
To try our best, to live our lives well,
In the ways they would have done.

I now invite Kathleen's grandchildren and great-grandchildren to come and light their own candles from their grandma's candle.

In this act you acknowledge that you will carry on the tradition, the values and life lessons learned and practised by your lovely grandma. All the wisdom, insight, love and goodness have been passed on to each one of you. In turn you shall now pass on these values and valuable lessons learned to your own children and so the lineage of love is passed from generation to generation.

You will carry the light of her love and her memory wherever you go in life.

(Light candles now)
(Rose petals now to be scattered on the coffin)

Family and friends, let us now gather our individual feelings and thoughts as we enter into this final rite of passage: The Committal.

Let us pray:

> Father God most high we humbly ask you to please send your Blessed and most Holy Angels to protect and guide our loved ones Bob and Kathleen as they leave this world and begin a new journey together in a realm unknown to us. We ask that your Angels protect, guide and lead them safely to your heavenly realm. Grant Bob and Kathleen eternal peace and rest oh Lord. We pray this prayer in the name of your son Jesus Christ. Amen.

I now invite Joanna, Rhoda, Kathryn and Amy to come and extinguish their lovely mum's and dad's candles.

(Place roses on the coffin)

Tenderly, loving and reverently we commit the body of Kathleen Reekie and the ashes of Robert Ritchie Reekie to the purifying fire. We commit their souls, their essence into the open arms of the Holy Angels who will present them to the Lord God most high. Receive them oh Lord. May the perpetual light shine upon them and may they rest in peace. Amen.

We are so blessed to have been a part of their lives and to feel the pressure and comfort of their hands and be warmed by their gracious, happy and generous smiles

We cherish the memories of their words, their deeds and their character.

We cherish their friendship and, most of all, we cherish their love.

Ashes to ashes, dust to dust. In the cycle of life and death, the earth is nourished, and life is eternally renewed. Let us live our lives with gratitude for the generous love of our parents, grandparents and great-grandparents.

Let us remember all that we have said and celebrated today. Kathleen and her Bobby are at peace. They are now at rest. Their physical bodies are no longer with us but their spirit and their love live on, in you, their beautiful and much loved and devoted family. The stories and the memories of them shall remain and be a comfort to you when the clouds hide the sun in your hearts.

You will grieve, and you will shed tears, however, also remember to smile and laugh as they would want you too.

Thank you family and friends for your presence and your support for one another this afternoon. May the peace that passes all understanding fill your hearts and remain with you.

I now invite you all to come forward to fulfil a last request of Kathleen's and that is to raise your glasses and drink a dram of brandy as a farewell toast to her and her Bobby as they journey on together. (All present to stand around the coffin and raise glasses as the coffin is lowered).

Song *Time to Say Goodbye*: singers Sarah Brightman and Andre Bocelli. (Coffin now lowered)

Song: *I'll Take You Home Again Kathleen*

REFERENCES

Books and articles

Ahern, Jennifer, '*Post traumatic stress disorder in Manhattan, New York City, after the September 11th terrorist attacks*' 2002

Albom, Mitch, *Tuesdays with Morrie*

Alzheimer Society of Canada, *Ambiguous Loss and Grief in Dementia*

Ashenburg, Katherine, *The Mourner's Dance*

Beasley, Julie, *It's Grief to me*

Cant, Sally, *The Heart and Soul of Celebrancy*

Carter, Abigail, *Alchemy of Loss*

Choron, 1964, *Modern Man and Mortality*, Macmillan

Friedman, Russell and James, John W., *The Grief Recovery Handbook*

Friedman, Russell and James, John W., *Moving Beyond Loss*

Gawande, Atul, *Being Mortal*

Grief Matters (Australian Centre for Grief and Bereavement)

Halifax, Joan, *Being with Dying*

Hellenbeck, James, *Palliative Care Perspectives*

Housden, Maria, *Hannah's Gift*

Houston, Jean, *The Search for the Beloved*

Karaban, Roslyn A., *A Practical Guide for Ministering to Grievers*

Kübler-Ross, Elisabeth *On Death and Dying*

Kuhse, Helga, Willing to Listen, *Wanting to Die*

Larkins, Robert, *Funeral Rights*

Levine, Stephen and Ondrea, *Embracing the Beloved*

Levine, Stephen, *Who Dies?*

Levine, Stephen, *Meeting at The Edge*

Levine, Stephen, *Unattended Sorrow*

Lewis C.S., *A Grief Observed*

Lewis, Scarlett, *Nurturing Healing Love*

McKissock, Mal and Dianne, *Coping with Grief*

McMordie and Kumar, 1984, '*Cross-cultural research on the Templer/ McMordie Death Anxiety Scale*', Psychological Reports, 54, 959-963

References

Marta, Suzy Yehl, Healing the Hurt, *Restoring the Hope*

Metcalf, P. & Huntington, R., 1991, *Celebrations of Death: The Anthropology of Mortuary Ritual*

Parkinson, Patrick, *For Kids' Sake*

Schumaker J. F., Warren W. G., Groth-Marnat G., 1991, '*Death Anxiety In Japan And Australia*', J Soc Psychol, Vol.131, No. 4

Solomon, Andrew, 2013, *Depression, the secret we share*, TED Talk, www.ted.com/talks/andrew_solomon_depression_the_secret_we_share

Syme Dr, Rodney, *A Good Death*

Teresi, Dick, *The Undead: Organ Harvesting, the Ice-Water Test, Beating Heart Cadavers — How Medicine Is Blurring the Line Between Life and Death*

Welshons, John E., *Awakening From Grief*

Welshons, John E., *When Prayers Aren't Answered*

WHO, 1998a, World Health Organization, The World Health Report 1998. *Life in the 21st Century: A Vision for Health for All*, Report of the Director General, Geneva

Wolfelt, Dr Alan, *Healing Your Grieving Heart*

Legislation

Cemeteries and Crematoria Act 2003 (Vic)

Medical Treatment Act 1988 (Vic)

Medical Treatment and Palliative Care Act 1995 (SA)

Inquiry into regulation of the Funeral industry, 2005, Family and Community Development Committee, Parliamentary Paper No 175 - Session 2003-05

Consent to Medical Treatment and Palliative Care Act 1995(SA)

Other

A Family Undertaking, <www.pbs.org/pov/afamilyundertaking/film_description.php>

Giddings, Lara, MP and McKim, Nick, MP, *Voluntary Assisted Dying – A Proposal for Tasmania*

Guest, Steve, interview on 774 ABC Melbourne <www.dwdv.org.au/RealStories.html>

Hickman, Leo, 'Should I ... be buried or cremated?', The Guardian, 17 October, 2005

Kripke, Kate, The Postpartum Wellness Center of Boulder, <katekripke.wordpress.com>.

Marshall, Nancy and Rounds, Rennie, *Green Burials in Australia and Their Planning Challenges*, UNSW, Sydney NSW, Australia

Parton, Glenys 2008, *Natural Burials*, Australasian Cemeteries and Crematoria Association

Raudon, Sally, *Contemporary funerals and mourning practices. An investigation of five secular countries*

Simpson, Susan <www.simbacharity.org.uk>

Tender – documentary – <www.tenderdocumentary.com.au>

Zagdanski, Doris, <www.allaboutgrief.com> and <www.mygriefassist.com>

Organisations and their roles

Government General organisations

Function	Organisation
Works to protect and promote the interests, rights and dignity of people with a disability.	Office of the Public Advocate Victoria www.publicadvocate.vic.gov.au
Cemeteries and crematoria	Department of Health, Victoria www.health.vic.gov.au
An active law reform and 'self help' organisation pursuing public policies and laws in the state of Victoria that improve self-determination and dignity at the end of life. Also has forms for Refusal of Medical Treatment Certificate, advanced healthcare directive (living will)	Dying With Dignity Victoria www.dwdv.org.au
Referral and advocacy organisation for natural death	Natural Death Advocacy Network in Australia www.naturaldeathadvocacy.net
Referral agency for natural end of life options for families and funeral directors	The Natural End Funeral Service Provider Network www.naturalend.com
Non-profit organisation working to encourage environmental sustainability in the death care industry	The Green Burial Council www.greenburialcouncil.org

References

Function	Organisation
Family directed funeral company – New Zealand	State of Grace – Deb Cairns www.stateofgrace.net.nz
Family directed funeral Company - Woodend	Natural Grace – Libby Moloney http://www.naturalgrace.com.au/
Resource centre that offers death education and empowerment	Natural Death Care Centre – Byron Bay, NSW – Zenith Virago www.naturaldeathcentre.org.au
Provides practical strategies and tools to create resilience and peace in your life	Quest For Life Foundation – Petrea King www.questforlife.com.au
Victorian Funeral Company	MacQueens Funerals, – Anne Gleeson and Steve Lamb, Terang, Victoria (03) 5593 1107
Offers death literacy preparation and support and funeral organising, home vigil and after death care	Liferites – Victoria Spence, Sydney NSW www.liferites.com.au
Develops innovative arts and health programs that create cultural change about death and dying	The Groundswell project http://www.thegroundswellproject.com/
National Peak organisation representing the interests and aspirations of all who share the ideal of quality care at the end of life for all	Palliative Care Australia http://www.palliativecare.org.au/
Organ and tissue donation register	Australian Organ Donor Register www.humanservices.gov.au
Information about organ and tissue donation in New Zealand	Organ Donation New Zealand www.donor.co.nz

Support organisations

Function	Organisation
Grief and bereavement	
Grief and bereavement education and support	Australian Centre for Grief and Bereavement www.grief.org.au
Grief and bereavement education and support, links to other sources of support	National Association for Loss & Grief (Victorian but has links to other states) www.nalag.org.au
Grief support for kids and families	Rainbows Australia www.rainbows.org.au
For children, young people and adults challenged by loss and change	Good Grief An initiative of the Sisters of St Joseph www.goodgrief.org.au
Helps to save the lives of babies and children during pregnancy, birth, infancy and childhood, and supports bereaved families.	SIDS and Kids www.sidsandkids.org/
Support people of all ages who are dealing with loss, trauma or grief	Skylight New Zealand www.skylight.org.nz
Counselling, support groups, information and resources	Grief Centre New Zealand www.griefcentre.org.nz

Function	Organisation
Free counselling for people affected by grief and loss	Grief Support Services Inc. New Zealand www.griefsupport.org.nz
Loss of a child	
Support for those who have lost a child	The Compassionate Friends www.compassionatefriends.org
Support for those who have lost a child	Grief Haven www.griefhaven.org
People who have lost a baby – miscarriage, neonatal death, stillbirth, ectopic pregnancy, termination	SANDS Australia www.sands.org.au
Services to children and their families living with disability	Novita (South Australia) www.novita.org.au
Suicide	
Support group for family and friends – suicide	Parents of Suicides (POS) - Friends and Families of Suicides (FFOS) www.pos-ffos.com
Support group – suicide As well as providing help in a crisis, Lifeline provides help in dealing with grief and loss	Lifeline www.lifeline.org.au www.lifeline.org.nz
Support group for family and friends – suicide	Survivors of Suicide www.sosbsa.org.au

Function	Organisation
Support group – suicide As well as providing help in a crisis, SuicideLine provides help in dealing with grief and loss	SuicideLine – as well as providing help in a crisis, SuicideLine provide help in dealing with grief and loss www.suicideline.org.au
Supports families bereaved by suicide and works to prevent suicide	CASPER www.casper.org.nz

Finding the right therapist

The largest professional association for *psychologists* in Australia	The Australian *Psychological* Society (APS) www.psychology.org.au
A registered health education charity, dedicated to making good therapy more accessible	Good Therapy Australia www.goodtherapy.com.au www.goodtherapy.org (USA only)
Provides research, education, and consultancy, support for bereaved people	Australian Centre for Grief and Bereavement www.grief.org.au
A national peak body for counsellors and psychotherapists in Australia	Psychotherapy and Counselling Federation of Australia www.pacfa.org.au
To foster and advance clinical practice and theory formation in family therapy	Australian Association of Family Therapy www.aaft.asn.au

Portal for finding a therapist in New Zealand	Mental Health Foundation NZ www.mentalhealth.org.nz
Provides support, advice and counselling to help those affected by loss and grief	Grief Centre www.griefcentre.org.nz
Encourages and promotes professional and community education in loss, grief, bereavement and trauma	National Association of Loss and Grief www.nalag.org.au

Coroners offices

State and territory coroners offices and courts

NSW	www.coroners.lawlink.nsw.gov.au/
NT	www.nt.gov.au/justice/courtsupp/coroner/
QLD	www.courts.qld.gov.au/courts/coroners-court
SA	www.courts.sa.gov.au/OurCourts/CoronersCourt
TAS	www.magistratescourt.tas.gov.au/divisions/coronial
VIC	www.coronerscourt.vic.gov.au/
WA	www.coronerscourt.wa.gov.au/

New Zealand
www.justice.govt.nz/courts/coroners-court

Cemeteries

To locate cemeteries in Australia, please go to www.australiancemeteries.com

Natural burial grounds

To locate cemeteries with natural burial options please go to www.ndan.com.au

Cemeteries Acts

Australia
The best place to start is the Australasian Legal Information Institute <www.austlii.edu.au>.

If you type in the search engine 'cemeteries and crematoria' you will locate all the relevant Acts.

New Zealand
www.legislation.co.nz/act/public/1964/0075/latest/DLM355079.html

INDEX

A

A Family Undertaking 111, 374
A Good Death 61, 67, 78, 83, 100, 268, 269
Albom, Mitch 209, 217, 371
Alzheimer's disease 15, 48, 59, 241, 242, 243
Alzheimer Society of Canada 242, 371
Ambiguous Loss and Grief in Dementia 15, 242, 243, 371
American Medical Association 86
A Practical Guide for Ministering to Grievers 135, 372
Ashby, Professor Michael 82
Ashenburg, Katherine 233, 371
Austin Health 73
Australasian Cemeteries and Crematoria Association 183, 187, 375
Australia Centre of Grief and Bereavement 235, 372, 378, 380
Australian Medical Association 85, 86
Australian Medical Association Code of Ethics 86
Australian Psychological Society 380

Awakening from grief 158, 373

B

Baby boomers 57, 72, 99, 100, 101, 195, 204, 212
Bearsley, Catherine xix, 272
Beasley, Julie 234, 371
Becker, Ernest 61
Being Mortal 78, 371
Being with Dying 17, 280, 372
Black Saturday fires 6, 45, 135
Brock, Ian 17
Burial xv, 6, 18, 23, 99, 104, 115, 117, 124, 159, 163, 172–176, 178–181, 183–192, 197, 198, 223, 263, 266, 300, 310, 314, 376, 382
Burial at sea 172
Burial on private property 175, 180
Burial sites 183, 185, 189, 190, 191
Bushland cemetery 185, 186, 187
Bydder, Ginny xvii, 47, 48, 49, 270, 271, 310

C

Cairns, Deb 109, 110, 377
Calm – App for phones 282
Carlile AM, Molly 73

Carter, Abigail 5, 315, 371
Celebrant xviii, 45, 47, 97, 104, 108, 109, 124, 125, 154, 159–167, 170–173, 212, 293, 301, 304, 308, 310, 312, 314, 315, 319–321, 354
Cell memory 293
Cemeteries 163, 175–178, 180–184, 186, 187, 374–376, 381, 382
Cemeteries bushland 185, 186, 187
Children death of 240, 246–249, 254–259
Chopra, Deepak 16
Cock, Peter 191
Coffins xi, xv, 23, 104, 112, 114, 118, 120, 162–164, 166, 170–172, 174, 175, 178, 179, 183–189, 192, 196, 209, 222, 311, 314, 319, 368–370
Compassion 37, 50, 72, 158, 169, 207, 223, 291, 320, 336, 340
Compassion book 50
Contemporary Funerals and Mourning Practices 197, 375
Conversation starters 267
Coping with Grief 238, 279, 372
Cornish, Keith 16
Coroner 89, 106, 107, 115, 126–133, 154, 224, 257, 381
Cremation xv, 23, 104, 106, 107, 108, 115, 124, 159, 163, 173, 174, 178, 192, 196, 197, 198, 263, 266, 310, 314

D

Dalai Lama 50
Death and Religion in a Changing World 231
Death anxiety 32, 33, 60, 61, 372, 373
Death – definition of (Ch2) 14, 15
Declaration of Geneva 85
Decomposition 117, 118, 188
Dementia xiv, 15, 18, 48, 59, 241, 242, 243, 365, 371
Denial 47, 77, 245, 247
Determining death 15
Diet 282, 286
Disposal of the body 104, 106, 115, 116, 172, 174, 188, 196, 197, 198
Dying With Dignity Victoria xviii, 47, 84, 92, 376

E

Eco cemeteries 184
EcoPrep 198
Edinberg, Mark 32
Embalming 110, 115–118, 133, 183, 187, 188, 196, 197
End-of-life directive 61, 80, 81, 85, 92, 376
Enduring Power of Attorney 58, 80, 88
Environmental Leadership Program 184
Euthanasia 58, 82, 83, 85, 87, 89, 93, 94, 95, 101
Exercise 138, 283
Exit International 83, 93, 94

Index

F

For Kids' Sake 251, 373
Fremantle Cemetery 187
Funeral advocate 99, 109, 167, 171, 172, 192
Funeral companies 105, 120, 158, 160, 163, 165, 169, 170, 196, 208, 209, 212
Funeral DIY xv, 167, 169–171
Funeral Industry Ministerial Advisory Council 122, 389
Funeral Rights 6, 21, 372
Funerals – cultures, xiv, 115, 157, 173, 307

G

GBC International 184
Get Low (film) 209
Giddings, Lara 95
Gilroy, Alex 149
Gilroy, Fiona xvii, 149
Gleeson, Anne xviii, 199, 377
Gratitude list 283
Gray, Ian (Judge) 131
Green burial 117, 174, 183, 184, 185, 187, 189, 197, 374, 376
Green Burial Council 117, 184, 197, 376
Green burials in Australia and their planning challenges 187, 374
Grief xvii, 2, 3, 5, 23, 32, 43–46, 52, 53, 60, 61, 63, 84, 90, 103, 113, 114, 134–136, 140–149, 156, 158, 160, 161, 198, 199, 202, 217, 218, 221, 222, 225, 229–247, 250–253, 258–260, 270, 273, 277–281, 287, 306, 308, 314, 317, 322–324, 329, 337, 338, 367, 371–373, 375, 378–381
Grief Matters 235, 372
Grieving – instrumental, intuitive, model of grieving 232, 233
Guest, Steve 83, 90

H

Halifax, Joan 17, 280
Hannah's Gift 239, 372
Harper, Jill xix, 336
Healing the Hurt, Restoring the Hope 251, 373
Healing Your Grieving Heart series 233, 373
Helbert, Karla 306
Hellenbeck, James 238
Hippocratic Oath 64, 65, 69, 70, 79, 85
Hooke, Michelle 63, 65, 74
Housden, Maria 239, 372
Houston, Jean 306, 372
Hughes, Phillip 46

I

Interlandi, Pia xvi, 104
Interment rights 176, 182

J

Journal – keeping one 281, 283

K

Karaban, Roslyn A 135, 372
King, Petrea 52, 377

Kingston Cemetery 186
Klass, Dennis 231
Kripke, Kate 246, 374
Krupp, Steve 293
Kübler-Ross, Elisabeth 3, 239, 336, 372
Kurweeton Road Cemetery 186

L

Lamb, Steve xviii, 199, 377
Large scale deaths 5, 45, 135, 142
Larkins, Robert xiv, 6, 21, 372
Lewis, Scarlett xvii, 142, 143, 162, 222, 223, 278, 295, 372
Lilydale Cemeteries Trust 186
Living wake 209, 210, 211
Living will 80, 81, 92, 376

M

MacQueen's Funerals xviii, 199, 377
Marshall, Nancy 187, 374
Marta, Suzy Yehl 251, 373
Mason, Rhiannon xvii, 142, 143
McKim, Nick 95, 374
McKinney, Cath 13
McKissock, Mal and Dianne 238, 279, 372
McMordie & Kumar 32, 372
Medical Treatment Act 57, 58, 87, 88, 374
Mental health 9, 85, 127, 195, 244, 254, 333, 381
Metropolitan Cemeteries Board 186
Mindfulness 270
Mitchell, Fran 110

Mitford, Jessica 6, 21
Moloney, Libby 105, 186, 377
Moora Moora cooperative 188, 189, 191
Moore, John Terry xix, 342
Mormon beliefs 17
Motor Neuron Disease (MND) 82
Music 44, 111, 124, 148, 155, 164, 282, 292, 312, 313, 389

N

Natural burial xv, 117, 172, 183–188, 197, 375, 382
Natural Death Advocacy Network xv, 105, 183, 191, 197, 376, 389
Natural End Pledge 187
Nitschke, Dr Philip 83, 93, 94
Nursing homes 112, 120, 121
Nurturing Healing Love 143, 223, 372
Nutik Zitter, Jessica 76

O

Oliver Wyman-Delta Organization and Leadership 293
On Death and Dying 3, 239, 372
Organ donation 23, 109, 112–114, 133, 266, 271, 377
Organisations, general 376–380

P

Palliative care 7, 24, 57, 58, 62–75, 77, 78, 81, 82, 83, 96, 101, 167, 238, 272, 372, 374, 377
Parkinson, Patrick 251, 373

Parton, Glenys 187, 375
Pehlivan, Paige xvii, 142, 147
Perrin, Marshall 89
Physician assisted dying, (PAD) 58, 82, 83, 87, 88, 89, 90, 93, 101
Pilates 283
Pre-paid funerals 121–123, 133, 203, 208, 209
Preparatory grief 238, 239
Private burial sites 190
Pryce, Amanda xvii, 103, 128–131, 223, 245, 325

Q

Quill, Timothy 90

R

Raudon, Sally 197, 198, 199, 375
Refusal Of Medical Treatment Certificate 80, 81, 86, 89, 92, 376
Regrets 46, 210, 259, 293, 303, 326, 333
Relationships Act 133
Resomation 173, 174
Restoration 116, 117, 184
Rights of the Terminally Ill Act 93, 94
Robbins, Anthony 52
Rounds, Rennie 187, 374

S

Sandy Hook Elementary school 135, 142, 162, 223, 278, 295
Sanitation 118
Savage, Jared 91

Schwartz, Morrie 2, 209
Seales, Lecretia 90, 91
Sehee, Joe 184
Shea, Sherinda and Lyndon xvii, 45, 97
Silverman, Phyllis 232
Silvester, Professor W (Bill) 70, 78, 79
Simpson, Susan xvii, 259
Sleep 140, 141, 222, 223, 253, 282, 284, 285, 286
Solomon, Andrew 60, 373
Soul, The 16, 17, 102
Spence, Victoria 97, 377
State Of Grace (organisation) 109, 110, 377
Stillbirth 230, 250, 255, 258, 379
Sudden death 79, 135, 136, 156, 157, 230
Suicide 8, 9, 87, 90, 91, 93, 94, 100, 135, 138, 141, 145, 148, 195, 230, 237, 243, 244, 246, 379, 380
Support organisations 250, 378, 379
Syme, Dr Rodney xviii, 47, 70, 71, 78, 83–85, 88, 90, 373
Symons, Bobbie xix, 301, 315, 354

T

Technology 36, 164, 208, 303
Tender (documentary) 7, 375
Teresi, Dick 373
Thackray, Jill 272
The Alchemy of Loss 5, 371
The Denial of Death 61

The Heart and Soul of Celebrancy 204, 371, 389
The Mourner's Dance 233, 371
The Natural Death Centre Inc. 96
The Natural End Funeral Service Provider Network 187, 376
The Search for the Beloved 306, 372
Tuesday's with Morrie 2, 371

V

Virago, Zenith 96, 377

W

Welshons, John E. 158, 373

Welsh, Tennille and Mark xvii, 254–259
Williams-Murphy, Monica 100
Wirra Wonga 185
Wolfelt, Alan D. 160, 198, 233, 373
World Medical Association 85
World Trade Center 5, 45, 135, 315
Worry list 282

Y

Yoga 283

Z

Zagdanski, Doris 217, 222, 375

ABOUT THE AUTHOR

Sally Cant is a Trainer, Author, Celebrant, Family Death Care Advocate, and a passionate advocate for end of life choices.

She is the author of The Heart and Soul of Celebrancy, owner of The Celebrants Training College, the owner of an IT Consultancy company, an inaugural board member of FIMAC (Funeral Industry Ministerial Advisory Council), a committee member of The Natural Death Advocacy Network (NDAN), President of the Celebrants Association of Australia, a University lecturer, an award winning artist and a mother of three.

Sally has a long and distinguished career in top level Management and Education, including teaching music for over 25 years. In her spare time she loves playing golf and singing. In 2015 Sally sang with the "Sing The World" choir touring Italy (singing at The Vatican, Santa Maria Sopra Minerva and the 2015 Milan World Expo) and the UK (singing at The Royal Albert Hall and Southwark Cathedral)

She lives in Rowville, Victoria, Australia.